WITHDRAWN
Learning Resources
838663

Inspired to Stitch

21 TEXTILE ARTISTS

Inspired to Stitch

21 TEXTILE ARTISTS

DIANA SPRINGALL

FOREWORD BY EDWARD LUCIE-SMITH

A & C BLACK PUBLISHERS • LONDON

First published in Great Britain in 2005
A & C Black Publishers Limited
Alderman House
37 Soho Square
London W1D 3QZ
www.acblack.com

ISBN-10: 07136-6986-1
ISBN-13: 978-0-7136-6986-2

CIP Catalogue records for this book are available from the British Library and the U.S. Library of Congress.

Book design by Paula McCann
Cover design by Peter Bailey
Copyedited and proofread by Carol Waters
Managing Editor: Susan Kelly

Printed and bound in China

A & C Black uses paper produced with elemental chlorine-free pulp, harvested from managed sustainable forests.

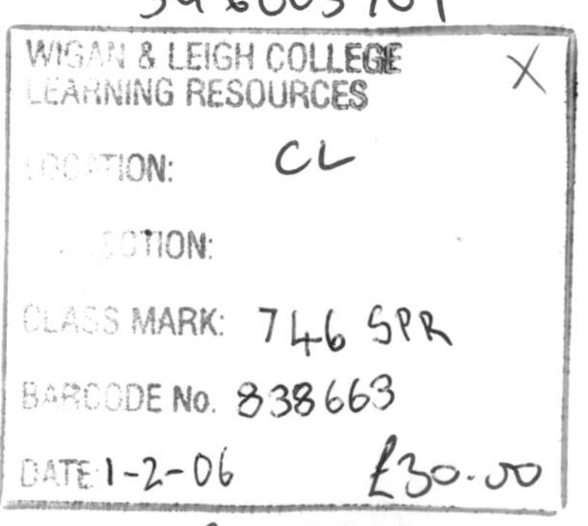

Contents

Acknowledgements

Special thanks to my publisher Linda Lambert for her vision in believing that my lifetime's study and appreciation of fellow embroiderers merited a book of this kind. From the outset of the making of this book thanks too must go to Andrew Salmon for his plan to support the launch of this publication at the Knitting and Stitching Shows. I also owe gratitude to my editor Susan Kelly for her constant support throughout the final realisation.

For all that I have learned about a computer I have Marie Boulton to thank. I must also record with gratitude the patience and support of my long suffering family and friends for whom this must have seemed a never ending assignment.

Above all I want to offer this book in praise of British embroiderers and of these twenty one artists who have so generously and enthusiastically embraced this project.

Diana Springall
Kemsing 2005

Foreword – Stitchery and Society

There are certain things that any attentive reader will immediately notice about the contents of this book. First, that the artists it celebrates are all female. Second, that – while many of them are justly famous in the contemporary arts-and-crafts community – quite a number confess to economic difficulties in pursuing their chosen form of creative expression. Third, the book reflects a real sense of community, with skills being handed on from one practitioner to another. All of these are topics that need to be addressed, however briefly.

The first and second are closely linked. Until very recently, women faced conspicuous difficulties when they tried to make their way in the world of the so-called 'fine arts'. The craft world was a great deal more welcoming, and indeed certain areas of activity have been regarded traditionally as the province of women. In the Western European world embroidery is one of these. Yet even in this area historical perception is slightly skewed. The great works of embroidery for which medieval England was famous – so much so that the general European name for them was 'opus anglicanum' – were often the product of male craftsmen, and not of women.

Gradually this situation changed, as the division between fine art – painting, sculpture and architecture – and other forms of creativity in the visual arts began to impose itself. Embroidery, even at its most skilled levels, became one of two things. Either it was a domestic activity, not undertaken for pay, but for its own sake and as a means of adorning a household; or else it was an activity connected with fashion – the adornment of things to wear. Here, too, there was a slippage from male to female. As the beautifully embroidered silk coats of 18th century court dress were replaced by the sober garments introduced by Beau Brummel, embroidered decoration became something largely confined to women's garments. Even the colourful hippie clothing of the 19th century could not entirely reverse this trend.

This meant that it lost status not only in purely artistic but also in economic terms. The great works of skilled medieval embroiderers were certainly, as surviving documents demonstrate, among the most costly luxury items of their time. Painters, still regarded as artisans on a level with a whole range of other craftspeople, were not necessarily paid more, and were sometimes paid considerably less, as their work was regarded as less labour-intensive and used, on the whole, less costly materials.

Once embroidery sank into the purely domestic sphere, the fact that it was a highly skilled area of creativity began to be discounted. The amount of labour it required was also discounted. It was seen as a female accomplishment, undertaken for its own sake – a subtle assertion of gentility, and a pleasant way for women of the leisured class to pass their time. In those spheres where it remained a professional skill, it was the province of poorly paid female workers – an ancillary of the fashion industry.

Within families, and also within communities, there was nevertheless both a strong sense of pride in the exercise of needle skills. Embroidery – working together, the sharing of techniques, and the small rituals involved in passing on these techniques from one generation to another – became part of a specifically female universe. This pattern was especially prominent in the pioneering communities of the 18th and 19th century United States where, for example, quilting bees often played an important part in social life, but it also showed itself in Britain.

It is this tradition that still, in part at least, informs contemporary needlework. Traces of it can be seen quite clearly in the life-stories of the embroiderers whose lives and accomplishments are chronicled in this book.

There is, however, another side to the story. We now live in a world where the boundaries between the various forms of artistic making are largely dissolved. The system of categorization set up by Renaissance theoreticians no longer applies to contemporary art, which can be made using any technique or any material or combination of materials. Unfortunately this wide-ranging eclecticism, combined with the cult of the 'readymade' [a concept invented by Marcel Duchamp in the second decade of the 20th century], has brought with it an increasing disrespect for, and indeed an ingrained suspicion of, obvious manual skills.

This has opened a new and different breach between the world of the fine arts and that of the crafts. It has led to a retreat into the world of the crafts of people who are fascinated both by the perfection of a particular set of skills, who also gain satisfaction from the production of actual physical objects.

Women have found additional reasons for identifying themselves with what is called craft rather than what is called art. The whole tradition of 'great painting' and 'great sculpture' is dominated by males. There is no female equivalent for Michelangelo. For this reason many women makers have opted to exercise their creativity in genres where a masculine history is less oppressively present.

The leading American feminist artist Judy Chicago has elaborated on this in a number of ambitious projects, such as the 'Birth Project' [1980–5] and the more recent 'Resolutions: A Stitch in Time' [1994–2000]. These, however, are not the work of a single individual, but are collaborations between an artist who does not sew and a team of highly skilled embroiderers. The work shown in this book, by contrast, is carried out by the same person, from first to last.

When we look at these processes – each embroiderer has her own individual method, so the plural form of the word is appropriate – unexpected elements emerge. It is interesting to see, for example, how many of these embroiderers were originally painters. It is also interesting to see how many of them make drawing an integral part of their preparation. Their drawings are fluent and show a high degree of skill.

Many of the finished works operate in precisely the same way as paintings and drawings – that is, they are intended to be hung on a wall, as art works independent of any practical function. There is a tendency, amongst avant-garde artists, curators and critics, to see objects that are clearly functionless, yet equally clearly craft-based, as unworthy parodies of genuinely experimental creative activity – in fact as a form of kitsch. Even this brings with it certain complications, since kitsch duly saturated with irony – the work of Jeff Koons is an example – now has an honoured place within the avant-garde pantheon.

What we have here seems to be the operation of an unacknowledged glass ceiling, a variant of the blockages women notoriously encounter when they embark on business careers. Contemporary embroidery has to struggle against art world prejudice for recognition and – not incidentally – for real financial status. Part of this prejudice is based on gender, and on historical perceptions linked to gender: the post-Renaissance image of embroidery as being primarily a domestic activity undertaken by women in the privacy of the home, usually without any real thought of material reward.

Part of it, however, and perhaps the larger part, is founded on the contemporary art world's extremely ambiguous attitude towards skill. Virtuoso skills, which is to say manual dexterity and technical ability well beyond the reach of most people, are especially suspect. This is particularly ironic, since the same qualities are worshipped in the professional sports that play so large a role in our society. In the case of sport, football for instance, skill clearly facilitates spontaneity. In the case of contemporary art, critics often seem to feel that skill impedes the spontaneous expression of true, visceral creativity.

Since the 1960s, art criticism has paid a good deal of attention to what is labeled 'process-based art'. Generally what commentators mean by this is a kind of art that is self-reflexive, in the sense that its subject is simply the process or set of processes through which it has come into existence. It is possible, I suppose, to appreciate embroidery in this way. Indeed, I suspect that some obsessives look at an ambitious example of embroidered work entirely from this very limited viewpoint. They want to work out exactly how it was done.

I don't think this is the audience that the embroiderers featured in this book really want. Their primary aim is to give delight by using skill combined with imagination to create things that will be immediately recognized as being beautiful. This book may help to get them the credit that is their due.

Edward Lucie-Smith
January 2005

Introduction

The most wonderful aspect of embroidery, when practised by those who can take it to the highest level, is its status as both an art and a craft. In the hands of some, who adopt it for leisure, it may remain a craft; for others who choose to adopt it in search of peace, courage and so many other aspirations, it is often therapeutic and constructive.

Above all, in Britain, embroidery is a subject unique in bringing professionals and amateurs together as equals.

This is the story of some of the most outstanding embroiderers to have emerged, in the last half century, from a higher education system that valued the significance of observational drawing.

It is about artists who have become committed exponents of the use of needle and thread and of their skill in raising this craft to an art form. It is no accident that they are all, without exception, the result of an art school system that founded all material skills on the principles of art. They are before the time of the late twentieth century pre- occupation with theory and academia and remain largely untouched by the new educational importance placed on the use of new technology. They remain outside the realms of the fashionable conceptual approach.

It is a period that starts with a dearth of embroidery materials and ends with present day consumer over-abundance; it starts at a time that was devoid of specialist textile exhibitions and ends with expectations of shows that encompass massive enterprise; The Knitting and Stitching Shows attract in excess of 100,000 visitors annually.

This is a book about people; of how and why they come to do what they do so spectacularly. Influences, often from an early age, are revealed in order to demonstrate the relevance of.circumstance in the destiny of individual achievement.

Through their self-generating approach to both circumstances of life, and to their highly specialised training in the concepts of art, many have reached world leadership in the subject.

This collection of very personal and innovative journeys, in the use of materials and techniques, shows the extension of the creative process.

This appraisal is also intended to contribute to the existing long history of embroidery in the British Isles dating back to medieval times.

It may also serve to break down the artificial boundaries between art and craft; the work of those described within amply demonstrates that they are but one. Embroiderers of this calibre are worthy, not only of the definition of artist and craftsman, but in time, deserve to be revered with the same awe that we today hold for the best of what has gone before.

This is a book about the significant and very different direction that embroidery took following the end of the Second World War. The main reason for this being that from 1945 its inspiration and development was art school led. The momentous year was 1954, when embroidery first became the subject of a formal qualification, the National Diploma in Design (NDD); alongside Painting, Sculpture and Illustration.

Inclusion as one of the fine arts, as with other craft based subjects of the time, was however transparently tenuous. Ironically too, just when embroidery appeared to be joining the fine arts, government funding for the arts was to be dispensed by two separate bodies, The Arts Council and The Crafts Council. A line firmly separated arts from crafts creating a situation that had not existed before and one that only now, at least in terminology, was reversed in April 2003.

In a single volume one cannot hope to include everyone who sews artistically. What is hoped is that it will serve to highlight a belief in the worth of the subject when practised at a rare and individual level.

Those with exceptional talent may be few but their importance places them very firmly in the world of Art – they have certainly made the world a richer place and created a heritage, which will surely stand the test of time.

It is a book written out of respect, admiration and some understanding of what has been achieved.

Above all, in the absence of being able to do anything to redress the twentieth century art/craft divide it seemed essential to document works of this calibre in a contemporary *salon des refusés* – albeit in book form.

Photo: Diana Springall

MARGARET NICHOLSON

1913	Born Sheffield 13 March
1928 – 1933	Sheffield College of Art Industrial Design Cert (later NDD) Received City and Guilds Gold Medal Evening teaching assistant Sheffield College of Art Teaching Chesterfield College of Art/Embroidery/Crafts Student Member Embroiderers' Guild
1930 – 1933	West Riding of Yorkshire Wombwell Institute, teaching miners' wives
1933 – 1939	Dress designer for Brook Manufacturing Co – producing large multiple orders for Marks & Spencer, C & A and British Home Stores. Company later taken over by The Calico Printers and finally by Courtauld. Designed copies of the famous black circular skirt and white blouse favoured by the Duchess of Windsor. Also the version of her wedding outfit for Marks and Spencer, which was sold in hundreds at the Marble Arch branch
1937	Married
1939	Outbreak of war and move to Evesham – husband worked for the BBC
1945	Anthea born
1946	BBC now back in Bush House London and with it family removal
1946 – 1954	Lived in Potters Bar
1954 – 1981	Move to Brookmans Park
1958	Herts W.I. Craft Committee and National W.I. Craft Committee with Avril Colby, Laura Ashley, Hebe Cox Member The Embroiderers' Guild teaching Wimpole Street Headquarters Executive Committee member
1959	Hammersmith College of Art and Building Refresher Course
1960	Author *Making a Quilt for Denman College* Spring issue Womens' Institute Magazine, *Home and Country*

1961	Author *A New Approach* Summer issue of *Embroidery*
1962 – 3	Teaching evening classes at Stanhope Institute
1965 – 1980	Lecturer Design Department at London College of Fashion
1965	Author *Appliqué Work* Spring issue of *Embroidery*
1966 – 1976	Stoke D'Abernon Teachers Courses for ILEA with D. Allsopp and I. Hills
1966	Author *St Clare Panels* Summer issue *Embroidery*
1967	Author *Embroidery in Fashion* Summer issue of *Embroidery* Author *Making a Notebook* Autumn issue of *Embroidery*
1970	Author *The Lady Banner at Coventry Cathedral* Autumn issue *Embroidery*
1974	Author *Decoration in Fashion* Winter issue *Embroidery*
1976	Author *From a Student's Sketchbook* Autumn issue *Embroidery*
1980 –	Designing and embroidering pictures, boxes, book covers
1988	Widowed
1995	Review in August issue *Needlework* Review Autumn issue *Embroidery* Author *Ideas for Necklets* Christmas issue *Embroidery*
1999	Review in June issue *Needlecraft*
2000	Author *Beaded Fringe Technique* June issue The Beadworkers' Guild Magazine
2001	Author *Creative Bead Work for Beginners* June issue of The Beadworkers' Guild Magazine
2003	Profile included British Library National Sound Archive Nation Life Story Collection - Fashion
2004	Review in first issue Yorkshire and Humberside Regional Magazine

Right: Detail, *The Sorcerer,* 2001, Or Nué, inspired by a visit to the Royal Academy of Arts exhibition on fairies in Victorian Art

Margaret Nicholson

Margaret is the epitome of what it is to be surrounded by art from birth.

Even more specifically, her passion for the use of gold cannot be anything other than directly inherited from her father, a noted guilder working in most of the great houses and churches. She says 'I was brought up with gold leaf – we *played* with gold leaf!'

Margaret's ninetieth birthday retrospective exhibition, at The London College of Fashion in March 2003, was an awe-inspiring experience, largely because of her unique artistic handling of both real and synthetic gold thread. Her achievements, in panel after panel of *or nué*[1], securely place her in the realms of both artist and master craftsman.

Encouraged by her grandfather the family lived in a world of art; all their magazines and books were about art. As a consequence by the time Margaret had reached the age of fourteen she recalls friends saying to her parents 'your daughter really ought to go to Art College.' With no thought to do anything other than to study art, the inevitable move came at the age of sixteen with admission to Sheffield College of Art.

In 1929 the five-year Industrial Design course began with a first year which was entirely based on drawing of every kind –' there were always things to draw – it was very much a Fine Art course'. Two years of different crafts followed and finally a chance to choose to specialise in dress and embroidery. She was one of the few students at that period to view this medium as a serious living; instead most girls regarded fashion and needle skills as an opt-out from work.

These years were further enhanced by attending an additional course in embroidery in order to achieve her City & Guilds of London Institute status, for which she was awarded the 1933 gold medal.

Opposite: *Girls Head,* Or Nué. Collection of The Constance Howard Resource and Research Centre, Goldsmiths' College, London

Right: *Mother and Daughter,* Or Nué

Skills of basic sewing and embroidery were clearly intrinsic to her but these were extended and complemented by the experience of working for her first employer, Brook Manufacturing Company, in Northampton, for whom, until her marriage, she designed both garments and embroidery. For a period of about six years she was involved in producing large orders for Marks & Spencer, C&A and British Home Stores. She clearly recalls that a frock cost five shillings in the shop and four shillings and one penny ex-factory. Working from newspaper photographs of the black circular skirt and white blouse favoured by the Duchess of Windsor, together with those of her wedding outfit, Margaret was asked by the company to design garments that were, as near as possible, exact copies. These sold in their hundreds at the Marble Arch branch of Marks & Spencer. She continued to work for the Company until two years after her marriage and the outbreak of the Second World War.

Second World War 'call up' meant five years domestic removal to Evesham. Her husband, an engineer for the BBC section of the War Office, had to accept a posting outside London. The birth of her only child Anthea[2] meant a further eight years until her career could resume; embroidery and fashion were now on hold.

A return to London at the end of the war created an opportunity to join the Women's Institute (W.I.), something that, in career terms, would not normally be considered particularly significant. However, in this context it proved to be the catalyst for the professional life that followed. She met Dorothy Allsopp[3] who, she says, 'became the greatest friend to me'. Through her she also met Iris Hills[4] who, on her retirement from examining the City & Guilds Embroidery course, asked Margaret to take over, which she did, from 1965-1975. More important was her recommendation in 1965 that Margaret should join the staff of the London College of Fashion. The next fifteen very full time years saw her reputation as a teacher grow hugely in stature. This was a remarkable achievement, bearing in mind that the only teaching experience, prior to this appointment, had been evening classes during college years. Two of these evenings each week were given to miners' wives, in a programme that would 'make them into better citizens'.

She says that the making of her own work was the springboard for student innovation and enterprise; she sees

the two as having been inextricably entwined. The samples and artefacts that are so simply described by her as 'making of her own work' are largely still available to see. She did sell a considerable number of her exquisite gold-work pictures but the quantity and quality of what remains in her possession is quite phenomenal.

Certain aspects of her art school training remain at the forefront of her thinking and form the starting points for a design, underpinning her choice of subject. She recalls that 'we were always taught to look at an object, to draw it, remember it and then work as many variations of it as possible'. Somehow this emerges in the series of sequentially developed pieces, so many of which are akin to the unique qualities of an icon.

The works are small scale, most often involving stylised heads and faces. At times the *or nué* is in reverse i.e. the laid thread is coloured and the couching is in gold. Shapes richly filled with laid gold thread are often further embellished with other embroidery stitches and beads, adding a heightened sense of reflection and richness. Beads were and are a great part of her expression. She has developed an unending range of encrusted neckpieces. At college she tried hard to get better respect and appreciation for professional beaders

Opposite top: Study from *An Iris* Pen and ink

Opposite bottom: Study from *A Passion Flower* Pen and ink

Above: Study for *The Ancient Mariner* Pen and ink

Right: *The Ancient Mariner* 2000, Or Nué, worked on the bias to suggest the storm

Opposite: *The Little Angel,* Or Nué

Below: Study for *Kings and Queens,* pen and ink

Right: *Head of the Virgin,* Or Nué

and especially for those who did tambour beading[5], which she regards as very skilled.

She is still a lady of great style, usually adorned with one of her sumptuous beaded necklaces. Clear memories of so much that is relevant to the story of embroidery, and still with a love of embroidering, makes her a pleasure to be with. Her home, which is now with her daughter and son-in-law in north London, shows that for a lifetime she has collected objects for pleasure. Walls of objects abound. Artists that have particularly influenced her include Klimt[6] and Ravillius[7]. Two sides of the bathroom that Anthea painted for her are covered with an enlargement of a Klimt painting. The other two walls, being mirror and glass, envelop a vast collection of plain glass scent bottles of every size and shape; absolutely stunning and so typical, not only of other parts of the house but, of the unique partnership of a creative mother and daughter.

When asked what enables her to start a new piece of work she always says it is the research into a subject she has seen. When asked what she would consider to be her finest

Left: *Book Cover,* Or Nué embroidery. A guest book for The Embroiderers' Guild. Binding by Heidi Jenkins

Below: *Face of a Woman,* Or Nué

Bottom: *Girl with a Blue Cap,* Or Nué

Opposite: *Josephine's Coat,* 2002, Or Nué – pure silk thread over gold thread

work, not counting the hundreds of lives she has enhanced through her teaching, she says it has to be her Mothers Union banner for Coventry Cathedral.

She has no elaborate equipment, no sewing machine, just a particularly special slate frame left to her by Hebe Cox [8] and of course a vast collection of beads and threads, stored in a myriad of drawers and huge glass jars.

She says with great enthusiasm that 'embroidery has been a splendid life to me personally. I have met so many people; I can't call them all friends but I've been to their funerals, memorials, and I've done such a lot'.

Left: *Mothers' Union Banner,* Coventry Cathedral 1968. Hand embroidered in many gold work techniques using numerous types of thread including cord and purl. Appliqué includes gold kid and beads

Below: Detail of embroidery, *Mothers' Union Banner*

Opposite: *Gemini Panel,* Or Nué embroidery with additional beading for panel. Note the two faces back to back

With reference to her continuing energy to embroider every day, she says she does sometimes long for an elixir but never the less is extremely keen 'to have things correct – as right as I can do it'. A great lady who has given so much to the world of embroidery.

Footnotes

1 Or nué *Method whereby gold thread is laid on the surface of the cloth and couched down; in the Middle Ages with silk threads and in more recent times with floss or cotton. These stitches, often coloured, were spaced according to the desired effect of surface pattern.*

2 *Anthea Godfrey, BA Embroidery/Textiles, ATD. 1945-*
Fellow of the Royal Society of Arts. Past Chairman and Emeritus member of the Embroiderers' Guild. Highly respected teacher/lecturer worldwide. 1980-London College of Fashion. 1988 Nomination for Woman of the Year. Examiner for MA and BA Textiles. City & Guilds chief examiner for 'O' and 'A' level embroidery

3 *Dorothy Allsopp ARCA ATD 1911-1999*
Work in the collection of the Victoria & Albert Museum. 1929-1931 Trained Chelsea School of Art 1931-1935. Royal College of Art. 1935-1949. West Hartlepool College of Art. Lecturer in women's crafts. 1949-1954 Expert in charge of Needlework Development Scheme – see note 22. 1954-1961 Hammersmith College of Art (now part of Chelsea School of Art) Senior Lecturer in Fashion/Textiles/Embroidery. 1961-1976 Inner London Education Authority Inspector, Fashion and Creative Studies. 1978 Chairman, City & Guilds of London Institute examination board in Creative Studies

4 *Iris Hills ARCA 1913-*
1932-1935 Trained Royal College of Art – Illustration/Embroidery. 1935-1938 Bromley College of Art, part-time Lecturer in charge of 'Craft School'. 1946 Bromley College of Art, Lecturer in charge of embroidery. 1955-1961 Expert in charge of The Needlework Development Scheme-see note 22. 1961-1966 Hammersmith College of Art and Building, Senior Lecturer in Fashion/Embroidery/Textiles. 1965-1975 Chief Examiner for the City & Guilds of London Institute examinations in embroidery. 1967-1977 Worked for Inner London Education Authority.
Introduction to Embroidery, *published by Victoria & Albert Museum 1953*

5 *Tambour beading is produced on a round tambour frame consisting of two hoops of wood between which the fabric is stretched tight. It is necessary to support the frame to leave both hands free, one for operating the hook on top and one for controlling the thread beneath. The beads are first threaded onto a continuous thread and the work is done with the wrong side uppermost. The hooked tambour needle goes down through the ground fabric and each time it takes up a thread it leaves a bead secured.*

6 *Gustav Klimt 1862-1918 Painter of the Austrian Jugenstil*

7 *Eric Ravillious 1903-1942 Painter and designer*

8 *Hebe Cox 1909-1993*
1931-1934 Trained at Central School of Arts & Crafts. Adviser to National Federation of Women's Institutes. Founder member and trustee of the Crafts Centre of Great Britain (now the Crafts Council) Member of the Arts and Crafts Exhibition Society (now the Society of Designer-Craftsmen)
Simple Embroidery Designs. *Studio Vista 1948.* Embroidery Technique and Design. *Dryad 1954.* Canvas Embroidery. *Mills & Boon 1960. Contributor to,* Fifteen Craftsmen on their Crafts. *Sylvan Press 1945*

9 *Avril Colby 1900-1983*
Training in horticulture; interest in garden restoration; specialism in Patchwork: Worked for The Needlework Development Scheme22, National Federation of Women's Institutes and many private patrons and lectured widely
Patchwork. *Batsford 1958 (p/b ed. 1976).* Samplers. *Batsford 1964.* Patchwork Quilts. *Batsford 1965.* Quilting. *Batsford.1972.* Pincushions. *Batsford 1975.*

10 *Laura Ashley 1925-1986*
Noted for the fabrics and clothes marketed through the business set up with her husband Bernard in 1953. Laura Ashley Foundation continues

Photo: Denys Short

EIRIAN SHORT

1924	Born Pembrokeshire 9 January
1951	NDD Sculpture Goldsmiths' College School of Art
1951	Married Denys Short
1951 – 1953	Studied embroidery under Constance Howard
1953 – 1985	Teaching part-time at Goldsmiths' College and Hornsey College of Art (now Middlesex University) but with some shorter periods at Avery Hill and College of All Saints
1967	Author *Embroidery and Fabric Collage* Pitman
1970	Author *Introducing Macramé* Batsford
1974	Author *Introducing Quilting* Batsford
1979	Author *Quilting, Technique, Design and Application* Batsford
1981	*Readers Digest Guide to Needlework* technical editor Two person show with Gillian Still Welsh Arts Council Gallery Cardiff
1985	Retired from teaching Showed with Constance Howard and Christine Risley, Goldsmiths' College School of Art Gallery Group Exhibitions with Society of Designer Craftsmen. '62 Group. Quad. Travelling exhibitions include *Contemporary Hangings, Out of the Frame, Art Textiles.* Tolly Cobbold. *All about Wool.* Numerous mixed exhibitions
1993 – 7	Helped co-ordinate with Audrey Walker and Rozanne Hawksley the *Last Invasion* Tapestry in Fishguard
1995	Solo exhibition Museum of the North, Llanberis
1995 & 97	Profile *Embroidery* Summer and July editions
1997	Solo exhibition Oriel Myrddin, Carmarthen
1998	Profile *Crafts* January/February issues
1996, 1997 & 2000	Shows shared with Denys Short, Museum of the Woollen Industry, Model House, Llantrisant, Cardiff, The National Library of Wales

Work in the collection of The Embroiderers' Guild, the Welsh Arts Council, the National Library of Wales, education authorities, colleges and private collectors at home and overseas.
Commissions have, on the whole, been small scale for private clients – for example favourite landscapes or 'portraits' of people's houses.
Design commissions include work for The Sunday Times Magazine, The Daily Express, Golden Hands, British Ropes, Briggs and Co and John Lewis.
Exhibiting regularly, accepting invitations to speak and to make frequent television appearances

Right: *The Open Window* 1998 detail of hand embroidery

Eirian Short

Eirian is without question a major figure in the world of British embroidery. Her work spans the whole of the period of the second half of the twentieth century and, at just over eighty years old, she continues to produce work of great integrity and visual worth.

Her early training as a sculptor can be seen to underpin and link the hugely varied subject matter. What one witnesses today is a huge volume of work, which began, at the start of her career, with a ten year period of flat pieced works. She then progressed to a prolific production of hand stitchery, which combined either with softly sculpted areas of fabric or decoratively painted supporting wooden surfaces.

Every subject pursued has been observed in detail with countless drawings from life. These are followed by actual-size drawings for the work envisaged.

This level of achievement would not be possible without a lifetime's discipline and passion for the subject. This started early and nothing expresses this more aptly than the story she shared which relates to her wedding day, New Year's Eve 1951; (she is married to the sculptor Denys Short[11]). Following the simple family wedding lunch, she and Denys did not leave for a honeymoon but instead went off in the afternoon to deliver the work she had produced for the *Pictures for Schools*[12] exhibition.

It is also a salutary thought that for a period of about thirty years, up to 1985 when she retired from part-time teaching, her output of works of art were produced only in limited times during the week. It was quite usual at this period in Britain for artists to financially support their creative time by part-time teaching. In Eirian's case she and Denys planned that each should teach on average no more than two days a week, which provided the minimum

Left: *Woman with Lilies* 1998
Hand embroidery with painted MDF frame
120cm x 100cm (47in. x 39in.)
Private collection

Below: *Woman with Lilies* 1998 detail of hand embroidery

Below left: Working Drawing for *Woman with Lilies* 1998
Photo: Philip Clarke

Opposite page: Collection of studies on studio wall – various media
Photo: Philip Clarke

subsistence. This allowed them to devote the rest of the time to their own work. Although teaching was of necessity she says she did enjoy it. The research she did on students' behalf often fed into her embroidery and the contact with young people provided a pleasurable balance to her life.

Teaching commitments began modestly with two evening classes per week at Gravesend School of Art in Kent to which was added later, with great significance, one afternoon and one evening at Goldsmiths' College School of Art, London. Soon after, and for the next fourteen years, she taught at Hornsey College of Art, London. Here, on the Art Teachers' Certificate course, both Jan Beaney[13] and Julia Caprara[14] were among her students. This contract only ended when she took the side of the students in the infamous 'sit in' of 1968 and was sacked. During the dispute Lord Longford[15] came to arbitrate and offered her a voluntary social workers task to help deal with the homeless and those on drugs. This she found rewarding and something she would continue at times of social need such as Christmas, even though, after six months, she gained a seven year appointment to teach Home Economics at the College of All Saints, Tottenham, London.

From 1975, on the retirement of Constance Parker at Goldsmiths' College, and the succession of Audrey Walker[16], her teaching commitment by 1981 was arranged so that she could teach in alternate ten day blocks, which enabled her to leave London and return to Pembrokeshire from where she could reasonably commute.

Her life had started in Pembrokeshire where she was born and from where her father originated. It is where she returned to on retirement, to work with even greater dedication. Her mother came from the Welsh mining valleys. The family were musical and poetry was also a prominent talent. There was, however, no evidence of a heritage of textiles that could account for Eirian's love of the needle. In fact art was entirely absent from her childhood due to her secondary school not offering the subject.

An awareness of art did not emerge until joining the army at the age of nineteen where she met many artists of all disciplines. Following the end of the war she was determined to learn more and joined evening classes in Life Drawing together with a month's painting course in an army 'Formation College' This was followed in 1949 by a full time course in Sculpture, taking the National Diploma in Design

Above left: *Primmy's Dog* 2003/4 Hand embroidery in wool mounted on wood profile. Overall size 100cm x 82cm (39in. x 32in.) Private collection. Photo: Philip Clarke

Opposite left: *Primmy's Dog* 2003/4 Preparatory pencil drawing Photo: Philip Clarke

Opposite right: *The Table* 2000 Flowers, fruit and carpet hand stitched; vase, bowl and table painted hardboard: table cloth, real. One of a series of vignettes. Photo: Philip Clarke

Top: *The Parlour* 1995 Hand embroidery. 92cm x 148cm (36in. x 58in.) Private collection

Above: *Garn Mebion Owen (The Rock of the Sons of Owen)* 1985 Hand stitched Pembrokeshire landscape 76cm x 153cm (30in.x 60in.)

(NDD) at Goldsmiths' College School of Art under the tuition of the sculptor Harold Parker [17].

This was followed by the teacher-training year, Art Teachers' Diploma (ATD), which encouraged the learning of new skills and where, in Eirian's case, joining the embroidery class under Constance Parker [18], one evening per week, was a life changing experience. She says 'I just picked up a needle and put it in the fabric and I was hooked – I just loved the act of sewing'. The discovery of the medium encouraged her to abandon the teachers' course and instead spend the next two years at the college as a student of embroidery.

Left: *The Open Window* 1998 120 cm x 130 cm (47in. x 51in.) Hand embroidery set in three dimensional painted window frame (Medium Density Fibre Board) Photo: Philip Clarke

Above: *Come Dancing* 1985 Hand embroidered entirely in French Knots. Art Deco style frame in chenille and lurex. 69 cm x 91 cm (27in. x 36in.) Embroiderers' Guild collection

Right: *Dream Cottage* 1977 Hand embroidery in padded fabric frame 90cm x 110 cm (35in. x 43in.) Private collection Photo: Philip Clarke

The era in which her embroidery career was emerging was one of considerable note. Embroidery style throughout the 1950s at Goldsmiths' was strictly governed – all motifs had to be flat, with no perspective, self-contained on backgrounds that could be either plain or decorative. Only certain fabrics were considered suitable and any thought of using paints or crayons on cloth was absolutely out. For years Eirian felt the influence of these rules, as did many others also studying with Mrs Parker at this time. Eirian recalls the response of shock and horror when she cut a bit of shiny black plastic from a mackintosh to add to the wings of a butterfly. She describes this early period of her work as 'twee' and always depicting 'acceptable' subjects such as birds, trees and buildings such as Welsh chapels and houses.

Left: Crows 1987 Hand stitched in crewel wools on flannel 150cm (59in.) square Collection National Library of Wales

Below: Preparatory sketch for *Crows* from artist's sketchbook c. 1987

Below right: Pen drawings of *Crows* from artist's sketchbook c. 1987

The work *Breaking Wave* shown in the *Materialists* exhibition of 1957 at Foyle's Art Gallery, London, was the start of a departure from the prescribed formula and something that would not have been possible at the start of the '50s.

Having said this it was nevertheless an era of enormous expansion of original embroidery as a medium for art and for creative pleasure. Christine Risley [19], who was a student at Goldsmiths' between 1946 and 1950, taking both her Intermediate and NDD Painting courses, saw an exhibition of embroidery mounted by Constance Parker in the main college corridor. Completely inspired by this she persuaded Mrs Parker to start a small class. From this grew the now famed evening classes of the period, which took place every weekday evening from 6-9pm and ran for years and years. These classes were largely responsible for the formation and dissemination of a nationwide interest in the practice of the subject at every level. Teachers, amateurs and students, were all coming and going from far corners of the country, spreading everything that had been gleaned from within the walls of this one large embroidery room within a small art school of no more than a hundred students in all departments. Despite its growing fame those involved with the painters, sculptors, illustrators, printmakers, potters and bookbinders did not consider the embroidery department as anything serious. In spite of Constance Parker being married to the head of the sculpture school; they remained simply intrigued.

Even by 1951 there were few 'creative' embroiderers – Margaret Kaye[20] was a name that stood alone for she was someone who was working very freely and boldly with fabric appliqué and indeed had several solo shows in London.

The only other oasis of creativity at this time was at Glasgow School of Art under the leadership of Kathleen Whyte[21]. Little else was happening of any significant educational or inspirational nature except for the Needlework Development Scheme (NDS) leaflets[22], the Embroiderers' Guild[23], and the Royal School of Needlework[24].

Sources for Eirian's embroidery have always been based on things seen around her. Careful initial drawings are meticulously squared up to exact size. Lines are transferred to the ground fabric by means of carbon, which in turn are made more specific with ink. Her thread is always Appleton's crewel wool (of which she stocks every colour) and her stitches are limited to French Knots and Straight stitches. For her these best express a mark or collected marks and are not selected for the sake of the stitch but to create gesture or texture.

She commences by placing a layer of stitches on the ground fabric thereby making marks much as might be done with a pencil or brush. These are further added to as the work progresses. The stitchery is not as predictably planned as one might think – she confesses to spending the first part of most days unpicking work done the previous day. Her subjects are varied – some she exhausts whilst others she revisits.

To visually assess her enormous achievement it is probably helpful to narrow our vision to the last thirty years. This enables an appreciation of the involvement and dedication to themes – when themes present themselves to her she has the inspiration and creativity to identify with them and transpose them to her own unique style. The 'Death' series, which commenced in the 1970s, being a strong example. It started by chance. Neighbours on their way home from a party had knocked on her door and said 'Come with us we are going for a walk in Nunhead cemetery.' This marvellous Victorian cemetery inspired her to look at gravestones, a subject which, in her hands, presented great opportunities for decorative and three dimensional reliefs in fabric and stitch. These were works that could as easily be referred to using the then new American expression of 'soft sculpture'; terminology that at this date was emerging quite separately from across the other side of the Atlantic. Very soon she was researching funerals in museums, watching funerals and enjoying the characteristically flamboyant style of those that took place in the south east of London; traditionally displaying huge floral memorial tributes, which could be likened now as precursors to the giant floral dogs produced by Jeff Koons[25]. This momentum within the subject was planned to continue into a whole further study of wreaths, but was halted in the late '70s by new and even more compelling subjects on returning to Pembrokeshire. She was faced with the sight of dead foxes hanging in the trees, which was none other than a farmer's attempt to keep other foxes at bay from his livestock. Though still on the topic of death, her focus changed to setting the subject within a landscape.

The move to Pembrokeshire to a cottage set in two acres, in stunningly beautiful remoteness, is a powerfully significant factor underlying her choice of subject and the quality and quantity of workmanship with which they are expressed. This distant location enables both her and Denys to have a pleasantly disciplined routine and a largely uninterrupted day. They both work all morning in separate studios. They break for a light lunch of homemade soup and bread; Eirian is a good cook. The afternoon includes a little gardening – she grows vegetables in abundance, which are enjoyed with good recipes at dinner. She does the crossword at teatime 'I feel the need to keep the brain working'. They are a close and supportive couple, each the mentor of the other. Work then resumes in the studio until it is time to cook in the evening. She has unbroken time to pursue and develop a topic, which she does with real craftsmanship.

Take, for example, snakes. Confronting her everywhere at Dinas Cross a major preoccupation arose 'I don't actually like snakes but there they were – so I drew them – and from this I moved to exploring them in myth and religion. This is a typical example of how I start with a matter of fact study and then develop through reading and research'. *Mandala* is the magnificent culmination.

Subjects such as The Creation never go away; a theme which in the 1960s was expressed by means of what she calls her 'jigsaw' technique. Hardboard was cut as a jigsaw pattern, which in turn was covered in fabrics of many colours and types.

The 1970s also saw a huge preoccupation with swans, many of which formed part of submissions to Vera Sherman's[26] *Contemporary Hangings* touring exhibitions.

Subjects of the 1990s 'series' include crows, doves, bowls of fruit, vases of flowers, landscapes and figures. Sometimes these are combined with painted surfaces thereby richly contrasting shine with the dullness of the wool thread. Frames are often planned as elaborate parts of the picture and other times disappear to reveal a powerful silhouette.

A lengthy project entitled *The Parlour* incorporates a meticulous composition of descriptive detail. A recent monumental work, *Woman with Lilies*, once again shows the artist's love of pattern and highlights her underlying ability to draw.

Works take anything from two to six months. The most recent piece completed in 2004 is *Primmy Chorley's Dog*. It took eight months to make, working six hours a day. It

represents everything that is remarkable about Eirian for it is a wonderful culmination of art, design and workmanship. It speaks too about her individuality and of her gentle, kind and non-material character. She says she has always made what she wanted to make in spite of criticism from the establishment. Possibly her fascination with things that relate to folk and peasant art, and of subjects that may seem hackneyed, were not understood by some people. Nevertheless the results of her independent endeavours in searching for merit in what she sees has yielded a rich body of work that commands admiration, respect and delight.

Above: *Mandala* 1995 Couched crewel wool, padded and mounted on board 122cm (48in.)diameter. Private collection
Photo: David Hankey

Opposite top right: *Rainbow* 1991 pencil and water colour pencils 26cm x 51cm (10in. x 20in.). One of a series of six.
Private collection
Photo: David Hankey

Opposite top left: *Ouroboros* 1991 Pencil drawing 46cm (18in.) diameter. One of a series of six. Private collection
Photo: David Hankey

Opposite bottom left: *Like the Waver of the Sea* 1991 Pencil drawing 43cm diameter. One of a series of six. Private collection
Photo: David Hankey

Footnotes

11 Denys Short Sculptor 1927-

12 Pictures for Schools Exhibitions In 1947, a painter, Nan Youngman, conceived the idea of regular exhibitions from which local education authorities and members of the public could be encouraged to purchase work for schools. The shows were organised by members of The Society of Education Through Art who were prepared to accept embroidery and collage alongside drawings, paintings and prints. These annual exhibitions were highly regarded as a major marketing outlet and the shows had venues as varied as the Whitechapel Art Gallery. Embroiderers included in the earlier years were: Eirian Short, Christine Risley, Esther Grainger and later Audrey Walker and Richard Box.

13 Jan Beaney NDD ATC 1938- See page 48

14 Julia Caprara NDD ATC 1939- Embroiderer exhibiting widely especially with '62 Group. Co Director and founder, with husband Alex, of Opus School of Textile Arts-

Distance Learning, London: BA Hons in Embroidered Textiles; City & Guilds Embroidery; City & Guilds Patchwork and Quilting.

15 Earl of Longford 1906-2001

16 Audrey Walker 1924- See page 36

17 Harold Parker 1896-1980 Sculptor and Head of Department of Sculpture Goldsmiths' College School of Art. Most especially noted for the design of the farthing coin. Husband of Constance née Howard

18 Constance Parker (née Howard) MBE ARCA ATD FSDC 1910-2000 World-renowned teacher and lecturer of embroidery. Author of nine B.T.Batsford publications: Design for Embroidery from Traditional English Sources 1956; Inspiration for Embroidery 1966; Embroidery and Colour 1976; Constance Howard's Book of Stitches 1979; Twentieth Century Embroidery in Great Britain 1981-86, four volumes

19 Christine Risley NDD MSIAD 1926 –2003 Well respected teacher and author specialising in machine embroidery. Lecturer, St. Martin's School of Art and Goldsmiths' College School of Art. Studio Vista Publications: Machine Embroidery 1961; Creative Embroidery 1969; Machine Embroidery – a complete guide 1973 (pb 1981).

20 Margaret Kaye ARCA 1912-1991 Her bold fabric collage pictures, exhibited in galleries and illustrated in numerous publications, influenced many embroiderers of the 1950s and 1960s. Altar Frontal for Epiphany Chapel Winchester Cathedral 1962

21 Kathleen Whyte MBE DA 1907-1996 Most noted Scottish embroiderer. Head of the Department of Embroidery Glasgow School of Art 1948-1974 and author of Design in Embroidery 1969 Batsford and three further editions. Founded the Glasgow School of Art Embroidery and Textile Group in 1956 eventually becoming the 167 Group now merged with Embryo and Seta Groups to become Edge (Textile Artists Scotland) in 2003. Obituary by Crissie White Crafts 1996 July/August issue

22 Needlework Development Scheme. Set up by J&P Coats Ltd of Paisley in 1934, and funded anonymously, for the purpose of improving technique and design through the loan collection, lectures and simple publications. Discontinued during the Second World War but re-opened in 1944 at the request of Glasgow School of Art. In 1946 an advisory committee was set up to ensure that embroidery collected was of the highest standard. The work was purchased both from pieces acquired from overseas as well as commissioned from Britain. Originally planned as a loan collection for the four Scottish art schools it was soon extended and by 1950 schools and colleges throughout Britain could borrow work free of charge. During 1949-1954 Dorothy Alsopp was 'expert in charge' and leaflets were published for all those who asked for them. She was succeeded in 1955-61 by Iris Hills. The scheme closed in 1961 and the collection divided between twenty-five institutions, including the art colleges at Dundee, Aberdeen, Glasgow and Edinburgh, the V&A, the Scottish National Museum, Paisley Museum & Art Galleries and the Embroiderers' Guild. Descriptions of all these disbursed collections are documented in the project database of Scottish Textile Heritage Online – see Chapter 'Where to see Embroidery' – which reunites the collection 'virtually' for the first time

23 The Embroiderers' Guild. Founded in 1906. Headquarters Apartment 41 Hampton Court Palace, Surrey, England

24 Royal School of Needlework. Founded 1872. Headquarters Apartment 12a Hampton Court Palace, Surrey, England

25 Jeff Koons 1955- American Post Modernism

26 Vera Sherman NDD 1917- Organiser of touring exhibitions of 'Contemporary Hangings', 'Fabric and Thread' and 'Contemporary Pictures in Fabric and Thread' from 1965-76.
Author of Wall Hangings of Today Mills & Boon London 1972

Photo: Denys Short

AUDREY WALKER

1928	Born Cumbria 3 July
1944 – 48	Edinburgh College of Art Diploma in Art
1948 – 51	Slade School of Art Diploma in Fine Art
1951 – 54	Leeds Girls High School Art Teacher
1954 – 57	South Hampstead High School Art Teacher
1959 – 66	Parliament Hill Comprehensive School Head of Art Department
1966 – 75	Whitelands College, Principal Lecturer in Painting
1975 – 88	Goldsmiths' College School of Art Head of Department of Embroidery/Textiles
1973 –	Speaker/Teacher at Conferences and Textiles Summer Schools including Aberystwyth Arts Centre, Barry Summer School
1973 – 91	Examining in numerous institutions of higher education for the BA Hons. and MA in Textiles/Embroidery/Tapestry; B.Ed Art; City & Guilds Advanced Diploma
1975 – 94	Visiting Lecturer at colleges, polytechnics, and universities throughout the UK, including: University of Ulster. University of London Institute of Education. Royal College of Art.Glasgow School of Art. Exeter College of Art. In the USA: Boston University. Washington University St Louis. Cranbrook Academy Detroit
1979 – 86	Member CNAA Fashion/Textiles Board Vice Chair 1984-86
1980 – 82	Member, Crafts Council Textiles Panel Member Crafts Council Education Panel
1983	Profile *World of Embroidery* Summer issue
1884 – 86	Chairman, Association of Heads of Textiles & Fashion Degree Courses
1985 – 87	Governor, Loughborough College of Art and Design
1991	Haystack Mountain School of Crafts Maine USA Resident Artist
1993	MBE for Services to Art especially Embroidery
1993 – 97	Chair Fishguard Arts Society Co-ordinator, *Last Invasion Tapestry* Project Fishguard
1994 – 98	Member Arts Council of Wales Crafts Board
1997	Crafts Magazine March/April issue *Sources of Inspiration* by Pamela Johnson
1988	Retirement from Goldsmiths' College and move to Pembrokeshire
1998 – 99	Chair Arts Council of Wales. Crafts Advisory Panel. Member Arts Council of Wales. Artform Development Committee
1998 –	Chair Fishguard Invasion Centre Trust Ltd
1999	Profile *World of Embroidery* March issue
1999	Shared in three person *Insights* exhibition Barbican Centre London and Shipley Art Gallery Gateshead *Fiberarts* USA Nov/Dec issue
2002	Honorary Fellow of University of Wales Cardiff
2000 – 02	Solo exhibition The Gallery Ruthin Craft Centre and U.K tour accompanying publication *Audrey Walker* Ruthin Craft Gallery
2002 – 03	Specialist Advisor textiles Arts Council of Wales
2003 –	Chair '62 Group of Textile Artists
1966 – 2005	Monumental number of group exhibitions in Britain and overseas
	Work in Public Collections Australia, Canada, Eire, Italy, USA and UK

Right: *Who's There?* (detail) 1999 Hand and Machine embroidery. Private collection 24cm x 15cm (9in. x 6in.)

Audrey Walker

There is little doubt that Audrey Walker's artistic achievement in stitched textiles - embroidery - equals or surpasses much that is applauded and exhibited as Fine Art. Her work is, however, not eligible for most exhibitions because it is made with needle and thread on cloth rather than with paint on canvas. An ironic situation given that, along with others included in this volume, her training was in Fine Art – she has simply added the riches of an alternative expression to this initial pursuit.

The enduringly powerful embroidery that we see today has evolved from childhood influences and a significant art school education, which have been directed into a totally focussed way of life. The trigger for all her work is direct observation of a landscape, a still life or the human form. It may be just a fleeting moment observed or a sensation of light or even sometimes words or phrases all quickly scribbled or written down – all saved in a pool of memory until revived and gathered together.

An only child born into a working class home in Cumbria to a mother who made everything, from their clothes to the rugs on the floor and, most significantly, embroidered beautifully. A lasting example is a set of four large silk pictures worked during the last World War by her mother for her trousseau to adorn the family living room. These now have pride of place in Audrey's sitting room. It was an age of thrift and she recalls being surrounded by people making things. Even her invalid father who died when she was eleven was a keen amateur watercolour painter.

So to up to the age of sixteen, when Audrey embarked on her four year Diploma at Edinburgh College of Art, she regarded embroidery as firmly in the category of a domestic hobby and at that time saw her mother's pieces as being of no great importance. The first two years of study, much like the courses in England at this time, covered general art

Opposite: *Walk to the Quiet Valley* 1991. Hand and machine embroidery on an old Welsh quilt. Private collection USA

Below: *Still Life* 1993. Hand embroidery on mixed fabrics. Private collection Photo: Michael Wicks

and design followed by two specialist years; for Audrey these were in Painting. The first child on either side of the family to go away to college and, though often accompanying her mother to her evening classes, she had never been inside an art gallery and says 'I had no idea how to behave in one'.

Clearly the results of the Edinburgh years were above average because she won a scholarship to the Slade School of Art to paint. Incidentally in her final year, 1951, she won the prize for the best painting of a head. She was just a little over twenty. For the next three years she was embarking on the rigorous five days a week discipline of drawing and painting from a model. This fundamental study of the figure, though appearing to lie somewhat dormant in her full-time teaching years, re-emerged with captivating power in the 1990s on early retirement. What one witnesses today is an unending flow of highly individually perceived life studies. She draws insatiably, in particular the figure, resulting in a huge resource of drawings. In spite of all her deadlines for commissions, for exhibition pieces, for her committee work as Chairman of the '62 Group[32]; she says she joins a drawing group every Friday in order to draw the figure. Standing in her small but well lit studio – no more than a large garage - she brings out sheet after sheet of figure studies which she mentally 'banks'. When planning an embroidery she never works directly from a particular drawing but instead retrieves images from her subconscious, re-depicting, in order to take on the subject of the piece. She especially loves to explore expressions which suggest 'secretiveness, a sense of unease or something hidden' and will also study avidly how past masters such as the Dutch, for example Vermeer, convey senses such as concealment. In her words 'seen and remembered' would seem to sum up the stages of her work; perception, drawing, mental and physical storage of the image, and finally the rebirth for a subject such as *No Evil* 2003.

What is also evident is a very personal stylisation of scores of drawings owing great allegiance to the early Italian renaissance painter Piero della Francesca[27] whose work she saw and studied whilst at the Slade. Drawings of heads that precede the glorious Gaze series of 1999 provide a fine example.

If her use of the drawn line is sensitive so too is her use of colour. It is extraordinarily delicate and magically composite.

Left: *Beach Woman,* 1995-96. Hand and machine embroidery on calico. Private collection

Below: detail of *Beach Woman* 1995-96. Hand and machine embroidery on calico

Opposite above: *Life is Just Another Bowl of Cherries,* 1996. Hand embroidery on 1930s tablecloth worked by artist's mother. Collection Bedfordshire County Council

Opposite below: detail of *Life is Just Another Bowl of Cherries*, 1996. Hand embroidery by the artist on a table cloth worked by the artist's mother

Layers of cloth are applied, sometimes over-laid with chiffon, into which she works with hand and or machine stitching. Every thread mark forms part of a surface of subtle combinations of colour construction. During her Slade years she was particularly influenced by William Coldstream's[28] highly disciplined approach to drawing. She also remembers Victor Pasmore's[29] talks to students, as he was making radical changes to his own work, from his seductive domestic interiors and landscapes towards abstraction and construction; the great colourist who, in her words, 'was young and extraordinary'. He was using paint at that time to depict his domestic interiors with layers of thin oil colour resulting in surfaces of captivating beauty.

She left art school as a painter with no practice of textiles. She retired after thirty-seven years of full time teaching with, not only her own strength as an artist undiminished, but to which she had added a fully recognised reputation as an embroiderer. The inclusion of textiles into her life came with her first post as the junior art teacher at Leeds Girls High School where she had to teach weaving and some embroidery as well as painting.

She reminds us that throughout the 1950s and much of the early 1960s there was very little teaching material available in embroidery and most teachers were heavily dependent on sources such as The Needlework Development Scheme[22] and the Embroiderers' Guild[23], both of which she says 'enabled the teacher to be one step ahead of the pupils'.

The real moment of seduction for the craft of embroidery came as a result of a move to teach in London. After a post at South Hampstead High School came the second appointment at Parliament Hill School which proved to be the catalyst where, not only was the subject included within the art department, but the school received students in training from the department of embroidery from Goldsmiths' College School of Art. In its turn this also brought the college assessor who happened to be none less than the now legendary Mrs Parker[18]. Like Eirian Short[30] and many others at this time, she found the fabric collage pictures produced by Margaret Kaye[20] to

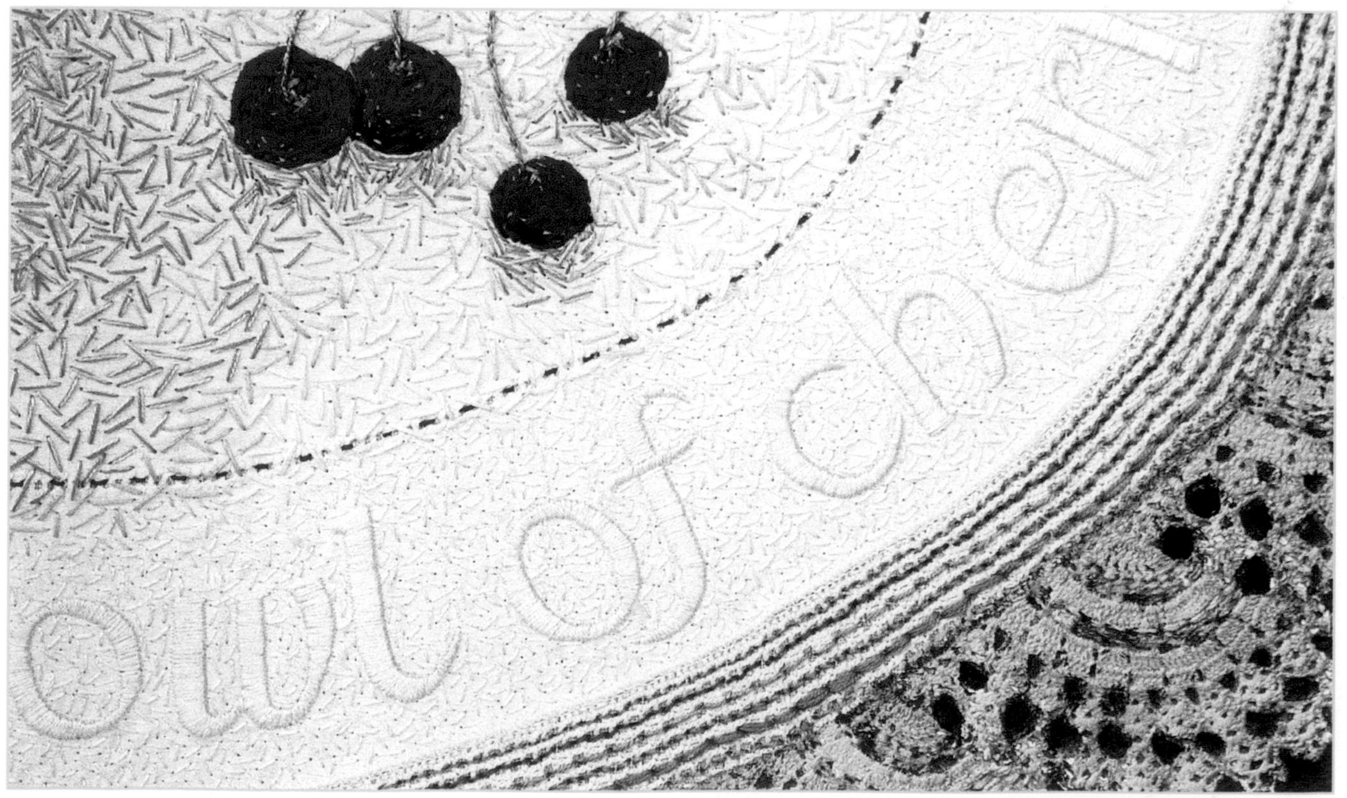
owl of cher

have a freedom of both subject and style unlike anything prescribed in the Goldsmiths' courses or the Slade dogma 'where you did as you saw'. The excitement of this refreshingly different approach was such that Audrey recalls going into John Lewis on the way home and buying every colour of net in order to start making her own bold gestural statements in fabric; often too breaking away from her well practiced world of the figure or the portrait in favour of landscapes and the abstract. Early results were not for exhibition but were given to friends.

Wishing to add the techniques of embroidery to her skills she joined a weekly evening class for two years taught by Margaret Nicholson[31]. These classes were held at the Embroiderers' Guild Headquarters and were her introduction to the resources of the Guild. It was there that she first saw work by professional embroiderers – the members of the '62 Group[32].

The next catalyst was the conclusion of teaching at Parliament Hill School and the start of a Lectureship in Painting at Whitelands College of Education, London. Significantly the curriculum included the teaching of embroidery under Jan Beaney[23]. In spite of this teaching role her own work continued depicting landscapes, still lifes and the major 1973 commission '*1000 Years of Monarchy*' for the Pump Room in Bath. Thoroughly researched, beautifully worked in appliqué and hand embroidery, it still attracts a great deal of admiration and gives much delight.

Then starts a period of considerable change in the embroidery world. Not simply that Constance Parker retires from leading the department of embroidery at Goldsmiths' College in 1975 and Audrey Walker is chosen to succeed her, but it is a time when the qualification of Diploma in Art and Design is superseded by the BA(Hons). Encouraged by this new degree status for embroidery and supported by her Principal she seized the opportunity to look afresh at possible ways of pushing out the boundaries of a craft discipline which to date had been technically, classically and historically contained. This move was also taking place to a lesser degree in the other three BA validated colleges in England; Manchester College of Art & Design (now Manchester Metropolitan University), Loughborough School of Art (now known as Loughborough College of Art and Design) and incidentally with the embroidery department (now renamed Mixed Media), Birmingham Polytechnic (now Birmingham Institute of Art & Design); and in Scotland at Glasgow School of Art and the one in Northern Ireland now under the aegis of University of Ulster at Belfast.

There were times during this period of thirteen years at Goldsmiths' College that she admits to envying the students at times 'they had time to do it and I didn't' yet on the other hand she recognises that teaching did feed into her own work. Students explored subjects that she would not have considered. This was also the beginning of an era when the Crafts Council[24] was backing craft as an art and objects no longer had to be 'useful'.

The publication in 1982 of *The Subversive Stitch* by Rozsika Parker was instrumental in directing Audrey to look again at her mother's embroidery, which years ago she had dismissed and for which she felt a sense of guilt. These were pieces that had been done at a time when she could recall her mother enquiring why it was that Audrey always had her head in a book when she could instead be doing something useful like embroidery. The combination of these two influences resulted in pieces which very often included applying an actual piece of her mother's embroidery to her own work. For instance embroidered table linen was incorporated into a picture and Audrey would add her own embroidery with great visual effect while at the same time making a mild

Above opposite: Drawings on Studio Wall. Mixed media. Various years. Photo: Philip Clarke

Opposite far left: Study for *The Pieta* 1998. Graphite. Photo: Philip Clarke

Opposite left: *Portrait of Rozanne Hawksley,* 1999. Graphite 76cm x 56cm (30in. x 22in.)

Right: *Gaze,* 1999. Hand and machine embroidery on mixed fabrics. Private collection Photo: Philip Clarke

Opposite left: *Gaze IV*, 1999. Hand and machine embroidery on mixed fabrics. 35 x 30 cm (14in. x 12in.) Private collection Photo: David Hankey

Top left: *Getting In*, 2002. Hand and machine embroidery on mixed fabrics. Private collection Photo: Philip Clarke

Top right: *Night Window*, 2001. Hand and machine embroidery. 92cm x 67cm (36in. x 26in.) 'Red – the colour of lips, nails, nipples, all prompting ideas of seduction and temptation'. Private collection. Photo: David Hankey

Above: Study for *Observed Incident*, 2001/2. Graphite and chalk. Photo: Philip Clarke

political comment. Delightful works such as her 1982 *Life is Just a Bowl of Cherries* belongs to this period.

There is no doubt that she is an organised person dealing day to day with diverse requests to make or do things, such as taking a major role in the funded community project *The Last Invasion Embroidery* at Fishguard. Appearing calm and always kind and gentle, she manages to prevent these demands from diminishing the true uniqueness of her art.

The surfaces flow; they are stitched as if she is drawing. The direction of each stitch coming only from someone who has used pencil and brush so extensively. Most work depends on a combination of both hand and machine stitching. Looking at the vastness of the task of building up an area with stitch she says she sees a positive side to what may appear boring because this gives her time to reflect on the work as she progresses. For her it is a necessary and fascinating process. She is completely engaged when the work contains a figure or face. Holidays in Greece provided her with two thousand year old incomplete figures and scraps and fragments of the human

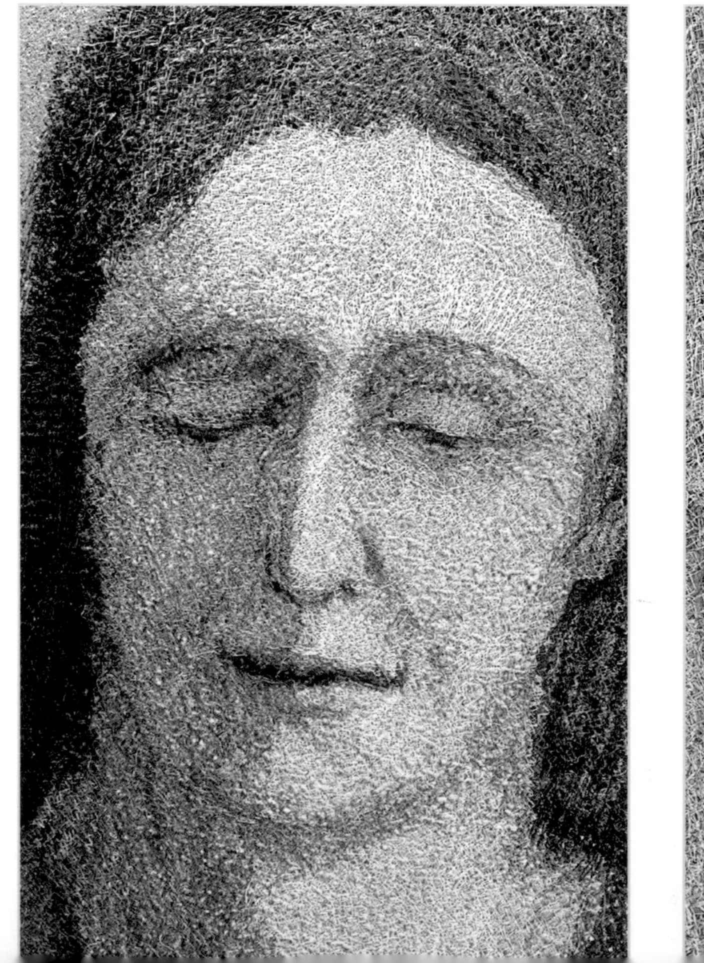

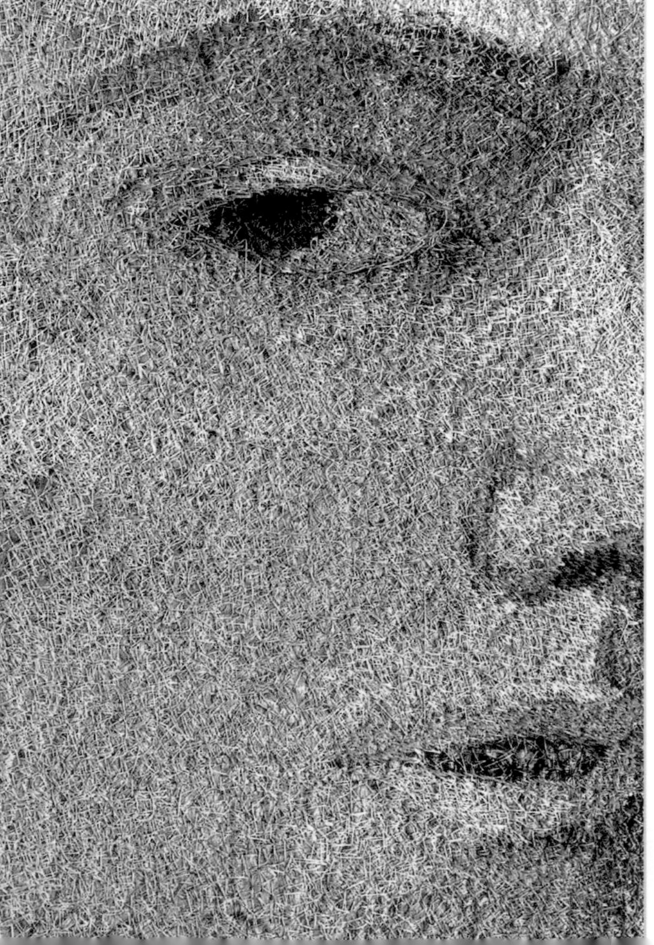

Opposite above: *Hear No Evil* 2003. Hand and machine embroidery on cotton fabrics. Private collection Photo: Philip Clarke

Opposite far left: detail of *Hear No Evil* 2003. Hand and machine embroidery on cotton fabrics. Private Collection Photo: Philip Clarke

Opposite below right: detail of *Hear No Evil* 2003. Hand and machine embroidery on cotton fabrics. Private collection Photo: Philip Clarke

Right: *At the Window* 2004. Hand and machine embroidery on mixed fabrics. 140cm x 75cm (55in. x 30in.). Photo: Philip Clarke

Below: detail of *At the Window – Dusk* 2004. Hand and machine embroidery on mixed fabrics. Photo: Philip Clarke

face or form, which she says 'all these years later still look at you'. For her the strong light always gave great meaning to the relevance of tonal separation.

Time spent with her and her work can only leave the viewer with great respect for her integrity. She has built upon her own endeavour. She is gifted and self generating in every respect. The recurring narrative throughout her work is the result of reading and observing; the entirely personal interpretation expressing so much with the minimum of material and technical means. She is not one who is caught up with the product rather than what the work is about.

The first solo exhibition in 2000 at the Ruthin Craft Centre, North Wales, of work produced since the summer of 1999, firmly acknowledges Audrey as a deeply thinking maker with a profoundly important place in the history of embroidery.

Footnotes

27 *Piero della Francesca 1410/20-1492 Most popular painter of the quattrocento*

28 *Sir William Coldstream 1908-1987 Studied Slade School 1926-29. Founder member of the Euston Road School 1937-39. Official War artist 1943-45. Slade Professor University College London 1949-75. Responsible for the Coldstream report which radically changed Art education in colleges*

29 *Victor Pasmore 1908-1998 Painter of the most subtle landscapes and interiors seen in England since Steer or Whistler. Later to embrace constructivist movement. Influential teacher*

30 *Eirian Short 1924- See page 24*
31 *Margaret Nicholson 1913- See page 6*

32 *The '62 Group. Founded in 1962 with the intention of providing a professional addition to an organisation of predominantly amateurs and viewed at the time as an exhibiting branch of The Embroiderers' Guild, now a separate group*

33 *Jan Beaney 1938- See page 48*

34 *The Crafts Council 44a Pentonville Road London N1 9BY*

Photo: Michael Wicks

JAN BEANEY

1938	Born Surrey 31 July
1954 – 55	Southampton College of Art
1955 – 58	West Sussex College of Art NDD
1958 – 59	Hornsey College of Art ATC
1959 – 64	Elliott's Grammar School
1963 –	Joined '62 Group exhibited widely in Britain, Japan and Israel.
1964 – 1968	Lecturer Whitelands College
1966	Author *The Young Embroiderer* Nicholas Kaye
1967	Married Steve Udall
1969	Birth of son Nicholas
1970	Author *Fun with Collage* Kaye & Ward
1971	Birth of daughter Victoria
1966 – 2004	In service training courses for teachers. Lectures/work-shops for the Embroiderers' Guild and other organisations
1976 – 2000	Associate Lecturer in Embroidery East Berkshire College
1975	Author *Fun with Embroidery* Kaye & Ward
1976	Author *Buildings in Picture, Collage & Design* Pelham Books
	Author *Landscapes in Picture, Collage & Design* Pelham Books
1978	Author *Textures & Surface Patterns* Pelham Books
	Author *Embroidery:New Approaches* Pelham Books
1978 –	President Windsor and Maidenhead Branch of the Embroiderers' Guild
1980	Presented the ten part BBC TV series *Embroidery*
1985 – 87	Presented *Creative Embroidery Strands* Pebble Mill at One BBC TV
1985	Author *Stitches:New Approaches* Batsford Books (Reprint Classic 2004) Presenter Strands on Bazaar BBC1. *This Morning* ITV. *Lifestyle, Wool Craft. Good Morning & Good Morning with Anne and Nick*
1981 – 93	Joint Chief Examiner for City & Guilds Embroidery
1988	Author *The Art of the Needle* Century Hutchinson. Video *Stitched Images*
1991 – 97	Verifier for City & Guilds Embroidery
1991	Co-author with Jean Littlejohn *A Complete Guide to Creative Embroidery* Century (Reprint.1997 Batsford Books) Video *Design into Stitch*
1991 –	Extensive overseas lecture tours and workshops include USA. Canada. Australia. New Zealand. Israel and Germany
1993	Awarded the Broderers' Prize
1993 –	Exhibiting Holland. France. Ireland. Japan. UK
1994	Awarded Licentiateship City & Guilds of London Institute(LCGI)
1995	Degree of Master of University, *honoris causa* Surrey University
1996	Honorary Membership of City & Guilds
1997	Co-founder of Double Trouble Enterprises (DTE) with Jean Littlejohn
1997	Author *Vanishing Act* DTE
	Honorary Membership of The '62 Group
1998	Co-author with Jean Littlejohn *Stitch Magic* Batsford Books
1999	Co-author *Bonding & Beyond & Transfer to Transform* DTE
2000	Co-author *Gardens & More & Conversations with Constance* DTE
2000 –	Artist in Residence Course Tutor East Berkshire College
2001	Honorary Membership of the Embroiderers' Guild
	Co-author *Trees as Inspiration & Giving Pleasure* DTE
2002	Co-author *New Dimensions & Double Vision* DTE; *A Tale of Two Stitches* & *A Sketch in Time* DTE

Work purchased for public and private collections in Britain, Canada, Australia, New Zealand, USA, Germany and Japan.

Contributor to numerous journals: *Pins and Needles. Radio Times. Textile Fibre Forum* Australia. *Stitch. Flying Needle* USA. *Embroidery* UK.

Right Detail *Cliveden* embroidery series 1970s Ground fabric painted prior to layers of hand stitching. Private collection. Photo: Dudley Moss

Jan Beaney

Through successfully and productively balancing a world of the artist with that of teacher and lecturer, Jan must surely rank as one of Britain's most influential figures in the world of embroidery. She continues to inspire not only through her own artefacts but by the continuous demand for her classes and educational publications.

Some fifty years have passed since she entered art school at sixteen - early entry made possible by immediate post war conditions – grammar schools in her area largely having been bombed - she was permitted to trade two 'A' level school years for the two Intermediate years of art school.

To a child whose major interests had been dance and athletics, even declining the role of prefect in order not to dilute her ambitions, the notion of going to art school was not a considered aspiration. Inspiration for a change of direction was largely due to her uncle Russell Brockbank the cartoonist [35]. He must have identified her early potential; and how right his encouragement and vision has proved to be. Her parents, of modest means, were very brave too for this was an only child whose headmistress, on hearing of the plan to leave school early, summoned them – and who in those days went against a Head's advice? – to say that 'they had to realise that the girl would be going to a life of sin and poverty'.

The initial art school year was in Southampton where the family had lived since she was nine. This was to open her eyes for she says that 'a first boyfriend was very important. He took me to the Tate Gallery where I discovered Matisse[36]. He also introduced me to the concept of tonal value – he would take me to the end of the pier and make me half close my eyes in order to identify shapes and tonal separations – I do still thank him for that.' Alas family circumstances were to alter the course of this momentous beginning.

'My wonderful parents did the most terrible thing. Father, who worked for Southern Railway, was promoted to Assistant Chief Accountant and we had to move to Horsham.' So at the end of this first blissful year she recalls being torn from all that seemed exciting. However, by the second year of her Intermediate course, her artistic progress was sufficient for her parents and uncle to support her endeavours in proceeding to Painting and Lithography for the next two years. Their only condition was that she should conclude these studies with a teacher-training year 'so that at the end of it all I did not starve in an attic'.

Painting and teaching remain central to her function but clearly painting was the catalyst for the way her embroidery was to develop. She says that 'one of the Painting tutors introduced me to the idea of thickly layering the paint as well as applying colour in glazes - just exactly what I do now with my threads'.

At this time too she became aware of the work of Chagall[36]. His work has continued to inspire and to move her not least when recently teaching in Israel and saw his *Twelve Tribes of Israel* in a hospital chapel in Jerusalem.

Also at this period, and typical within all one year art teacher-training courses, students were obliged to add a range of supporting art or craft skills to their timetable. To help in selecting this prerequisite number of subjects, it was the custom for staff to make presentations in order to 'sell' their specialism and gain recruitment. Hornsey College of Art was no exception. Fully engaged in her passion for lithography and screen-printing – layers of colour upon layer – Jan only reluctantly attended Eirian Short's[30] embroidery presentation and only then because she thought she might loose her grant if she did not do the rounds. Unable to resist she found herself enrolled in a craft discipline that would be with her for the rest of her life.

Jan's art teaching career commenced with the inclusion of a small component of both embroidery and sport. Of this first five years she recalls the most unique aspect being that the senior mistress was also head of the art department – a fact that brought huge respect for the subject. 'I thank her again and again for I really enjoyed teaching something which initially I had viewed as only a means to earning a living'. Eirian Short continued to be an encouraging influence and suggested undertaking the City & Guilds

Above: *Cliveden Water Garden* 1970s Ink & Pencil

Below: *Cliveden Water Garden* 1970s Ink drawing

Opposite: Colour sketch for *Burgh Island* series 1977-82
Photo: Dudley Moss

Embroidery course, which she achieved with Distinction, becoming ever more 'hooked' on the whole subject. From here it was embroidery all the way. Joining the Embroiderers' Guild[23] in 1962 she was greeted by the secretary of the day who exclaimed 'Oh! you are just the sort of person we need', as she enthusiastically welcomed her into the Wimpole Street headquarters. A focussed world of embroidery had certainly taken root and she went on to take Part Two of City & Guilds Embroidery and soon joined the '62 Group[32]. Today she is an Honorary Member having survived the rigours of membership for over forty years.

In the early 1960s she stopped painting as an end in itself instead allowing it to become a compulsive means to observe and record visual information. Lithography ceased from the practical aspect of lack of space in a small flat.

Today she has no lack of space. A beautifully organised workroom within her home in Maidenhead, overlooking a tranquil, well formed garden, it has specifically designated zones that enable separation of tasks; one large desk is for the computer and paperwork/administration whilst another

Opposite: *Passages of Time I Israel* series 1998 Appliqué, hand and machine stitching 51cm (20in.) square. Private collection. Photo: David Hankey

Top left: Pencil drawing *Crete* series 1990-92

Top right: Aquarelle crayon drawing *Crete* series 1990-92

Above left: Aquarelle crayon drawing *Crete* series 1990-92

Above right: Aquarelle crayon drawing *Crete* series 1990-92

is for the Pfaff 2054 machine and all fabric and thread activity. A third area is for designing whilst all supplies are neatly housed in bespoke drawers and shelves.

Also stored is an archive of material relating to work past and present. Viewing the quantities of sketchbooks, samples and teaching aids, spanning almost five decades, can only be described as incredible. It is a monumental output of visual and practical accomplishment, far greater in every respect than could be imagined.

From observed subjects she builds layer upon layer of hand and machine stitchery, each piece of work being a

sequential development of the last; evoking the nuance of her visual response.

Like many artists who combine teaching with marriage and motherhood – she has been married to Steve Udall for nearly forty years and of whom she says everything she has achieved she could not have done without him – inevitably there has to be compromise. However, taking as an example, an early series such as those inspired by Cliveden, there is no evidence of difficulty. Membership of the National Trust enabled her to walk a small son and daughter, countless times, around its landscapes. She could observe differences between mornings, afternoons and evenings and observe the changing light and colour.

Through her own words it appears that landscapes are her abiding passion. She will use phrases such as 'because of fleeting light' and 'because somehow I always come upon it with fresh eyes. Light on a surface or the tone of colour on a road when it has just rained makes me quite emotional'.

Whichever sets of sketchbooks or drawings are looked at, it is obvious that these are never literally interpreted. Perhaps this is most easily understood on looking at the huge series that lasted a few years in the 1980s based on journeys to Crete. 'It took me many visits to capture the essence of the place – there was so much different light to catch'. Or more recently in *Fleeting Moments* from the Tunisian series 2002.

Whether it is work inspired by the Red Centre in Australia or a journey to Israel – in order to undertake teaching invitations – she always feels the need to return in order to select and simplify again. She is very humble about the

Above: *Bright Morning* Crete series 1990-92 Machine stitching on soluble cloth to form a new fabric which is then hand embroidered. Private collection. Photo: Dudley Moss

Below: Gouache sketches Tunisian series 2000-2002. Photo: Michael Wicks

Opposite: *Fleeting Moment* Tunisian series 2000-2002 Machine stitching on soluble cloth 80 x 147cm (31in. x 58in.). Photo: Michael Wicks

Top left: *Australian* series 2000-2002. Typical sketch book pages Aquarelle crayons. Photo: Michael Wicks

Middle left: *Australian* series 2000-2002. Typical of the numerous sketches produced before commencing a theme. Aquarelle crayons. Photo: Michael Wicks

Bottom left: *Australian* series 2000-2002. Further Aquarelle sketches in continuous exploration of a theme before commencing the embroidery. Photo: Michael Wicks

Above: *Searing Heat, Australian* series 2000-2002. Machine stitching on soluble cloth thereby creating a new fabric. Size 82cm (32in.) square. Private collection. Photo: Michael Wicks

quality of her work saying 'I know I am not a Modigliani or a Picasso but I'd dearly love to draw and draw so that what I can see is reduced to a few lines which say it all. Then I might be able to eventually capture it in thread with the minimum of means.' The hand and machine-embroidered panels that emerge are the very essence of the image seen and assimilated.

Her visual search continues unabated. Her working partnership of over twenty-five years with Jean Littlejohn[37] (see page 72) continues with ever greater harmony and result. What comes next, makes one feel that she is right when she says, she has not reached her peak.

Left: *Edge of Shade* Australian Series 2000-2002. Machine stitching on soluble cloth thereby creating new surface 41 x 48 cm (16in.x 19in.). Private collection. Photo: Michael Wicks

Right: *Five Minutes from Home* 2004. Preparatory Sketches for new work. Gouache and Aquarelle crayons

Far right top: *Five Minutes from Home* 2004. Typical sketchbook page. Gouache and Aquarelle crayons

Far right below: *Five Minutes from Home* 2004. Typical page from a well filled sketchbook. Gouache and Aquarelle crayons

She now needs a bigger space of time to work on the new series '*Five Minutes from Home*' - the drawings are powerfully perceptive and indicate a new spirit for the embroidered landscapes to come. The dream to explore and derive a new body of richly layered stitched surfaces would mean cutting back on some of the teaching. She still makes about four overseas journeys per year, teaches one day a week at East Berkshire College, contributing to the three year Diploma in Stitched Textiles, together with numerous workshops around Britain. She is a skilled teacher, in great demand, and still getting great pleasure from the reactions of students. Her years of producing books, teaching aids and training teachers at Whitelands Teacher-training College, are all elements intrinsically rooted within her and give no sign of vanishing. She even recounts that when her own children were small she would offer to look after other people's in order to have more children drawing and creating landscapes – how else could she have filled her first series of books for Pelham!

In those early days she had made contact with a friend and headmaster, Philip Littlejohn, giving her access to another school and even more children.

The integrity and generosity of her character are borne out by the walls of her house, which are filled with the works of others; a testimony to sincere concern for the value of her contemporaries and the joy of embroidery.

Footnotes

35 *Russell Brockbank 1913-1979 Art editor and cartoonist for* Punch *1949-60. Regular contributor to* The Motor

36 *Henri Matisse 1869-1954 French painter and sculptor. Principal artist of the Fauve group*
Marc Chagall 1887-1985 Russian painter whose main works in Britain, a complete series of stained-glass windows, can be seen in the church at Tudely in Kent

37 *Jean Littlejohn 1945- page 72*

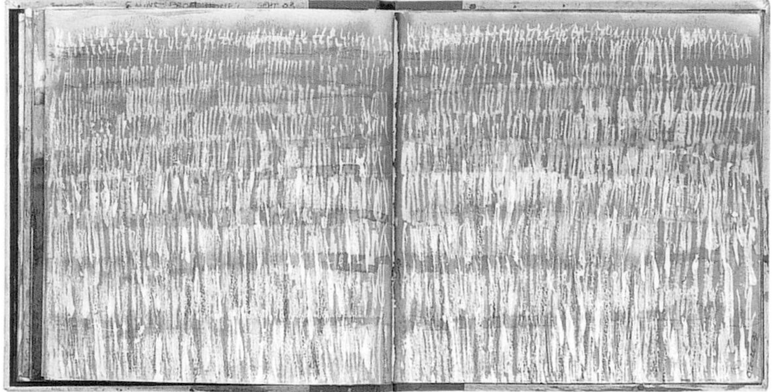

JUDY BARRY

1941	Born Derby 10 January
1954 – 58	Attended Joseph Wright Junior School of Art
1958 – 60	Derby and District College of Art and Design
1960 – 62	Hammersmith College of Art and Building, National Diploma in Art and Design Hand and Machine Embroidery at Special Level
1962 – 63	University of London Institute of Education ATC
1963 – 65	Full time Lecturer Derby and District College of Art and Design
1965 – 66	Year travelling in North Africa and Middle East
1967 – 72	Part-time Lecturer Manchester Polytechnic Department of Textiles/Fashion
1973	Married Paul Callaghan
1973 –	Established freelance design partnership – Judy Barry and Beryl Patten Commissioned works include: set of five Copes for Chester Cathedral; set of three Copes and High Altar Furnishing Schemes for Manchester Cathedral; series of twelve hangings Yeshurun Hebrew Congregation Synagogue Gatley Manchester; series of three hangings for the Royal Naval Training College Chaplaincy Tor Point Cornwall; series of four hangings for the Fire Service Memorial Chapel Morton-in-Marsh Oxford; also vestments, copes, ecclesiastical furnishings, throughout the UK
1973 – 75	Full-time Lecturer Manchester Polytechnic Department of Textiles/Fashion
1975 –	Senior Lecturer Manchester Polytechnic/Manchester Metropolitan University
1976	Author *Embroidery for the Church* Autumn issue *Embroidery*
1978	Author *Scheme for Manchester Cathedral's High Altar* Winter issue *Embroidery*
1980 – 89	Visiting Lecturer: Trent Polytechnic, Carlisle College of Art, Wakefield College of Art, Embroiderers Association of Canada Ontario, Royal College of Art, London
1984	Sabbatical term with Beryl Patten, ecclesiastical and other textile collections visited + machine embroidery companies in France/Germany/Switzerland.
1990 – 96	Fractional post one day per week Deptartment Textiles/Fashion and Multi Media Textiles Course, Royal College of Art London and fractional four days Senior Lecturer post Manchester Metropolitan University Department of Textiles and Fashion
1992	Widowed
1995 – 96	Co-author with Beryl Patten *The Rediscovery of Ritual in the Nineteenth Century* Slide Pack, the Manchester Metropolitan University
1999 – 2001	External Examiner BA.Hons Embroidered & Woven Textiles Glasgow School of Art
1999 – 2002	Jointly with Christine Weston, established learning manuals for embroidery machines, available for Manchester Metropolitan University undergraduates
2000	High Altar frontal to celebrate the Millennium for Auckland Castle/Bishop of Durham's residence Co. Durham
2000	Completed Research Supervision M.Phil/Ph.D *Machine Stitched & Applied Machine Stitched Decoration on Dress 1828-1910 Found in Museums in England* – Ann Gibson (see Bibliography)
2000 –	Member of Fabric Advisory Committee Manchester Cathedral
2001	Author *An Appreciation of the Work of Beryl Dean* September issue *The World of Embroidery*
2000 – 2003	External Examiner BA.Hons Embroidered Textiles and BAHons Woven Textiles, The National College of Art and Design, Dublin
2002 – 2003	External examiner MA Embroidered Textiles The National College of Art and Design Dublin
2003	Festal High Altar Frontal and Furnishings Church of St Peter Bolton-le-Moors
2004	Trinity Vestment St John the Baptist Barlaston Staffordshire

Works have been exhibited in major exhibitions of contemporary Church Art and are included in key publications on Ecclesiastical Textile Art

BERYL PATTEN

1951 Born Salford Gt. Manchester 22 January

1969-70 Bolton College of Art Foundation Course

1970-73 Manchester Polytechnic/Manchester Metropolitan University Dip.AD Textiles/Fashion/Embroidery

1973- Established freelance design partnership with Judy Barry
Commissioned works include: set of five copes for Chester Cathedral; set of three copes and High Altar furnishing schemes for Manchester Cathedral; series of twelve hangings Yeshurun Hebrew Congregation Synagogue Gatley Manchester; series of three hangings for the Royal Naval Training College Chaplaincy Tor Point Cornwall; series of four hangings for the Fire Service Memorial Chapel Morton-in-Marsh Oxford; Cope for Bolton Parish Church;also vestments, copes, ecclesiastical furnishings, throughout the UK

1974 Altar Frontal with Judy Barry, St.Stephen's Elton Bury Lancs

1974-1984 Visiting Moderator for City & Guilds Examinations in Embroidery

1974-2004 Lecturer/Senior Lecturer Bolton College of Art. Senior Lecturer Bolton Institute of Higher Education embroidery, visual research, and critical studies to Foundation, HND and BAHons Textile/Surface Design students, Admissions Tutor, Pathway leader BAHons Textile/Surface Design

1975 Red set of vestments with Judy Barry, St Mark's Oldham

1975-1979 Altar frontal with Judy Barry All Saints Elton Bury Lancashire

1976 & 1980 Three altar panels and East Window hangings with Judy Barry, St. Andrew's Droylesden Manchester

1979 Altar Frontal with Judy Barry, Summerfield School Oxford

1980 In service course for Wigan and Bolton Metropolitan Borough

1982-1989 GCE Examiner Joint Matriculation Board

1984 Royal Society of Arts Award 'Lecturers in Design' for study of historic and contemporary textiles in Switzerland, France, Germany

1985 Mothers Union Banner with Judy Barry, St.Luke Weaste Salford

1986-87 Birmingham Polytechnic Postgraduate Diploma in Art & Design History with Dress History as major study

1987-88 Four stoles with Judy Barry, Holy Trinity Berwick-on-Tweed

1988-1995 Consultant for British Council and Ministry of Education, Egypt in the development of the Girga five year technical training college in Sohag, Upper Egypt.

1995-1996 Co-author with Judy Barry *The Rediscovery of Ritual in the Nineteenth Century* Slide Pack, Manchester Metropolitan University

1995-2003 Cope, festal frontal, pulpit fall with Judy Barry, Bolton Parish Church

1996-1997 Manchester Metropolitan University MA History of Art and Design

1998 Contributor *The Watts Book of Embroidery, English Church Embroidery 1833-1953* by M Schoeser

Joint exhibitions with Judy Barry include *Contemporary Ecclesiastical Embroidery* Hereford Cathedral. *Crafts in Question* Whitworth Art Gallery Manchester. *Spectrum* Cookham Festival. *The Fabric of the Church* Bristol Museum. *Church and Secular Embroidery* York City Art Gallery. *International Festival of Embroidery* Clarendon Park Salisbury. *Artworks for the Church* Buxton Festival. *Celebratory Exhibition* Prestwich Manchester. *British Ecclesiastical Embroidery Today* St Paul's Cathedral.

Right: Four Dossal hangings for the Fire Service College Chapel Moreton-in-the-Marsh Gloucestershire 1987/88. Machine appliqué and machine embroidery 4m x 60cm (13ft. x 2ft.). Photo: P.S.A. Architects

Opposite: Detail of painted design for hangings for the Royal Navy Church of St Paul, Tor Point, Cornwall. 1982

Judy Barry & Beryl Patten

For over thirty years Judy Barry and Beryl Patten have responded to commissions to produce vestments, altar frontals, hangings and banners for places of worship. This unique partnership has consistently produced work that is totally appropriate for the setting. Their designs have always responded perfectly to the style and age of the building in question thereby achieving complete visual appropriateness. Any one of their scores of projects could illustrate this but perhaps none better than the *Dossal Hangings* for the Fire Service College Chapel at Moreton-in-the-Marsh, Gloucestershire, where the commissioning client is also so aptly represented.

They always visit the site together and share in the numerous preliminary consultations before jointly committing their initial response to paper in the form of drawings and painted designs. Typical design sheets, such as *Orphreys and Hoods for the Chester Copes*, give a visual indication of the proposed appliqué and intricacy of the machine embroidery that might follow.

Realising these ideas in cloth however is not a matter of slavishly transposing the working sketch to a larger scale. In Beryl's words 'it is not a case of taking a tiny thing and enlarging it. Students think that they can successfully take a small print and digitally increase it to fifteen times only then to wonder why it doesn't work. The subtlety is lost and very few people address this'. In the case of Judy and Beryl, once the design is accepted, they proceed by working directly on fabric to full size. A ground cloth of STAFLEX, for an altar frontal or a hanging, is temporarily pinned in place and worked on in situ using the working drawing for reference. Fabrics for appliqué are taken to the site where the backing will act as a temporary base while pieces are pinned in place. Shapes are freely cut and pinned according to the main compositional directions. When all the principal areas are arranged the work is taken

Above: Three hangings for HMS Raleigh, Royal Navy Church of St Paul, Tor Point, Cornwall. 1982. Artists working *in situ* on day two – placing of fabric pieces prior to machine appliqué; each 4.3m (14ft.) high. Widths 1.3m (51in.), 1.7m (66in.), 84cm (33in.)

Opposite top: *Altar Frontal* 2003 Bolton Parish Church. Fabrics mainly silks, cottons and wools, and some synthetic metallic fabrics, on a ground fabric of heavyweight hand woven Indian raw silk. Machine methods include Cornely, Irish and 12mm (1/2in.) wide Industrial Bernina stitching techniques. Photo: Stephen Yates

Opposite below left: St Peter's Cope 1995 Bolton Parish Church, Lancashire. Ground of Merino wool with appliqué of various fabrics – decorated with machine embroidery. Photo: Stephen Yates

Opposite below right: Detail of machine embroidery *St Peter's Cope* 1995 Bolton Parish Church, Lancashire. Threads include machine embroidery cottons, rayons and synthetic metallic yarns. Photo: Stephen Yates

back to the workroom where, with the pins carefully removed, it is then ironed ready for machine stitching. 'We use scissors as our drawing tools – directly cutting shapes to build a composition, like painting'. These simple gestural beginnings could be likened to putting down very broad brush-strokes. This stage can involve many visits to the site as did the preliminary work on the *HMS Raleigh Hangings* for the Royal Navy's Church of St Paul at Tor Point, Cornwall.

Not only do they share ideas but also all of the processes. A piece of work could pass between them many times during a working session; both of them extending the creative journey. They use the Bernina and Irish machines as well as the Cornely which gives a characteristically specialised form of chain stitch.

It is an amazing marriage of styles brought about by having the same colour sense and compositional eye.

The idea of sharing work began in 1973 when Beryl had just completed her Post Graduate course at Birmingham Polytechnic. It was when Judy needed help to carry out two major commissions simultaneously that the partnership began. A chasuble for Bolton Church and curtains and altar frontal for St. Andrew's Church Droylesden were the first two projects tackled jointly; these were large enough to merit setting up a working partnership. A perfect solution for two people with full time lecturerships, yet both with the artistic ability and motivation to apply their talent beyond the academic day; Beryl was teaching at Bolton College of Art and Judy at Manchester Polytechnic. It is worth noting that this was still a period in higher education when lecturers were not merely supported in the personal practice of their subject but were expected to be continuously proving themselves outside college.

Besides commissions for work all over the U.K., Bolton Parish Church has continued to commission the pair throughout their years of shared work. This demonstrates the value of a client who has repeatedly returned to appointing

THE DESIGN COULD INCORPORATE AN INSCRIPTION RELEVENT TO THE SCHOOL. LATIN. ETC. IN THE UPPER AREA. – PROBABLY IN GOLDS. LETTERING WOULD NOT BE OBVIOUS IN ANYWAY, BUT WOULD ONLY BE APPARENT IF ONE REALLY LOOKED FOR IT.
IN THE IMAGERY, WE WERE THINKING ON THE LINES OF SEEDS OF KNOWLEDGE GROWING – IN FERTILE SOIL ETC. IE. EDUCATION. THE "GROWING" THINGS COULD BE READ AS CORN OR IN SOME PLACES AS TREES – WHICH IN TURN COULD ALSO BE SEEN AS CROSSES.

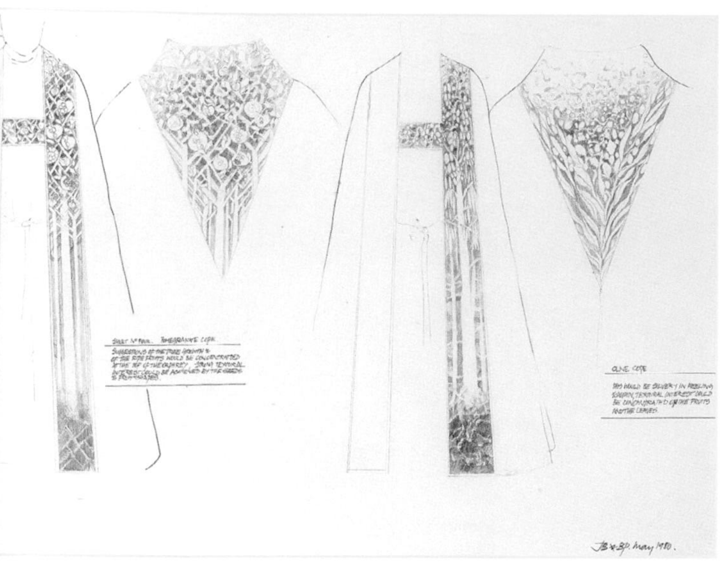

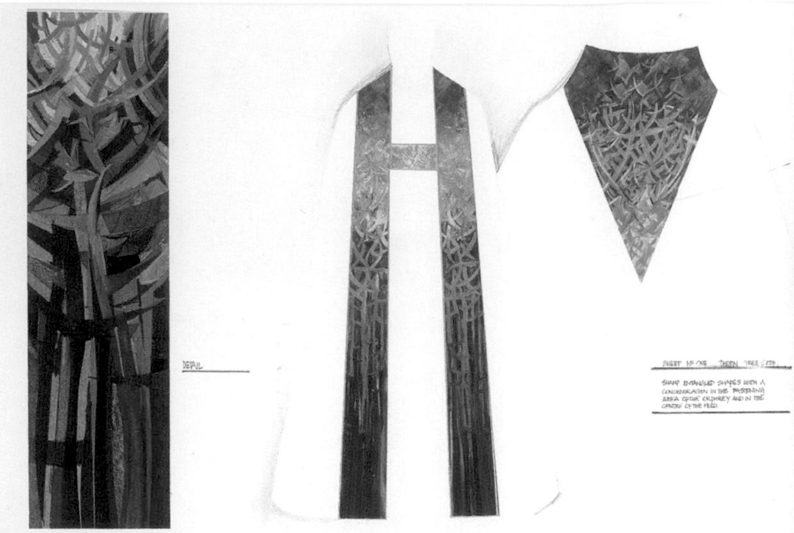

Opposite above: Design for *Altar Frontal* 1979 Summerfield School, Oxford. Photo: David Hankey

Opposite below: *Altar Frontal* 1979 Summerfield School, Oxford

Above left: Preparatory drawings for Orphreys and Hood for the '*Pomegranate*' Cope. 1982 Chester Cathedral – one of a set of five copes – the other four themes being *The Thorn, The Vine, The Corn* and *The Olive*. Photo: David Hankey

Above right: Preparatory paintings for Orphreys and Hood for '*Thorn*' Cope 1982 Chester Cathedral – one of a set of five copes – the other four themes being *The Vine, The Olive, The Corn* and *The Pomegranate*. Photo: David Hankey

Right: Detail of machine embroidered Hood of '*Thorn*' Cope, 1982, Chester Cathedral. Photo: Stephen Yates

the same artists. Over a period of some twenty years, starting from the 1973 chasuble referred to above, projects have included the *Bolton Cope* in 1995. This cope is particularly exceptional being based on research and development arising as a direct result of a sabbatical term undertaken by both of them some twelve years earlier. It contains the sum of their product based approach to teaching and design. They wished to re think the traditional shapes of vestments and bring them into the present. The cope offers an ingenious solution to providing a much wider use for an otherwise often limited vestment. The design solution in this case is a basic semi circular cloak which can be used on its own or can have the back and front orphreys attached; the hood is also planned to be optional. The co-ordinating *Altar Frontal* followed in 2003.

They work in a light, well organised, workroom in Judy's house which contains a work table large enough for assembling altar frontals, an Irish machine, two Cornely machines, two Bernina machines not to mention stacks of coloured

fabrics, threads and the vast archive of completed projects.

Together they have developed and sustained a consistency in both design and workmanship that ensures that each textile relates, not only one to another, but more critically, relates to the whole nature and spirit of the space they inhabit. Everything they make is always totally appropriate for the site.

This strength and the sheer number of works undertaken places their achievement firmly alongside other great names in church embroidery in the last fifty years; Beryl Dean[38], Pat Russell[39] and Hannah Frew Paterson[40], all of whom have also succeeded, in producing enduring great works of art for places of worship.

For Judy the route to embroidery is unusual. Failure to pass her 11+ exam resulted in a special opportunity, via the 13+ exam, to finish her secondary education at Joseph Wright Junior School of Art. Here pupils experienced rather more periods of art than would be usual and, more significantly, were introduced to craft subjects including embroidery.

On leaving school, due only to the encouragement of a local dentist for whom she was working, her art studies continued. He both took her to see the principal, who offered a

Opposite above left: Design sheet for *Altar Frontal* 1977 All Saints Church, Bury, Lancashire. Photo: David Hankey

Opposite above right: Detail of *Altar Frontal* 1977 All Saints Church, Elton, Bury, Lancashire. Photo: Stephen Yates

Opposite below left: *Altar Frontal* 1977 All Saints Church, Elton, Bury, Lancashire. Appliqué and machine embroidery in silks and wools with some synthetic, metallic fabrics. Stitching with Bernina, Cornely and Irish machines Photo: Stephen Yates

Right: Design for *Trinity Super Frontal,* 1985/6, Church of The Holy Trinity Berwick-upon-Tweed. Photo: David Hankey

Below: Detail of machined appliqué from central section of *Trinity Super Frontal* 1985.
Church of the Holy Trinity Berwick-upon-Tweed

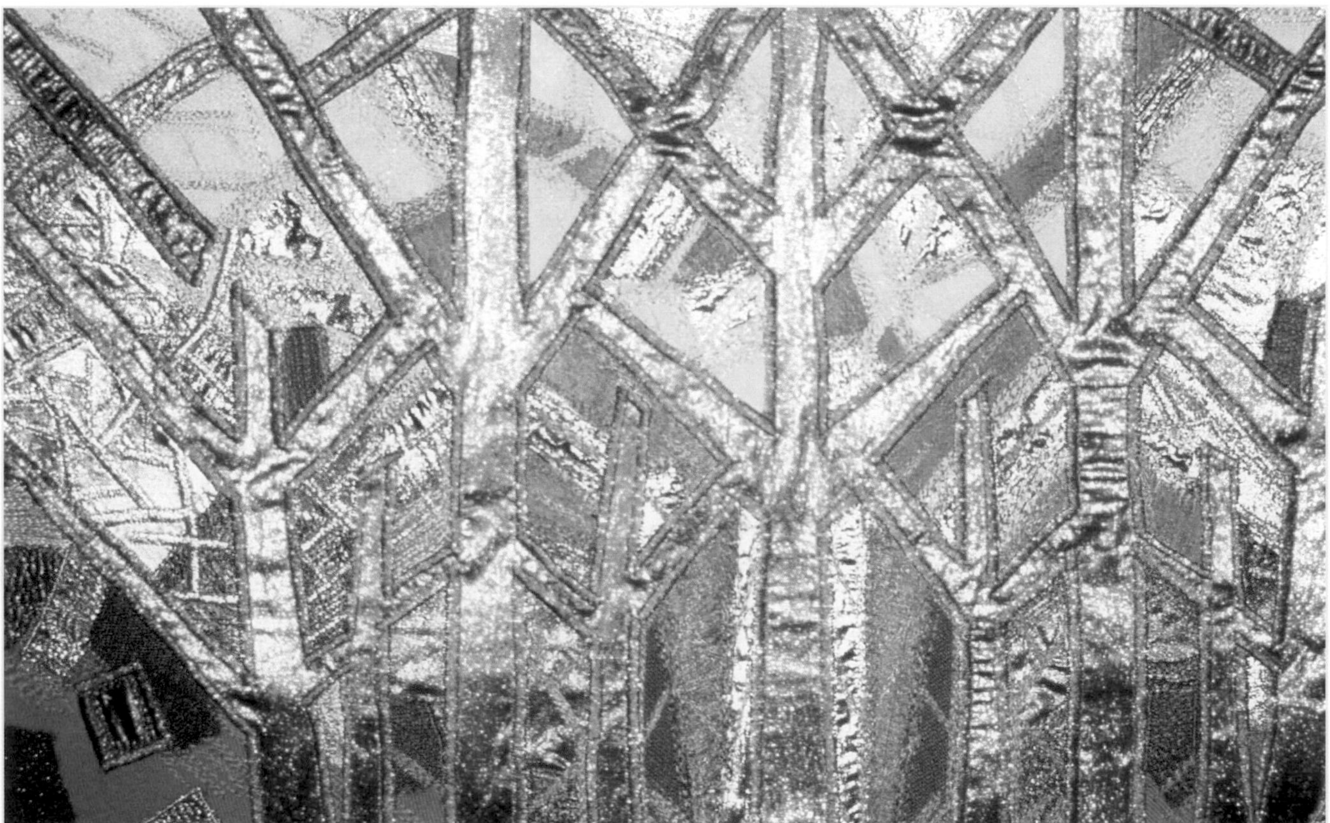

late place, and then persuaded her father that 'talent should be encouraged'. Subjects she most favoured such as lithography and pottery were already full; only dressmaking and embroidery remained with vacancies. She accepted both but disliked 'the discipline of those quarter scale dress blocks. Embroidery I accepted as I thought it had to be easy just making pictures out of material'.

Vacation jobs revolved around scenic art, which proved to be a strong enough attraction for her to seek a Theatre Design course for her NDD. Disappointed at the constraints imposed by the content – history of costume, architecture and scale models, she endured half a term realising what a mistake she had made. Seeing an exhibition in London of the best NDD work from all the colleges, and in particular the embroidery shown by Hammersmith College of Art and Building, she was determined to change courses. This she did and joined the small group of four or five embroidery students, under the tutelage of both Dorothy Allsopp[3] and Iris Hills[4]. Also of enormous long term influence was the major ecclesiastical figurehead, Beryl Dean[38].

Following her teacher-training year at the London University Institute of Education, she returned to the art school in Derby to teach embroidery for two years until leaving for a year of travel in north Africa and the Middle East.

Her long term involvement in embroidery started in 1967 when she began to teach one day a week at Manchester Polytechnic. She speaks of this inclusion in the new DipAD art education as giving her an enormous buzz. 'The polytechnic was wonderful and the students' work was hugely exciting. I felt alive to be part of the sixties'. It was here that she developed and extended her ability and interest in machines. The college owned two Cornely machines which were never used. Due entirely to her Hammersmith training, she was able to get them going again. Skills, which at the time had seemed unimportant, now not only became significant in her job but an enormous asset in responding to commissioned projects. A further consignment of old Cornely machines of different kinds was acquired by the college; at which point they released Judy for a week's intensive instruction at the London College of Fashion.

Encouraging the students to use the machines became central to her teaching at Manchester Polytechnic.

Her interest and expertise in ecclesiastical embroidery was also increasing. From the late sixties to 1984 students such as Beryl Patten, on the Diploma in Art and Design (Dip.AD) undertook an ecclesiastical 'site' project as part of their three year course. The years of teaching have been continuous inspiration to her but the most formative and long term influences on her work have been her eighteen-year marriage to industrial designer Paul Callaghan and the thirty year partnership with Beryl Patten. 'We respect and complement each others strengths and weaknesses.'

Beryl's artistic destiny was also less than assured. With no artistic member within her close family she was extremely fortunate to have an exceptional art teacher, Margaret West, at her grammar school, Pendleton High School for Girls. She recalls that she was at the forefront of art education in Manchester and had not only noticed Beryl's ability to draw but observed that in free time she was always in the art room rather than the common room. Identified as having talent at this stage meant progression to art school was now inevitable.

Content with her Foundation course in Bolton she assumed a continuation to the Dip.AD course at the same college. However, her tutor Chandra Chopra formed the next catalyst by encouraging Beryl to make an application to Manchester Polytechnic. Successfully enrolled, her future path now had its

Below left: Design for *Mothers' Union Banner* 1985 for St Luke's Church, Weaste, Salford, Lancashire. Photo: David Hankey

Below right: *Mothers' Union Banner* 1985, St Luke's Church, Weaste, Salford, Lancashire. Photo: Stephen Yates

Opposite above: Detail of machine embroidery on *Trinity Super Frontal* 1974/5. St Stephen's Church, Elton, Bury, Lancashire. Photo: Stephen Yates

Opposite below: *Trinity Super Frontal* 1974/5. St Stephen's Church Elton, Bury, Lancashire. Worsted wool ground fabric with appliqué of silk, wool and rayon fabrics. Machine decoration with Cornely, Irish and Bernina. Photo: Stephen Yates

final stepping stone. However her academic beginnings, never far away, have continued to underpin her teaching and her church embroidery. Not merely with the study of Design History but in the accolade awarded to her by the Royal Society of Arts in 1984. This travelling research bursary she generously chose to share with Judy who in turn gained additional support from Manchester Polytechnic. There is no doubt that this dedicated endeavour proved to be crucial to the breadth and success of her years of tutoring Foundation students.

Equally significant, in terms of a life changing experience was her five-year consultancy in Upper Egypt at Girga. The British Council, as one of the Aid Agencies, was contracted to support the building of a 'five year school'; in turn they commissioned Bolton Institute of Higher Education (being one of a small number of institutions that offered technical teacher-training) to plan from scratch – they in turn appointed Beryl for this unique responsibility. A 'five year school' means a secondary school with an extra two years added to the basic three; children of eleven would normally leave at about fourteen. The extra two years were to become a teacher-training school for those who would be expected to go out to instruct in colleges of Technical or Further Education. Over a seven year period she watched the building grow from foundations to a fully equipped building; and in which would develop her responsibility for a very important part of the curriculum 'Decorating and Advertising'. A modest title for a huge range of technical and art skills incorporating every kind of decorative wall finish (graining, marbling and painting for Mosque walls, to name some – no wallpaper – too warm!). It was a case of upgrading the course without being too European; conferring with the Department of Education in Cairo and requisitioning everything from drawing boards and photographic equipment, to screen printing materials. (Most of the papyrus used for tourist knick-knacks is screen-printed). There is no doubt that she contributed greatly in redressing the need for technical education alongside the stronger elements of training for business or the medical profession.

Without her quiet kindly disposition and a total ability to share, the legacy of some of the most aptly designed and beautifully made church embroidery to be seen anywhere would simply not have occurred.

Footnotes

38 *Beryl Dean 1911-2001 MBE,ARCA, highly esteemed designer/maker of church vestments and renowned teacher.* An Appreciation of the Work of Beryl Dean *by Judy Barry, September issue* The World of Embroidery *2001. Profile* Twelve British Embroiderers *by Diana Springall 1984 Gakken Tokyo. Trained at Royal School of Needlework. 1930- Teaching Bromley College of Art; Royal College of Art; 1939-46 Eastbourne School of Art; 1952-Hammersmith College of Art and Building; Stanhope Institute London. Numerous major commissions most notably five panels Royal Chapel Windsor. Author many books most notable* Ecclesiastical Embroidery *1958 Batsford.* Ideas for Church Embroidery *1968 Batsford.* Embroidery for Religion & Ceremonial *1981.Batsford. ISBN0 71343325 6.*

39 *Pat Russell 1919- Prolific designer maker of church vestments, altar frontals and banners most usually carried out in fabric appliqué. Renowned for superb site-specific design and workmanship. Profile in* Twelve British Embroiderers *by Diana Springall Gakken Tokyo 1984. Author* Lettering in Embroidery *1971 Batsford ISBN 7134 2642*

40 *Hannah Frew Paterson 1931- Trained and lectured at Glasgow School of Art. Respected for her teaching and for many embroidered works of art for both ecclesiastical and secular application. Author of* Three-Dimensional Embroidery *1975 Reinhold. Profile in* Twelve British Embroiderers *by Diana Springall 1984 Gakken Tokyo*

Photo: Michael Wicks

JEAN LITTLEJOHN

1945	Born Maidenhead 21 March
1963 – 66	Certificate in Education specialising in Art and Textiles
1966	Teaching Bracebridge Heath Middle School
1969 – 76	Teaching Alwyn Primary School 1975 deputy Head
1973	Married Philip Littlejohn
1976	Birth of daughter Hannah
1977	Part-time Lecturer East Berkshire College
1983	Associate Lecturer East Berkshire College
1985	Author *Every Kind of Smocking* Search Press
1986	Solo show *French Images* Docklands Cannon Workshops *Fabrics for Embroidery* Batsford
1988	Included in Video *Stitched Images – Find a Fact*
1990 –	Exhibiting *Art of the Stitch* Embroiderers' Guild
1991	Included in Video *Design into Stitch – Find a Fact* Co-author/Jan Beaney *A Complete Guide to Creative Embroidery* Century Joined the '62 Group of Textile Artists
1991 –	Talks Presentations Workshops throughout the UK and overseas including Israel, USA, Canada, Sweden, New Zealand, Australia, Germany.
1992 –	Exhibiting with '62 Group 30th Anniversary touring: USA. Canada. New Zealand. Ireland. Holland. France Japan Exhibiting *Out of the Frame* Crafts Council
1994	Licentiate of the City & Guilds of London Institute
1995	Daler Rowney Award for outstanding working drawings *Art of The Stitch* Kreinik award for outstanding use of metal threads *Art of the Stitch*
1996	Anchor Award for European travelling Design Exhibition Included Video *Inspirations – Find a Fact*
1997	Co-founder of Double Trouble Enterprises with Jan Beaney Author *Voluptuous Velvet* Double Trouble Enterprises
1998	Artist in Residence East Berkshire College Co-author/Jan Beaney *Stitch Magic*, Batsford
1999	*The Splendid World of Needle Arts* Group exhibition touring Japan Co-author *Bonding and Beyond* Double Trouble Enterprises Co-author *Transfer to Transform* Double Trouble Enterprises
2000	Four person show *3 J's and an A* Cojobah Gallery Birkenhead Co-author *Gardens and More* Double trouble Enterprises Co-author *Conversations with Constance* Double Trouble Enterprises
2001	Co-author *Trees – as inspiration* Double Trouble Enterprises Co-author *Giving Pleasure* Double Trouble Enterprises
2002	Duo show with Jan Beaney *Double Vision* Knitting and Stitching Show Co-author *New Dimensions* Double Trouble Enterprises Co-author *Double Vision* Double Trouble Enterprises
2003	Duo show with Jan Beaney *Double Vision* Cajobah Gallery Birkenhead Exhibiting Art of the Stitch
2004	Honorary Member Embroiderers' Guild Former joint Chief Examiner, assessor and verifier for City and Guilds

Works in many public and private collections including Southampton City Council

Right: Sketchbook page detail, showing *Cactus Study* 2000

Jean Littlejohn

The citation for the award of Honorary Membership of the Embroiderers' Guild, delivered at the 2004 Annual General Meeting, was for Jean Littlejohn, and read as follows:'In recognition of her outstanding service to embroidery as an artist, teacher, lecturer, advocate and as an Artist in Residence at Windsor School of Textile Arts.' To these words should be added any that express wholehearted generosity. Together they so perfectly sum up what Jean's embroidery has meant to a great number of people and form the significant platform from which her own work emerges.

It is of huge importance to note that she began her career as a teacher; teaching skills remain intrinsically part of her. Clearly she loves the world of education and was someone with an exceptional natural talent for the life of the primary school, achieving a deputy headship by the age of thirty. For ten years the school environment was her whole life, becoming even more so in 1973 when she married a fellow teacher from the neighbouring junior school. He later became a headmaster and currently is an OFSTED inspector. When she left full-time teaching to raise a daughter she saw it also as a chance to have time to develop her early love of stitching. This reawakening of a desire to sew imaginatively had its origins in Saturdays spent with her grandmother but had eluded her since both grammar school and college days. Her grandmother often used to take her to buy half a yard of fabric and a selection of carefully chosen stranded cottons. More importantly, she also gave her a small manual sewing machine when she was about eight years old; which remains a prized possession. This stimulation was a perfect adjunct to her week at a small church school, which she recalls as being a place full of poetry, dance, imagination and self-expression. She remembers enjoying reading or writing her own little plays and then making crêpe paper costumes for the characters. This inventiveness was to be somewhat put on hold during grammar school and college years. Needlework was a craft discipline with prescribed tasks and her wish to do art, as an exam subject, albeit with no element of stitch, was not permitted until 'A' level, along with History and English.

Art was the main subject during her teacher-training years but she recalls it as being a period with little instruction.

View from Elizabeth's workshop window – April 7th
Milkweed stem with fibrous qualities and dark discolouration silver grey with pink.
The milkweed stem splits in a wondrous fibrous way
Hints of pinks, hints of yellow and silvery blue which breaks down into almost silk like filaments.

Opposite top: *Hedgerows* sketch, 1979/80. Pen/ink/pencil. 15cm x 21cm (6in. x 8in.). Photo: Michael Wicks

Opposite bottom: *Hedgerows* sketch, 1979/80. Pen/ink/pencil. Photo: Michael Wicks

Left: Preparatory sketch for *Normandy Remembered.* Pencil & wash

Below left: Sketch for *Normandy Remembered.* Mixed media waxed scraffito

Below: *Normandy Remembered,* 1986. Hand stitchery on painted ground and applied fabrics. 76cm x 21cm (30in. x 8in.). Private collection. Photo: Dudley Moss

Left: *Bayeux* 1986. Machine stitchery on hand painted ground. 110cm x 70 cm (43in. x 28in.). Private collection. Photo: Dudley Moss

Below: Sketchbook open to show *Palm Study,* 2000

Bottom: Sketchbook open showing design from *Cactus Studies*. 2000. Wax resist, water based dyes, incised wax.

Right: *Istron Carpet – Magre series.* 1992. Machine embroidery. Applied fabrics on a velvet ground with couching and hand stitching. 96cm x 41cm (38in. x 16in.). Private collection. Photo: Dudley Moss

'Students were offered the facilities for painting and drawing but were expected to "just catch" techniques as if they were a cold. With the proximity of the materials, whether they be literary or artistic, it was hoped you would simply absorb the skill.' However she loved preparing for college plays and can remember spending a whole term making properties for *A Winters Tale*.

Making things came naturally. Her father was a precision toolmaker so she grew up with the attitude that you made everything and that always 'there must be a way of making it'.

Realisation of her dream to creatively pursue embroidery came about by a chance meeting. Whilst still in her primary school post, Jean was teaching teachers in evening classes at a local teachers' centre, in subjects such as how to improvise in the making of puppets. Also teaching was Jan Beaney[13] who was giving classes in embroidery. Once on maternity leave and into motherhood she was free to join Jan's day classes to embark on City & Guilds Part I. Thus began the now well-known professional partnership and subsequent friendship across both families, and for Jean and Jan. They are each the hugely valued and important inspiration for the other. Jean describes her parents as 'generous spirited' caring for their new granddaughter one day a week to enable her to pursue the course with dedicated attendance. She says Part I afforded her the chance to re-learn what, in her opinion, had been a lack of

structure at college. Part II was achieved in a year motivated by the need to work ever harder in order to cope with the sudden death of her younger sister.

Theme-based learning and motivation, that had so inspired her infant teaching, was to return. The topic of Hedgerows was the first subject that attracted her attention and in which she became totally absorbed. They were all around her as she pushed the pram around the country roads. Small sketchbooks and pens and pencils at the ready resulted in the most delightful and accurate recording of detail. These would then be brought home as inspiration for stitchery. As she says 'I really don't give up if I want to do something'. Though she thought her plan was to give up teaching, she found herself invited by Jan to help with City & Guilds classes whilst still studying herself and, after completion of the exam, to being committed to undertaking tuition for the same course two evenings a week for the next six years.

Teaching requests resulted from an even more unexpected direction. Lynette de Denne, the well-known teacher and secretary to the Embroiderers' Guild, had been asked by Marks and Spencer to find someone to write a chapter on Smocking for a book they were producing. Jean

Opposite: *Forbidden Fruit,* 2002. Machine embroidery on top of hand stitchery with wire and bead additions, 38cm x 29cm (15in. x 11in.). Private collection. Photo: Michael Wicks

Top: *Forbidden Fruit,* 2002. Machine embroidery applied to hand embroidery with addition of beads, 25cm x 32cm (10in. x 13in.). Private collection. Photo: David Hankey

Right: *Forbidden Fruit,* 2002. Machine embroidery applied to hand embroidery with addition of beads, 27cm x 32cm (11in. x 13in.). Private collection. Photo: David Hankey

Left: Sketchbook page for *Twilight Pall* 2003 Gesso, wax resist, pen and wash. Photo: Michael Wicks

Below left: Detail *Twilight Pall*, 2003. Discharged velvet with appliqué, hand and machine stitching

Below: *Twilight Pall,* 2003. Discharged velvet with appliqué, hand and machine stitching 2.5m x 1.5m (98in. x 59in.). Photo Michael Wicks

Opposite: *Zip Fastener,* 2004. Graphite/pencil on gesso textured ground. Photo: Michael Wicks

accepted the commission and worked diligently to produce a lot of ideas, demonstrating by means of drawings the many ways the technique could be adapted. She recalls that invitations to speak on the subject took on a domino effect.

There is no doubt that teaching is the *raison d'être* for so much of her own work. She has to be filling sketchbooks wherever she goes. Scores of them can be seen piled on her workroom shelves. One sees that the energy to perceive and record is driven by her teaching philosophy;'the need to enthuse and generate in others the spirit to pursue a subject or current topic for visual ends.' The pages are part observation and part refinement or exaggeration of the place or the experience. They form her main vehicle for exploring the essence of observation and memory. In some cases they are akin to a diary and she says,'the teaching part of me has to put the diaries into narrative'. She still teaches at East Berkshire College on the Diploma course and in addition accepts commitments to give workshops in countries that are culturally varied, geographically distant, and as artistically diverse as Australia, Alaska and Israel.

Holidays in particular have always played a big part in forming the basis of her subject matter, for in these small interludes she could find time to look and to sketch. Her first solo show in 1986 provides a good example of the results of a trip to France. A series, *Normandy Remembered*, of architectural façades, of jewel like intricacy, are depicted in machine and hand stitchery and form a related set of enduring images.

Delicate and sensitive handling of thread continued into the 1990's with a return to the subject of trees; this time ornamental and in some senses akin to ancient textiles and carpets in which she says she has always had a great interest. Titles such as *Turkey – Rose Evening* evoke the traveller's view of the country at this period. A more recent series entitled *Forbidden Fruit* falls into a period of low relief wall panels inspired by the prickly-pear cactus of the Arizona desert. Delicate surfaces of hand stitching in silk are then further worked with machine stitching and finally enriched by the reflective qualities of projecting beads.

Her personal output is teacher driven 'inventiveness of necessity' as she says. For instance a syllabus requirement could conjure up thoughts of fastenings and fabric joins. Her mind would then revert to all those laboured efforts of Run-and-Fell and French seams so rigorously learned at school and yet, suddenly, they are the solution to a student project. Jean's response would typically be pages of vigorous pencil drawings of actual zips and seams depicted by bold lines and patterns across a sketchbook page.

The embroidery that one sees is inspired not just by what she has seen in Tunisia or Greece but by the needs and demands of students. She says she never planned to go on teaching beyond the primary school years but pupils are as necessary to her drive to perceive as a visual subject in front of her. One needs little imagination to see that before she begins a new topic she is already visualising a sharing and imparting of the latest visual discovery.

Her workspace is small but crammed from floor to ceiling with materials of the trade and no elaborate equipment beyond both a Husqvarna and a Pfaff machine. That said the rest of the house is not dissimilar with every shelf and wall being completely filled with everything and anything that could possibly become a teaching aid or the springboard for a piece of visual energy – what else could one expect with a long marriage of two teachers?

Photo: Trevor Griffiths

DIANE BATES

1946	Born S. Yorkshire 18 April
1962 – 65	Barnsley School of Art
1965 – 69	Goldsmiths' College School of Art BA Fine Art/Textiles
1969	Liverpool College ATD
1969 – 70	Part-time lecturer Bradford College
1970 – 80	Member of '62 Group
1970 –	Full-time lecturer Bradford College
1971	Part-time lecturer Bretton Hall
1972 – 89	Barry Summer School
1978	Part-time lecturer Bramley Grange Leeds
1979	Part-time lecturer Woolley Hall Wakefield
1983	Part-time lecturer Goldsmiths' College School of Art
1987 – 88	University of Central England, Birmingham PG.Dip. Industrial Design Solo exhibition *Find the Painted Lady* Solihull Library Birmingham Fellow Royal Society of Arts
1989 – 91	University of Central England, Birmingham MA Industrial Design (extra mural)
1997 – 98	Numerous joint projects include *Fabric of the North*, *East Meets West/Drape and Shape*, *Speaking Out*, *Fibre and Fashion into the Millennium*
1998	Solo exhibition *Flights of Fancy* East Riddlestone Hall Yorks. Machine Magic of The Painted Lady *World Of Embroidery* November issue *Work Box* August/September issue
1999	Contributor to *F.E.NOW* summer issue Invitation Madeira Threads show Harrogate Dress for Marie Curie Charity Fashion Extravaganza
2000	Solo exhibition Dean Clough Halifax Invitation Madeira Threads show Harrogate Contributor to *Conversations with Constance* published by Jan Beaney and Jean Littlejohn Guest Designer at Halifax Courier Fashion Show Victoria Theatre Halifax
2001	Work featured on *Twisted Thread* website www.twistedthread.com *Live Lunch* show Yorkshire Television Guest speaker Goldsmiths' College School of Art *Celebration of Constance Howard's Life* Guest Designer at Wakefield Express Fashion Show Painthorpe Country Club Wakefield
2001 – 2003	Invitation to exhibit *Knitting & Stitching* Shows
2002	Solo exhibition Cannon Hall Cawthorne S. Yorkshire Exhibition stand ICHI Harrogate Hallmark Cards project
2003	Opus School of Textile Arts Summer School
2004	Profile *Workbox* June/July issue

Work in both private and public collections of The Rachel B.Kay Shuttleworth Collection, The Embroiderers' Guild, The National Association of Teachers in Further & Higher Education, and Bradford & Ilkley Community College

Work included in numerous publications. Lectures and workshops given to a wide variety of groups including The Embroiderers' Guild

Right: *Tinted Drawing* (detail), 1987, based on observation of dragonfly movements – one of a number of studies that became the inspiration for *The Painted Lady Collection*. 76cm x 56cm (30in. x 22in.). Photo: Trevor Griffiths

Diane Bates

Diane describes her work as 'sculpted body pieces'. In fact they can be seen also as exquisitely beautiful, wearable, embroidered garments and accessories. To be in the tiny rooms of her south Yorkshire home, where these jewels of creativity come to reality, deserves description. Dressmaker's dummies, clad with sections of richly encrusted machine embroidered lace-like fabric, inhabit every space where a human might have dared momentarily to dwell. When at home it is obvious that she has no other desire but to work. Boxes and boxes of threads and fabrics and beads and braids and out-of-season Christmas decorations bought from car-boot sales and plastic snowflakes from Poundstretcher and silly second-hand hats and crinoline net from Chapelier in Ossett and florist's cellophane and B&Q's industrial plastic tags and general paraphernalia bought from London's House of Troy and second hand doilies and so much, much more that the eye cannot take in. There is no room to leave your cup and saucer! What the eye can take in is her ability to do something so aesthetically pleasing and so immaculately worked from items of seemingly so little worth.

Maybe this comes from her parents who had to make a life from almost nothing. Born illegitimate to doting parents, she was raised until the age of seven in a converted double-decker bus which was parked on top of The Ram Jam near where she now lives. Her father, a farmer, had also been a wood carver for various Lincolnshire churches. Her mother, generous to a fault, knitted, sewed, cooked, gardened and competently handled the modest finances. Although Diane always says that her childhood was privileged because of the love bestowed by her parents she counters this by saying 'I learned so much so early about values, money, friends, relatives and how cruel people could be. I am sure that is why I have stayed away from marriage'. For example, as a child she could be in a world of her own dotingly taking her rabbits for rides in a toy pram, having first dressed them in clothes she had made, yet at the same time would have to cope with

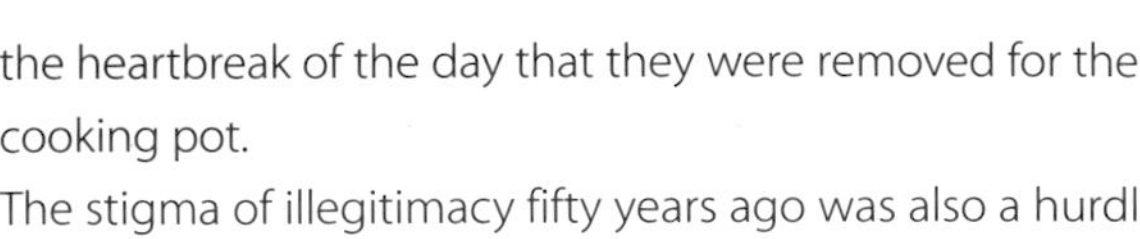

the heartbreak of the day that they were removed for the cooking pot.

The stigma of illegitimacy fifty years ago was also a hurdle. One story she recounted was about one of her primary school teachers who wished to adopt her. This lady hoped to succeed by making out to the local authority that she was a malnourished child and lacking in care, when in fact she was a naturally thin active youngster enjoying a healthy, carefree outdoor existence. Also, the head of her primary school went so far as to say it would be a waste of paper to let her take the 11+ exam.

The move to a secondary modern school saw her fortunes change. Her keenness to draw was encouraged and the entrance exam for Barnsley College of Art was supported. While at Barnsley School of Art she achieved her 'O' level exams. Her sights were focussed, however, beyond this. From the age of seventeen her heart was set on going to London either to Goldsmiths' College School of Art or Hammersmith College. Particularly favouring the former she remembers writing to the head of the embroidery department Mrs Parker[18] every week for weeks. 'Determination and my drawing got me in but only for the Vocational course.' The transfer to the Dip.AD. course came later only by chance. The Principal of the art school happened to see her drawing in a corridor, clearly impressed, said 'Go and get your A-level art and,

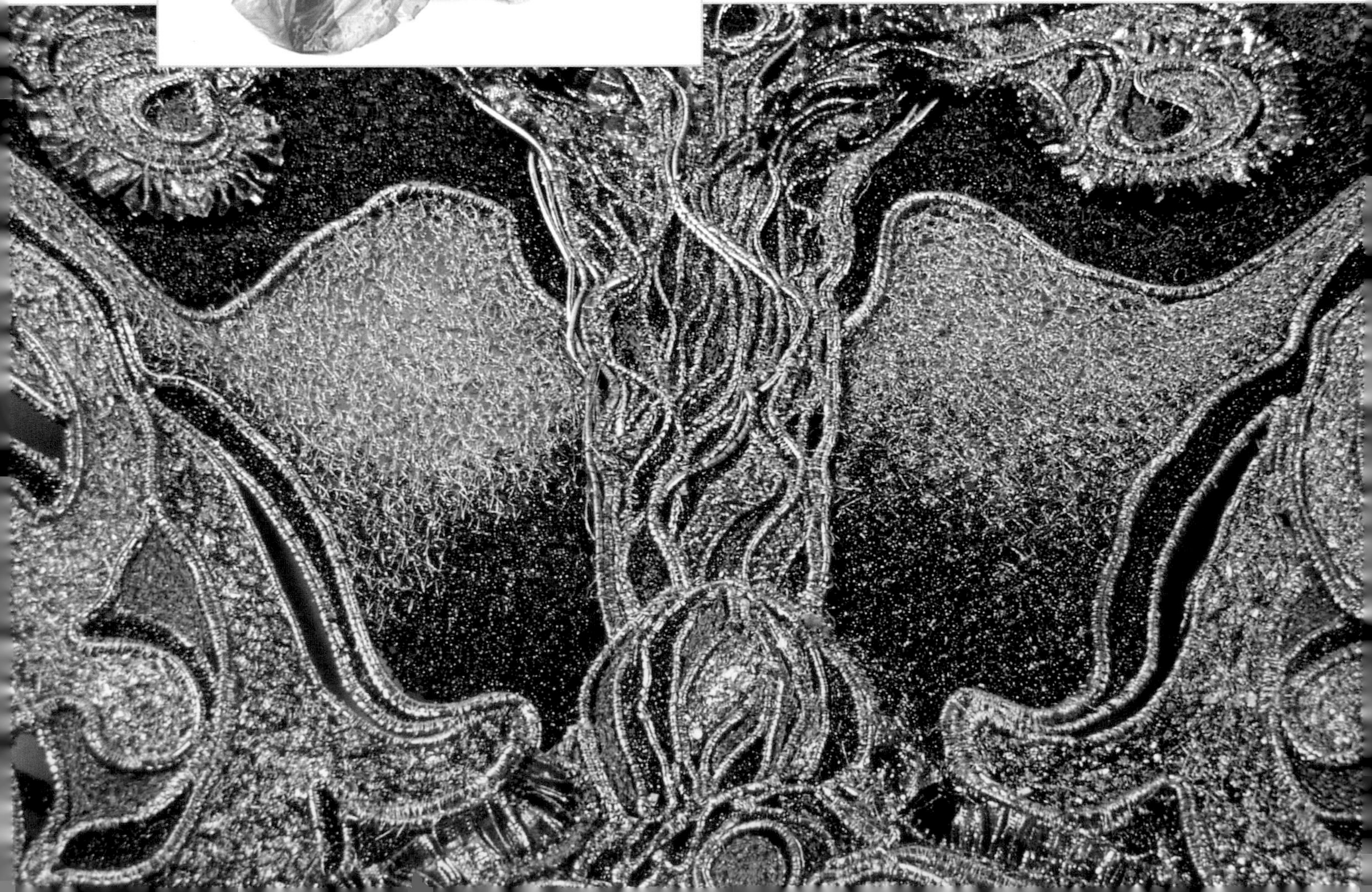

Opposite above: *Through The Lace Gates 1*. Blue and gold free machine embroidered bodice. Matching colour long tissue silk skirt. Photo: Trevor Griffiths

Opposite below: Detail of bodice for *Through the Lace Gates 1*. Photo: Trevor Griffiths

Below: Bodice *The Keeper of the Water Lilies 1*. 1997. Gold and bronze free machine embroidery mounted on a gold and purple short silk tissue skirt. Photo: Trevor Griffiths

Right: Tinted drawing one of a series of studies for *The Keeper of the Water Lilies*. 76cm x 56cm (30in. x 22in.). Photo: Trevor Griffiths

Right below: Design sheet for *Keeper of the Water Lilies*. Pen and gold ink. Photo: Trevor Griffiths

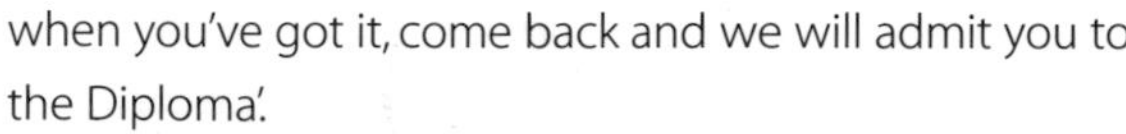

when you've got it, come back and we will admit you to the Diploma'.

Of the Diploma years she especially enjoyed being a student of Barbara Dawson[41] 'I so loved everything that sparkled and shone. I was fascinated by her techniques and how she did it. I still think of all that padded gold and curly purl'.

Never bitter about missing out on things and always ready to turn adversity into fortune she was prepared at all times to take on modest work to pay for her needs. 'I could

Left: *Through the Lace Gates 2* 1997. Free machine embroidery in gold and turquoise with garlands of gold beads twisted through the lattice work, mounted on a short gold metallic mesh skirt. Photo: Trevor Griffiths

Above: Bodice detail of *Through the Lace Gates 2.* Photo: Trevor Griffiths

Opposite top left: *Twenty Six Below* 1998. Made from a thousand plastic snowflakes which were cut up, placed as a repeat pattern on to a base of cold water dissolvable fabric and used as the basic structure for free machine embroidery. A thousand Austrian crystals were studded into the bodice, collar and the upper part of the full-length transparent skirt. Photo: Trevor Griffiths

Opposite top right: Back view of *Twenty Six Below.* Photo: Trevor Griffiths

Opposite bottom left: Detail of embroidery *Twenty Six Below.* Photo: Trevor Griffiths

Opposite bottom right: Tinted drawing for *Twenty Six Below* 1998, Pen and Tipp-ex, 42 x 30 cm (17in. x 12in.). Photo: Trevor Griffiths

not possibly write home for money so, Constance Parker[18], knowing my resources were minimal, paid me to clean her house and Barbara Dawson invited me to assist with her Chelmsford vestments.'

Of Christine Risley[19], another of her tutors, she says 'I loved her.' Christine, being so slim and fashion conscious, always wanted to bring better clothes for Diane. She and Constance Parker were always very kind and supportive knowing that she was missing home. Still very overweight from the primary school days, in their mistaken belief that she should be given extra food, she did succumb in her fourth year to buying a chic black gros grain suit from Deptford market with the will to slim into it 'I loved it – it had fabulous jet buttons'.

Christine's Friday evening classes meant that all her classmates were combining embroidery with fashion but she shied away from clothes feeling she was not the right shape. She felt that others, particularly Anthea Godfrey (née Nicholson)[2], Verina Warren (née Lynne Jones)[42], Carol Naylor (née Jackson)[43], had more of a fashion look about them. Though not in the same year group, she particularly recalls the talent of fellow student Margaret Hall-Townley[44].

Whilst taking her teacher-training year she discovered that she loved teaching. Ever since qualifying she has balanced a heavy teaching schedule, with the development of her own work and, not least, commuting daily for fifteen years to care for her sick widowed mother. This exhaustive balance continues today. She is a dedicated artist and teacher with holidays usually also spent teaching. Nevertheless, the wide number of people she meets through her work bring her enormous pleasure.

Before her mother's death in 1992 she had been given a sabbatical year 1988/9 and spent it achieving an MA in

Top left: *Camouflage 1*, 1999. Bodice in black and silver threads. Free machine embroidery. Note the gatekeeper butterflies with crystal eyes Photo: Trevor Griffiths

Below left: Detail of embroidery, *Camouflage*. Photo: Trevor Griffiths

Below: Study in pen and wash for *Camouflage*. 42cm x 30cm (17in. x 12in.). Photo: Trevor Griffiths

Opposite top left: Study in pen and wash for *Constellations*, 2000, Constructed from black sequin waste with the addition of black feathers and crystals. 42cm x 30cm (17in. x 12in.). Photo: Trevor Griffiths

Opposite bottom left: *A Little Black and Pink Number*, 2003. Corset and neckpiece both constructed from two layers of machine embroidery and embellished with shiny black beads. Photo: Trevor Griffiths

Opposite bottom right: Drawing with embroidered sample for *A Little Black and Pink Number* showing richly encrusted surface 42cm x 30cm (17in. x 12in.). Photo: Trevor Griffiths

Industrial Design at the University of Central England in Birmingham. Her final project resulted in the invention of a fastening system which lead to a successful patent application.

This new energy coincided with a particular drawing experience in 1987 gained whilst taking students on a field course to Duffren Gardens as part of the Barry Summer School in South Wales. Her own work culminated in a series of small drawings which she later developed into very large airbrush paintings; sometimes accompanied by text, which

she called *Find the Painted Lady*. Together with her students she witnessed a mass of water lilies and the timely arrival of dragonflies when the sun was at its hottest; their colour was electric blue.

These drawings lay dormant for almost ten years. The catalyst for their revival was turning down the chance of early retirement from Bradford College. She says it was like a 'wake up call'. Instead she was ready to rise to a new challenge and in March 1997 set out on a mission to produce 'a collection' based on the dragonflies, their secret garden, their journeys; slowly a fairy tale world was emerging in three dimensions. Making a conscious decision to use the machine, in spite of not particularly liking machine embroidery, she bought lots of threads and cold-water dissolvable fabric and made a start. Her personal method for interpretation of the large drawings meant working directly onto a dress makers stand drawing, not on paper, but onto the plastic base of the dissolvable fabric with a silver pen. Thumbnail fashion sketches follow from these modelled beginnings, allowing her to visualise the whole effect. In order to embroider, the fabric must be stretched in a circular tambour frame. She is the third owner of her Bernina Record 930 sewing machine, now more than thirty five years old and which still dutifully trundles through endless hours of straight and zigzag stitching.

As each section is complete it is removed from the frame, steeped in cold water to remove the plastic, leaving the rich surface of threads, cords and anything else applied.

Completion of the fourth garment in the series coincided with a great piece of luck. The college technician had just hired a photographic studio and a size eight, female model. His first project inevitably involved Diane's embroidery, draping it and providing a huge initial boost in confidence. Armed with these first pieces, she set off for the Madeira show in Harrogate to show the directors what she had done with their threads. They immediately offered to give her a stand of her own for the following year 1998. This also led to the 1998 article in Embroidery magazine. 'I started so humbly – Harrogate was the beginning for me. I had no great fashion show ambitions – I had not forced or manipulated anything; everything came naturally; things are simply growing and growing and it has surprised me.' By 2003 her range of swimwear was well received when shown at the Knitting and Stitching Show. This recent work differs technically from the earlier pieces in that she now works on a man made sheer fabric instead of the dissolvable ground. This enables her to heat seal intricate edges. The process of making small areas of embroidery and offering them up to the dummy is otherwise the same.

Even though she is now slim she has never wanted to wear any of her creations. The one exception is currently under construction; grey stitchery upon grey stitchery, encrusted with silver beads and awaiting accessories of a neck piece and matching bag.

Diane's 'collection' is underpinned by her ongoing research into the possibilities of inclusion of fibre optics into her use of yarn.

There are so many of her masterpieces in the house but probably the one that stays longest in the memory is the dress inspired by a Christmas visit to Austria *Twenty Six Below*. Constructed from 1000 Austrian crystals studded into the collar, bodice and part of the skirt together with 1000 plastic snow flakes (cut up and recycled in a repeat pattern to form the basic ground) evoke the sub zero temperatures. The cellophane skirt transports the mind to glaciers and the melting of ice.

Diane is never unhappy with her own company but being with others of a like mind will generally bring forth a torrent of conversation delivered in her inimitable broad Yorkshire dialect. Always characteristically delivered with a warm and wonderful smile from beneath yet another marvellous hat. She will tell you how much she still loves teaching and of how she spoils her students; how she does a lot of listening and of her enthusiasm for everything.

What everyone must love best is her honesty.

Footnotes

41 *Barbara Dawson 1922- Particularly known for her accomplished use of gold and metal thread embroidery. Author* Metal thread Embroidery *1968 Batsford*

42 *Verina Warren 1946- Noted machine embroiderer of landscape scenes. Author* Landscape in Embroidery *1986 Batsford ISBN 0 7134 4567 X*

43 *Carol Naylor 1946- Lecturer Bishop Otter College 1972-1997, noted machine embroiderer and Vice Chairman of The Society of Designer Craftsmen*

44 *Margaret Hall-Townley 1946- Embroiderer, lecturer at Goldsmiths' College School of Art Department of Textiles and curator at the Constance Howard Resource & Research Centre in Textiles, Goldsmiths' College, London*

Opposite left: *Babes in Beads 2*, 2003/4. Gold bikini and neckpiece freely machined stitched in gold and aubergine colour threads finally finished with crystals and other beads. Photo: Trevor Griffiths

Opposite right: Drawing and embroidery sample for *Babes in Beads 2.* Photo: Trevor Griffiths

Above left: *Silver Star Dress, Neckpiece and Bag* enriched with Haematite studs and silver beads. Photo: Trevor Griffiths

Above right: *Bag.* Machine embroidered in black thread decorated with Haematite and silver beads with a metal fitting and chain. Photo: Trevor Griffiths

Below left: Preparatory drawing for Embroidered Dress. Photo: Trevor Griffiths

Below right: *Drawing for a Bag* accompanied by gold beaded embroidered sample. Photo: Trevor Griffiths

Photo: D. W. Blanco

HELEN BANZAHF

1947	Born Llanwrtyd Wells Wales 16 March
1963 – 64	Italy *au pair*
1964 – 67	Foundation Course and City &Guilds Fashion Brighton College of Art
1967 – 70	St Martin's School of Art London Dip.AD Fashion/Textiles
1970 – 71	Designer for Dorville
1975	Married
1975 – 78	Teaching Sydenham School
1978	Birth son Oliver Teaching Eltham High School Adult education including 'special needs'
1982	Birth son Finbar
1990 –	Fashion Lecturer Lewisham College
1992	Solo exhibition Blackheath Concert Halls
1993	Selected for Chelsea Crafts Fair
1994	*Inspirations* March issue 'Variations on a Theme' Robin Bicknell
1995	Selected for Chelsea Crafts Fair. Crafts May/June issue 'Look Out'. Also included in exhibitions Clayton Gallery Newcastle-upon-Tyne. Model House Craft & Design Centre Llantrisant. Woodlands Art Gallery Blackheath London. Gardner Centre Sussex University
1996	Selected for Chelsea Crafts Fair. Included in exhibitions Bothy Gallery Wakefield. Woodlands Gallery Blackheath London. The Grace Barrand Design Centre Nutfield. Textiles show Marks & Spencer Baker Street London. Vena Bunker Gallery Bristol. Rufford Craft Centre Ollerton Nottinghamshire
1997	BBC2 Master Craftswoman on *The Craft Hour* Joined '62 Group exhibits regularly including Tel Aviv show Included in exhibitions The Grace Barrand Design Centre Nutfield. Pacific Heights San Francisco *Winter Show*. Crafts Council Foyer Showcases. San Francisco International Fair. Ruskin Gallery Sheffield. Wilcox Gallery Stratford-upon-Avon. Hithcocks Gallery Bath. The Devon Guild of Craftsmen Bovey Tracey. Royal Contemporary Art Gallery Eastleigh. Prize winner at exhibition National Eisteddfod of Wales. Crafts Council Index. Included in exhibitions Oxford Gallery. Brook Street Pottery Hay-on-Wye *Gone Soft Again*. Separation of marriage
1998	*World of Embroidery* A Personal Approach by Jae Maries Selected for Chelsea Crafts Fair. Crafts Council Shop V& A. Included in exhibitions Oriel Myrddin Galley Carmarthen. National Eisteddfod Wales. Vena Bunker Gallery Bristol. Rangers House Blackheath. Piece Hall Art Gallery Halifax Yorkshire
1999	Profile *Embroidery* magazine July/August issue
2000	New York International Fair
2001	Included British Council touring exhibition to Sweden, Denmark, Iceland, Australia *Home Sweet Home*. '62 Group Cajoba Birkenhead. Medway Galleries Rochester. *Art of the Stitch* London and Birkenhead
2003	Included exhibitions Rufford Craft Centre Ollerton Nottinghamshire. Bowie & Hulbert Hay-on-Wye
2004	Work included '62 Group show Millennium Galleries Sheffield

Right: *Distorted Vase*, (detail),1997. Raised machine embroidery. 16cm x 25cm (6in. x 10in.)

Helen Banzhaf

It is an uplifting experience to walk into Helen's home. Though small and unpretentious the whole place is a visual extension of the embroidery she produces. Light and bright and colourful and happy and small scale; made even more so, with her work hung on almost every wall. All artists' homes are an expression of their art but here the main sitting room doubles as her studio and is in itself a work of art. It rings of her delight and competence in making things: 'I am lucky I can make anything – I love working with cloth – that's where I came from - fashion and clothes as an art form. For me decorative stitch came later'. Even her tailored sofa covers are perfection – cream fabric fastened at the lower corners with large orange buttons giving an air of absolute visual finish and relating to everything she collects.

Inspiration for her immaculate machine embroidered pictures has always been vessels or fragments of them – jugs, beakers, jars, pots and the like, which she draws very simply with pencil and coloured pencils. Those she has chosen to collect are displayed around the walls and are largely decorated with the sunshine colours of 1930s plus black. The relationship between objects observed and the work clearly show the latter deeply infused by the former. Thread colours emanate from those that predominate in the glazed decorations and metamorphose into her characteristic little masterpieces of stitch.

She has not always embroidered. This began out of adversity. A teaching job came to an end in 1989 and in the intervening month before finding another post she started using her trusted old Bernina Sport sewing machine, not for clothes or furnishings, but for making tiny pictures. A colleague seeing these little 'jewels' commissioned an embroidered jacket and she says 'I found that my machine was going somewhere new'. She had always loved sewing and recalls sitting with her mother to make things. 'When I was nearly seven we made clothes for my sister before she

Opposite: *Lime Bottle,* 1994. Machine embroidery. Private collection. 17cm x 23cm (7in. x 9in.)

Left: *Mexican Pot,* 1996. Raised machine embroidery. Private collection. 19cm x 28cm (7in. x 11in.)

Below: *Abstract II,* 1995. Three-dimensional machine embroidery. Private collection. 23cm x 20cm (9in. x 8in.)

was born.' Her parents had a small farm and life was of a rural pace. By the age of eleven drawing was also a passion: 'I was always drawing and I also knew I wanted to do fashion.' Clearly at this early stage, also good with the sewing machine, she was making presents and experimenting with her own clothes. Fortunately her grammar school included needlework as a curriculum subject so she was able to develop the subject in preparation for art school.

The City and Guilds' course at Brighton included a pattern-cutting element which Helen maintains gave her the precision and skills that became second nature. Now teaching as a full time fashion lecturer, with many successes including the pleasure she gets from teaching people with learning difficulties, her own work is produced only in evenings and at weekends. Nevertheless her devotion to her sewing machine ensures a continuation of productivity and, as she says, 'it is a

Helen Banzhaf.

Opposite: *Ginger Jar*, 1998. Raised machine embroidery. Private collection. 22cm x 18cm (9in. x 7in.). Photo: David Hankey

Left: *Nineteen Fifties Pot* 1997 Machine embroidery. 15cm x 29cm (6in. x 11in.)

Below left: *There is a Vase,* 1997. Machine embroidery. 19cm x 17cm (7in. x 7in.)

Below: *Yellow and Lime,* 1998. Raised machine embroidery. Private collection. 18cm x 23cm (7in. x 9in.)

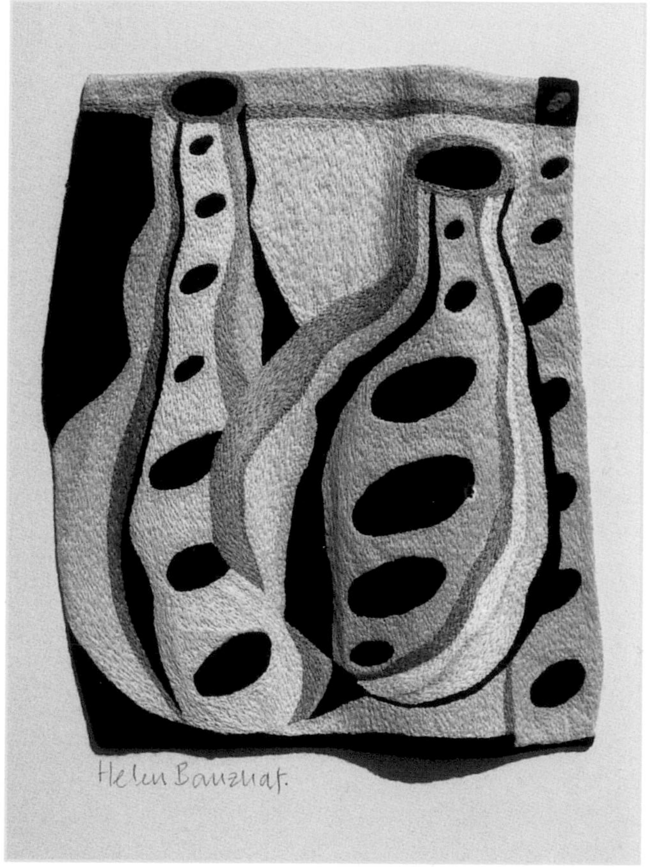

way of life – I love doing it and it crosses all sorts of boundaries'.

Helen's gentle nature hides the strength of motivation and commitment required to produce the exquisite quality and quantity of her stitched pieces. The process begins with observing a vessel, drawing it, tracing the main image onto calico. This is then put into a tambour frame ready for sewing. The solid coverage is achieved with straight machine stitching in either Mettler embroidery thread or Sylko. From start to finish attention to detail is paramount right up to the simple beautifully made glazed frames, which she constructs herself.

Over the years the imagery has been representational but of late it is moving towards selecting abstract areas of pattern which, whilst usually conforming to the organic, are a comfortable, designed, positive/negative, balance of space.

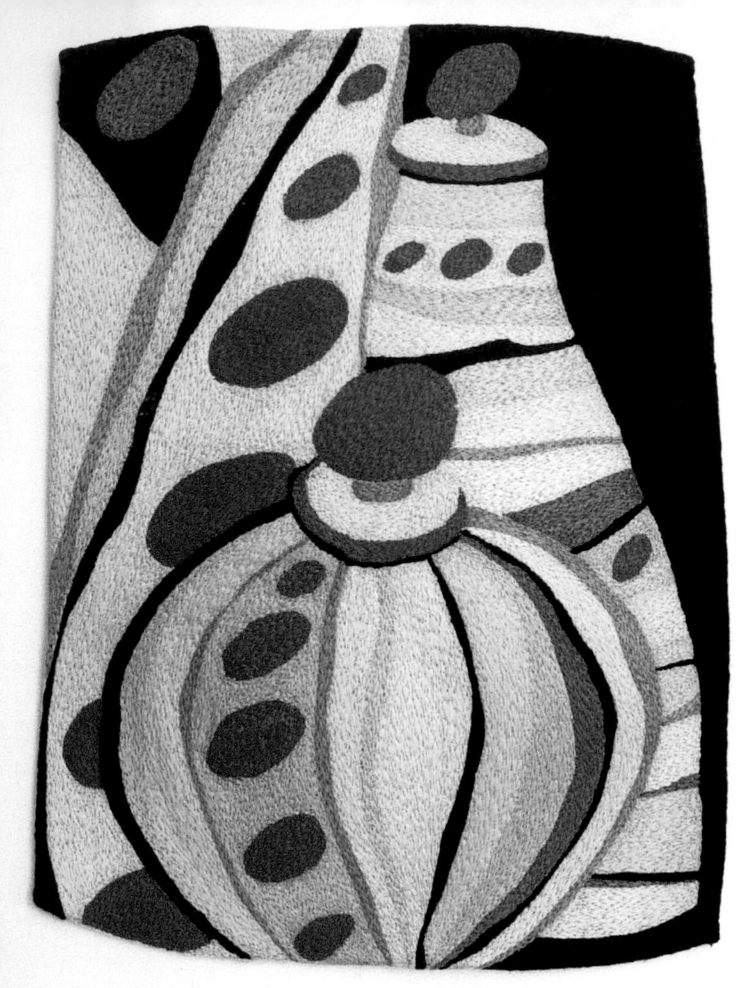

Left: *Clowning Around,* 1998. Machine embroidery. Private collection USA. 15cm x 24cm (6in x 9in.)

Above: *Busy Coffee Pot,* 1998. Raised machine embroidery. Private collection. 20cm x 22cm (8in. x 9in.). Photo: David Hankey

Below: *Abstract I,* 1998. Machine embroidery. Private collection, USA. 19cm x 16cm (7in. x 6in.)

Opposite top: *Two Fat Pots,* 2001. Raised machine embroidery. 31cm x 18cm (13in. x 7in.). Photo: Bill Blanco

Opposite bottom left: *Too Tall,* 2001. Raised machine embroidery. 15cm x 32cm (6in. x 12in.). Photo: Bill Blanco

Opposite bottom right: *Three Friends,* 2002. Raised machine embroidery. Private collection. 15cm x 17cm (6in. x 7in.)

Helen Banzhaf

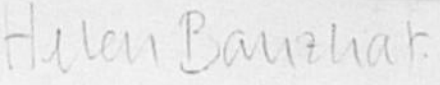
Helen Banzhaf

Helen Banzhaf

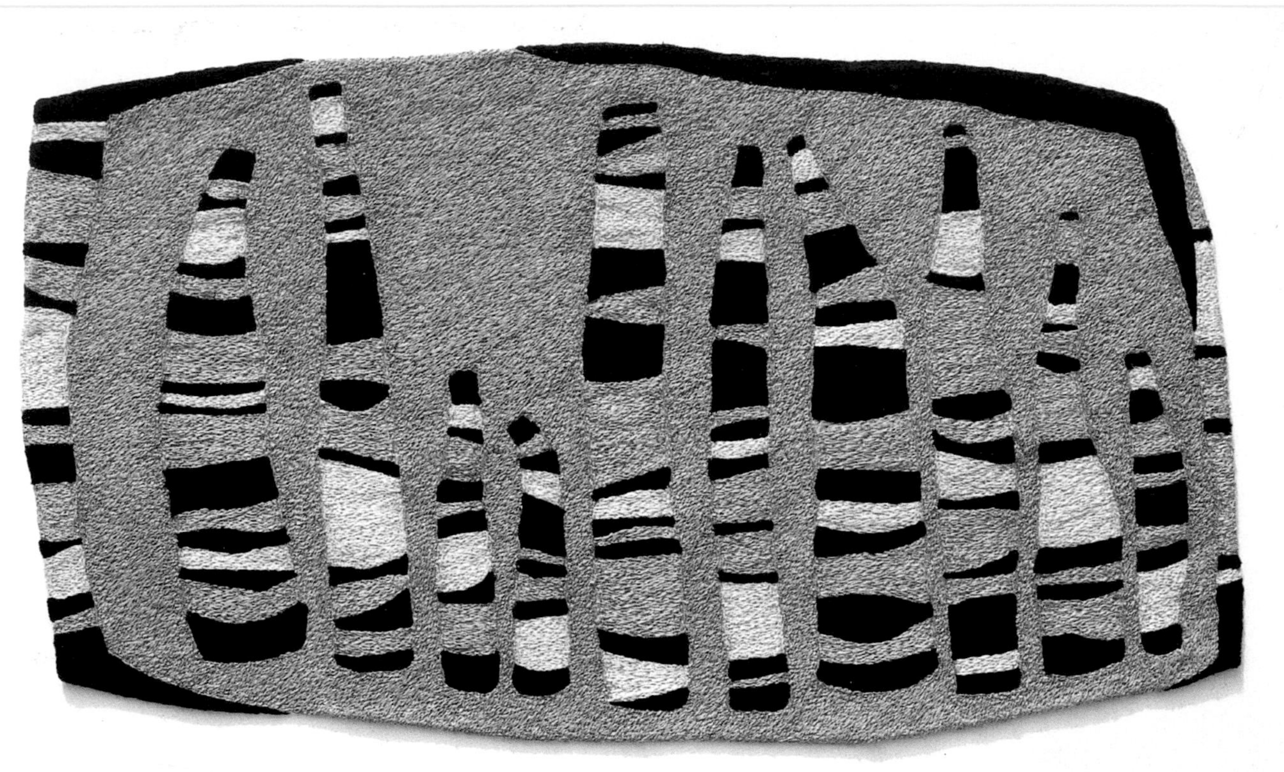

Opposite top: *Striped Crowd,* 2002. Machine embroidery. 31cm x 18cm (12in. x 7in.)

Opposite bottom: *Three Pieces* 2004. Machine embroidery. 22cm x 9cm (9in. x 3½ in.)

This page and following pages: Studies and designs for embroidery. Various media including pencil, crayon and watercolour

An early practical discovery came about whilst ironing a completed work. The piece, refusing to respond to becoming a totally flat surface, Helen decided to apply one of her tailoring skills. Taking a 'ham' she 'formed' the surface thus providing a subtle and beautifully controlled low relief. With the addition of wadding, a jug or a teapot was lifted just above the surface; a feature that has become very much her own style. Final edges or confines of the work are never regular and sometimes may be wired giving soft volutes.

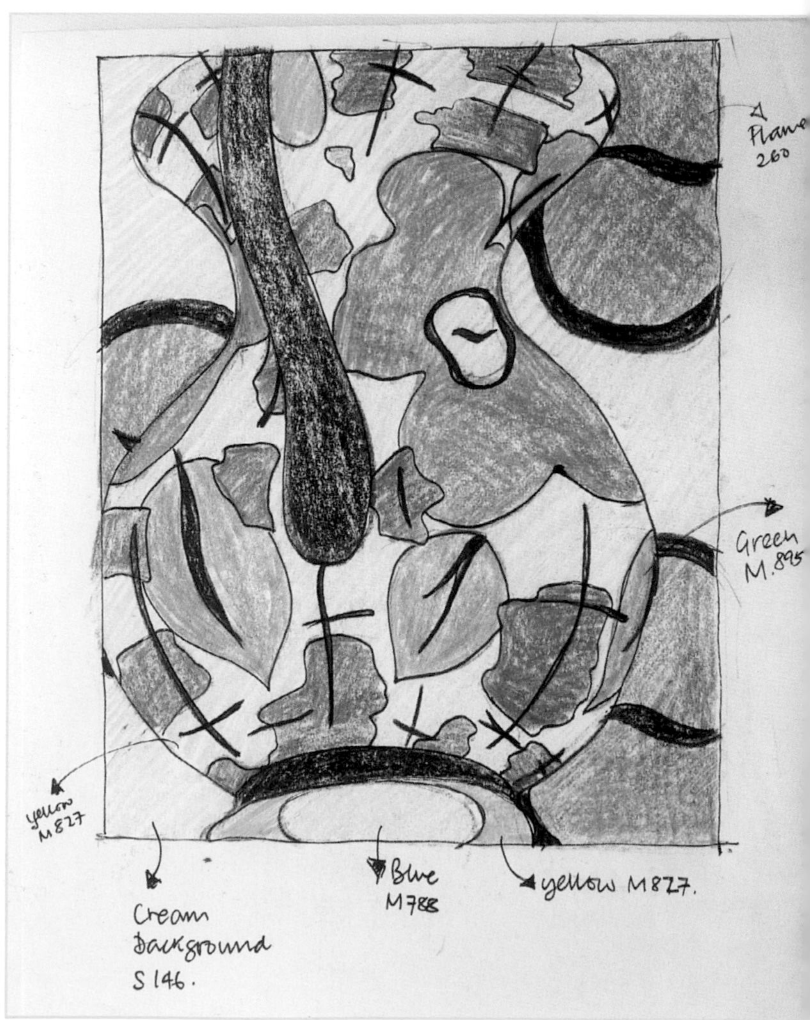

Orange M 953
yellow M 827
Black M.
Dream-de-nil 310. S.
Jasmine Gold S.414
Mid yellow S 19.

There are many embroiderers who are solidly stitching the surface of the cloth in their own individual way; Helen's way produces the character, or family of forms, that intrinsically suggest the crispness of the decorated clay that provided the origins of her momentum.

Her work is widely exhibited and purchased. Being selected for the Crafts Council Index has undoubtedly helped this process. It proved to be a significant accolade which later assisted in focussing the attention of selectors seeking exhibitors for projects such as the British Council travelling exhibitions and overseas Craft Fairs organised by the Craft Council.

She is someone who deserves more time for her work but, like others featured in this book, has, through financial constraint, to teach until retirement age. Maybe, as with them, work will then take off into new and greater heights.

Her home location in south London is very important. She says, 'This is my neighbourhood and where my friends are'. It is from here that this unassuming and sensitive artist works obsessively - so modest that she is almost apologetic at entering the world of Fine Art. She is mindful of not becoming so self absorbed that she should forget relationships with others; unlikely in one whose concern for her students is obvious.

Photo: Stephen Jacobson

JANET HAIGH

1948	Born Bebington Cheshire 4 July
1964 – 67	Liverpool College of Art Foundation and Dip.AD Fashion/Textiles
1969 – 70	Goldsmiths' College London A.T.C.
1970 – 75	Fashion/Textile Designer and Illustrator London Design Companies. Started to embroider
1973	Married Stephen Jacobson
1975 – 86	Senior Lecturer Bristol Polytechnic
1977	Mixed show *Flowers* Francis Kyle Gallery
1978	Mixed show Frances Kyle Gallery London Contributor *Good Housekeeping Encyclopedia of Needlecraft* Judy Brittain Ebury Press ISBN 0 85223164 4
1979	Solo show *Canvas Embroideries* Francis Kyle Gallery London
1980	Included in BBC2 series *Embroidery*
1981	Royal Society of Arts Travel Scholarship to Japan Group show *New Faces* British Crafts Centre London
1982	Solo show *A View of Japan* Francis Kyle Gallery London
1984	Included in BBC Doomsday Project
1985 – 96	Numerous commissioned Stitched Portraits undertaken *An Artist in the Land of the Flying Kimono* Caryll Faraldi *Observer* Magazine
1986 – 2001	Associate Senior Lecturer Bristol, University of West of England (B.U.W.E)
1987 – 91	Chelsea Crafts Fair
1989	Interview Prime Time B.B.C. TV David Jacobs
1992	Author *Cross Stitch for Knitwear* David and Charles Group show *The Embroiderer's Flowers* Museum of Garden History London
1993	Solo show *Museums and Makers* Bristol City Museum Artist Spotlight Roslyn Sadler *Modem Painters* Winter issue
1993 – 6	Freelance designer for Fabric 8 Fashion Fabric Agency
1996	*Gardens Embroidery* Burton Agnes Hall Yorkshire *Two Hangings* Lung Cancer Research Centre Liverpool *Frieze Frame: work in progress* Judith Hoskins documentary H.T.V. Profile *A Stitch in Time* Miranda Innes Country Living Magazine
1998	Author *Crazy Patchwork* Collins and Brown Artist in Residence *The Paradise Garden* Cardiff City Museum and Art Gallery C.D.Rom. Interview Cleo Witt National Electronic and Video Archive
1999	Group show *Gardens and Flowers in Embroidery* Tokyu Gallery Tokyo Japan Author *Japanese Inspirations* Collins and Brown *Hanging* Royal Caribbean Cruise Line m.v. Eagle II Chambers Night Club Solo show *Telling Tales With Threads Flora's Legacy* Holbourne Museum Bath Channel 4 Interview Howard Jacobson *Takes On the Turner Prize*
2001	National Trust National Garden Embroidery Prize 'The Spirit of the Garden' *Eight Hangings* Royal Caribbean Cruise Line m.v.Voyager III for Jesters Night Club & Cigar Club Designs for embroidered carpet and cushions for Ehrman Tapestry Co.
2001 –	Senior Research Fellow and Chair of Enamel Textile Clay (ETC) research group. B.U.W.E.
2002	Author *Embroiderer's Floral* Collins and Brown *Hanging* and *Six Collage Pictures* Royal Caribbean Cruise Line m.v.Voyager for Crypt Night Club and Windjammer Restaurant respectively Designs for embroidered carpet and cushions for Ehrman Tapestry Co.
2003	Author *Simply Stitched Series: White on White* and *Colour on Colour.* Coats Crafts UK Lectures/workshops/staff assessment Gottenburg University Stenebyskolan Sweden Group show *Brave Hearts* stitched enamel jewelry Studio Fusion London
2004	Author *Simply Stitched Series: Blue & White* Coats Crafts UK Commission for Home Ornaments developed by Daphne Wright for Art Works Programme for CZWG Architects Installation of twenty embroidered 3D Parrots for new Gorbals apartment block Glasgow Embroidered cushion collections Ehrmans Tapestry Co. for USA and UK market
2004 –	Chair of Steering Committee Textile Forum South West

Right: *The Harris Family,* 1980s. Silk, cotton and wool fabric; canvas work, crewel work, black work and appliqué. Crewel work and black work integral frame. Private collection. 60cm (24in.) square

Janet Haigh

By her own admission Janet has always been able to draw. She says all her family could draw but she was the only one that received a training; and goes further to say 'I was precocious at drawing'.

Volumes of large sketchbooks testify to this; she works on the premise that if you get your ideas down on paper you can return to those pages and be excited for ever. 'When I look at what I have recorded I feel a sense of energy'. These books provide the vigour on days when she may not have the time or the inclination to go out to draw; they form a bank of visual thoughts in readiness for the client who asks to see what ideas she may have. Her designs for cushions and carpets for Hugh Erhman[45] have often started in this way. Images are recorded in pencil, ink, paints, crayons and anything else that makes a mark; also, they are often, at this early stage, supported by stitched experiments.

Countless times these volumes have been responsible for either helping her to sell work or provided a starting point for clients placing an order. 'People love to see drawings – they feel a sense of substance'. This is borne out most clearly in the years she exhibited her personal style of stitched pictures at Chelsea Crafts Fair; where she received many commissions to undertake family portraits, houses, gardens, animals and big celebratory pieces. Examples of these are the *Harris Family*, the *Rendell Family* and the *Kardasis Family*; all intricately hand embroidered on various ground fabrics, which, as with all these early pieces, were made in separate sections and then assembled.

Until three years ago she balanced this world of her own workroom with part-time lecturing. She loved teaching in an art school, saying that it was one of the most rewarding jobs anyone could have. Having reached her mid fifties, and after more than twenty five years teaching on the B.A. Textiles course at Bristol U.W.E., she felt it was time to change direction.

Above: *'Robe of Precious Objects' Self Portrait,* 1983. Silk resist dying and silk embroidery based on the pose taken from *Modern Design in Embroidery,* 1936, by Rebecca Crompton. 30cm x 45cm (12in. x 18in.)

Above right: Pencil and wash drawing for *Self Portrait,* 1983

Right: Pencil drawing for *Self Portrait,* 1983

Opposite above left: Preparatory pencil drawings for *Kardasis Family,* 1985

Opposite above right: Painted sketches for *Kardasis Family,* 1985

Opposite below: *The Kardasis Family,* 1985. Embroidery. Private collection. 56cm x 60cm (22in. x 24in.)

Above: *Tulipomania,* 1993-9. Hand stitchery and appliqué. Photo: John Hezeltine

Opposite above left: Pencil and crayon drawings for *Burton Agnes Gardens,* 1995-6

Opposite above right: Pencil and crayon drawings for *Burton Agnes Gardens,* 1995-6

Opposite below: *Burton Agnes Gardens* hand embroidery, 1995-6. Collection of the house open to the public in the summer, 85cm x 90cm (33in. x 35in.)

However, the college had other ideas; not being prepared to lose 'a good all-round design tutor', suggested that she return as a researcher. One of Janet's great strengths is helping students to research and record creative ideas, which they can then develop individually.

She did not train as an embroiderer but started making small canvas work scenes as a reaction to years of being a frustrated fashion designer and illustrator. She says she was never really in touch with the embroidery fraternity so she taught herself from books and stitch dictionaries. The only exposure to the subject had been while she was at Goldsmiths' College for her teacher-training year. This was the first time she had seen embroidery as a creative art; up to this point she had been satisfied with embroidering or embellishing both her own clothes as well as those she designed for commercial companies.

Armed with a collection of these first early canvas embroideries, incidentally all inspired by either her parents' garden or those found in old garden books, she went to London and knocked on many gallery doors. The Francis Kyle Gallery responded with an offer of inclusion in a mixed show. The thrill was multiplied by having her name on the poster alphabetically just above that of David Hockney. On the strength of four sales they invited her to prepare for her first solo show.

for
Susan Cunliffe-Lister
to Record and Celebrate
Her New Elizabethan
Gardens at Burton Agnes
29 June 1995

IL TEMPO PASSA

Janet Haigh – Her Work
1994-96 + DJC + HJ

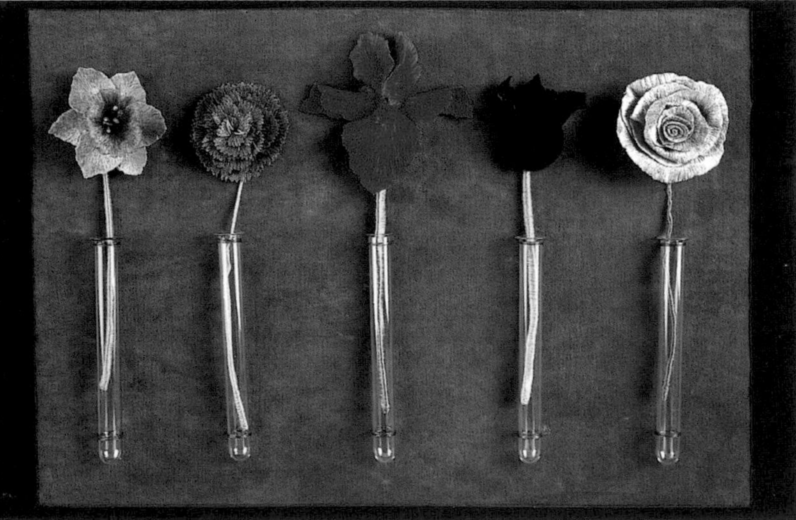

Top: *Paradise,* 1996. The composition is closely modelled on an illustration from an early herbal *Paradisi in Sole, Paradisus Terrestris* 1629 by John Parkinson. Small areas of hand embroidery applied to resist dyed background. Photo: John Hezeltine

Above: *Current Breeding Objectives,* 1999. Inspired by plant breeders' desire to reverse the art of nature – to breed colours that do not exist. Photo: John Hezeltine

Right: *Auricula Theatre,* 1998. Raised embroidery framed with original Spitalfields silk depicting auriculas. Photo: John Hezeltine

Right above: *Working drawings of Iris*, 1999

Right below: Colour sketch and embroidered sample of *Helebores,* 1999

Though continuing to sell successfully Janet was becoming aware of the difficulty of making a living from exhibiting hand embroidery. 'There is no comparison in price for what I could get from selling a drawing and what I received for an embroidered picture; the one may have only taken a day and the other a month and the price little different. Prices have only been more appropriate when work is commissioned.' She says that people have compared saving up for one her pieces with the price of an exotic holiday. Others who pay a fair price are big companies; her many hangings and panels for the Royal Caribbean Cruise Liners being one example. 'I could use whatever fabrics I wanted – the more expensive the better'.

Janet's artistic progress appears to have been one of natural evolution; something built on a natural course of events; expressed in her words it could be summed up thus 'Somehow I have developed – into an embroiderer – something that sustains and delights me'. Stemming initially from family roots in art; water colourists, sign writers and people who could draw, she was able to turn her 11+ failure to good result. Her parents were disappointed at the thought of her going to a secondary modern school but she feels that, for her, it was the best choice due to the amazing encouragement she received from the staff in the art department. She was one of the few who took 'A' level art and went to college early. Her mother would have preferred her to start with a paid job but her father said that it was better to delay earning a living in order that eventually she could work at what she liked doing; but prefaced it by saying 'at least until someone is soft enough to marry you'. She more than fulfilled his wish for she managed to combine the two.

She and her husband have happily founded their marriage on the understanding that their work is paramount. They have adjoining studios. Hers is dominated by a huge work table and a complete wall taken up by rows of magnificent small wooden open-fronted drawers of the type that used to furnish haberdashery shops. These are filled with threads, ribbons and every kind of trimming. The room is on the top floor of their house, three cottages imaginatively knocked into one, and overlooking the most incredible landscape. Positioned at the confluence of the river Avon and the river Severn, the mud flats and changing colours of this stretch of the Bristol Channel form an ever changing and virtual canvas. The importance of this location for Janet is that it is reminiscent of her origins in the Wirral. She also says

Above: *Lytes Carey Manor Garden,* 2001. Appliqué with embroidery in woollen yarns on a dyed wool crepe ground. Artist's collection. 137cm x 180cm (54in. x 71in).

Above right: Pencil drawings for *Lytes Carey Manor Garden,* 2001

Below right: Painted sketch for *Lytes Carey Manor Garden,* 2001

Opposite: Series of twenty *Parrots,* 2004. Three dimensional, free-standing silk embroidery on foam body, with hand painted faces. Apartment block Glasgow. 20cm (8in.).

there is nothing to do except look out of the window, walk the dogs, 'keep your eyes down and look in'.

'Eyes down' could often mean working on what she would call tiny and precious. In developing her techniques she made a conscious decision to look to the past and became enchanted by English seventeenth century raised work.

A good example of this is her series of nine works entitled Flora's Legacy, shown together as a series in 2000; each is a composite work comprising individual miniature pieces of embroidery. Intrigued by the countless plant shows she saw, which demonstrated the results of man's desire to control and 'perfect' nature, she was inspired to use the embroidered surface to draw attention to the seeking of perfection. Many of her works are underpinned with her need for symbolism.

Winning a Royal Society of Arts Scholarship to Japan in 1981 was also a significant help both technically and practically. The study of kimono crafts added to her visual language and needle skills, and heightened her love of all things labour intensive, time consuming and precious. *Self Portrait* of 1983 testifies to this.

The five week visit was a huge event. Serendipity played a part. Her friend and colleague Janet Arnold[46], had worked on an English translation of a book on Japanese dress for the curator of costume of the Japanese Royal Family. With this introduction Janet was not only able to stay with her daughter but to learn embroidery techniques from her. 'They were fascinated by my life-like drawings – so unlike those of the Japanese. I kept a day-book and swapped my drawings for wonderful fabrics and threads. Through the family's contacts I got to visit places of which I could only have dreamed.'

Her method of hand stitching differs for larger work such as *Lytes Carey*, depicting her special love of topiary. Though bold in colour, it is worked in small, straight, stitches; cross-hatched, that she calls her darning technique. She says this same use of the stitch could also work on the subtle colours that lie outside the window but feels that this landscape is just too big – she would want to produce the whole view – a case of all or nothing. Her husband on the other hand, busy with a furniture business to run at the time of moving house, had no creative thoughts about location - yet it is he who in his personal work paints nothing but the view.

Janet is primarily a hand embroiderer whose themes are always illustrative and decorative. Her sense of colour is inspired by both objective observation as well as a major preoccupation with traditional textiles. Her only use for her New Home sewing machine is for plain and zig zag strengthening stitches.

Janet has never taught the design or the practice of embroidery but, through her many contributions to books on patchwork, appliqué and other techniques, has disseminated information. Designing and making prototypes, to accompany embroidery publications, she has also formed a considerable instructional element within the craft.

In her non-commissioned work she enjoys invention and digression within a chosen theme sometimes taking several years to finalise a piece. She enjoys the labour intensive nature of hand worked research giving her 'time to think, take a chance, try something new, make a mess, get it wrong and still have time without constraint'.

Her commissioned work on the other hand awakens the other part of her nature; responding to a design brief; problem solving; working to a budget and a deadline and employing extra hands when needed.

Her most recent work is based on research into other media and techniques; paper, ceramics, glass, metal and, in particular, enamel, to which she can add embroidery techniques.

A generous teacher but one who may well respond, in the following way, to those with a tentative approach to the practice of drawing 'When people say to me that they can't draw and can't design, I say to them – if you can write your name the same way twice, you can learn to draw – it is just a matter of practice'.

Footnotes

45 *Hugh Erhman of Hugh Ehrman Kits, 28a Kensington Church Street London W8*

46 *Janet Arnold 1932-1998 Noted Costume Archivist. Costume: volume for Janet Arnold 2000 published by the Costume Society Journal no.32. ISSN 0590 8876*

Photo: Michael Wicks

SUE RANGELEY

1948	Born Rugby 16 December
1966 – 67	Loughborough College of Art and Design Foundation Course
1967 – 70	Lanchester Polytechnic Coventry Dip.AD Painting
1970 – 71	Brighton Polytechnic A.T.D.
1971 – 74	Teaching Art and Design Highdown School Reading Berkshire Attended creative embroidery workshops with Constance Howard
1975	Set up studio *Sue Rangeley Embroidered Originals* First collection of quilted bags and cushions
1975 – 80	Fosseway House Workshops Stow-on-the-Wold Gloucestershire
1976 – 78	Designed and produced quilted silk appliqué jackets for Bill Gibb Collection
1978	Selected for Crafts Council Index UK Profile *Crafts* July/August issue. Profile *Embroidery* Spring issue
1979	Crafts Council Textile Tour UK. Exhibited V&A Crafts Council Shop *British Craftsmen of Distinction* Charles de Temple exhibition Paris
1980	Set up new studio in Charlbury Oxfordshire
1980 – 98	Visiting lecturer UCE/Birmingham Polytechnic
1982	Awarded Southern Arts Bursary Group show *Fashion as Art* Westminster Gallery Boston USA
1987	Commission Bridal gown and accessories. National Gallery Victoria Australia Group show *Hatches Matches Dispatches* National Gallery Victoria Australia Chelsea Crafts Fair
1989	Lecture/workshop tour Australia and New Zealand
1990	Lecture/workshop tour Canada Evening bag raised £1500 at charity auction Mansion House London Artist-in-residence *Embroidery in Kelmscott*
1991	Included Embroiderers' Guild touring exhibition Tokyo and Osaka Japan
1992	Lecture/workshop tour Denmark
1993	First solo show of 100 works Tokyo Japan
1994	Video *Business is the Common Thread* made by the Banking Information Service for GNVQ students Author *Guilded Splendour* Spring issue *World of Embroidery*
1995	Included Exhibition at Yarlington House Somerset Work featured in *Needlecraft & BBC Homes & Antiques*
1997	Organised first *Contemporary Crafts in the Cotswolds* continuing till 2003
1997 – 98	Artist-in-Residence at Botley School
1998	Lecture/Workshop Tour Vancouver and Seattle Featured in Carlton TV *The Heart of the Country* August
1999	Included exhibition *The Embroiderers' Garden* Tokyo Japan Feature *The World of Embroidery* May issue. Artist-in-Residence St. Mary's School Chippenham Wiltshire
2000	Lecture/Workshop for EGA Coupeville USA and Vancouver Canada
2000 – 03	Member steering group Contemporary Crafts, Abingdon Museum Oxfordshire

Commissions have included large scale hangings, quilts, screens, cushions, bags and numerous accessories for dress. Bridal and eveningwear, waistcoats, jackets, man's elaborate dressing robe, film set including bespoke shawls.
Works in public and private collections worldwide.
Lectures, workshops and study days are undertaken worldwide and include the Embroiderers' Guild and The Victoria & Albert Museum in the UK
Work exhibited in numerous galleries include Prescote Gallery Oxfordshire; Charles Temple Gallery London; Gallerie Kraus Paris; Ehrman Gallery London.

www.suerangeley.co.uk

Right: Detail of *Silk Jacket* made for Bill Gibb Spring/Summer Collection 1977 showing the emergence of the artist's now familiar style of quilting and three dimensional appliqué for dress and accessories. Over eighty of these jackets, which co-ordinated with a delicate Liberty print fabric in different colourways designed by Susan Collier, were sold in the UK and USA

Sue Rangeley

It is now some thirty years since Sue Rangeley began developing her personal style of functional embroidered artefacts. Items that today, range from belts and bags to complete garments, bridal wear, cushions, bedspreads and screens. The delicate spirit underlying each design exudes femininity and charm and every object carries her hall-mark of technical perfection. From botany to butterflies her visual study of the natural world is transposed to silk and chiffon. With extreme deftness, having first captured her images by means of pencil drawings, she translates this observed world of nature into ornament. Subtle colour is applied directly to the fabric surface with techniques such as air brushing of dyes or hand painting. Surfaces further evolve into low relief with the addition of meticulous quilting by machine, of which she has three. The very small 1870 Wilcox and Gibbs was actually bought by her to add interest to a room but on discovering that it actually worked she regularly puts it to use producing the tiniest and most perfect of chain stitches. Of her other machines she says she will never part with her trusted thirty year old Bernina Minimatic in spite of adding a Bernina Artista 180 to her fleet.

Thus by these simplest of means her stylised flora and fauna are often three dimensionally raised from the surface, bejewelled with beads and hand embroidery, epitomising the style for which she has become so well known.

More recently floral decoration has become less descriptive instead at times becoming sculptural and almost free standing against a simpler quilted ground. Her immaculate use of rouleaux[47] continues also to be a masterpiece of decorative finish.

As with many artists Sue's work has been produced within a largely solitary existence enabling her to become very focussed and prolific in output. Her time, apart from the first three years after college, has only been lightly interspersed

Leaf
belt.
Same design
as hibiscus
waistcoat
but in
chiffon
Orchid
design
Fragments
image

Opposite page: Design sheet of air brushed samples demonstrating thought process towards decoration for fashion. Photo: Michael Wicks

Above: Study of *Dog Roses,* 1990

Left: Study of *Yellow Scabious and Grasses,* 2004
Photo: Michael Wicks

with travel, teaching and giving workshops. Her first overseas invitation to teach did not take place until 1989. The only other visible diversion being her unique approach to the decoration of her house, and, in the last few years, to an expansion of her talents as a plantsman and gardener. Her new home includes a greenhouse where she raises many things from seed. She says she could not live or work in a city: 'I value space more than ever.' Space she certainly has as will be described later. She qualifies this by saying, 'Equally I could not operate from a remote location – my rural setting needs to be one with proximity to London and ease of international travel'.

From a very early age she loved making things. Born to farming parents she and her brother shared not only a very rural childhood but also a practical one. Attending the village church primary school, with an unbelievable school roll of only seventeen children, a large part of the curriculum was devoted to art and craft. This early practical experience was extended when moving on to a small boarding school where again art played an important part. She still speaks of her first art lesson as 'being a magical door that opened'. This was also

Opposite page: Twelve examples of floral motifs for accessories in black, white, metallic, pewter, silver and gold – stitched, quilted and beaded – 1990s studio collection. Photo: Michael Wicks

Above: Study of *Poppies and Fennel Flower,* 2004. Photo: Michael Wicks

Right: Four examples of spray painted floral motifs – machine stitched on painted or spray dyed silk ground. Some flowers raised three dimensionally either by applying thin layers of similar chiffon or by means of padding or quilting. Photo: Michael Wicks

a period when a close neighbour and friend, and great craftsman, taught her to embroider. A sensitivity to fabric was also clearly noticed by others who gave her old garments in which 'to dress up' and to satisfy her love of 'all things sparkly'.

Other really key moments responsible for decisive directions in her life were to follow her art school years. Whilst full-time teaching in her first post she also attended creative embroidery workshops given by Constance Parker[18]. 'I started with little padded people on panels and realised that embroidery was what I really wanted to do. I wanted to stop teaching and do my own work'.

Leaving teaching she set up her own workshop for a year but felt the need for a shared creative environment.

Above left: Bridal Sketches, 1993. Three typical drawings showing potential for fashion embellishment Photo: Michael Wicks

Above right: Sketch, 1980 – initial design for Primavera Dress. Photo: Michael Wicks

Opposite page right: *Chiffon Dress 'Primavera'*, 1980. Spray-painted layers of silk crepe de chine and chiffon with details of entwined rouleaux with flowers and leaves forming the shoulder strap and choker. Photo: Graham Howard

Opposite page left: Detail of *Chiffon Dress,* 1980. Photo: Graham Howard

Fosseway House, set up by Michael Haynes[48], was suggested by a fellow craftsman. She applied for a space and was able to live and work there for the next five creative years before feeling the need to move on. Indeed these years were to prove seminal to her career. Whilst there, it was a natural progression to consider presenting herself at the Vogue offices where Judy Brittain suggested shops that might be interested in her work. These included a visit to Bill Gibb[49]. She says, 'I found myself sipping tea with him accompanied by my picnic basket of embroidered samples. Things were very differently marketed in those days!' It was the start of yet another door being opened. 'He was ecstatic about my work'. So started her run of appliqué quilted silk jackets for his collections for the next two years.

This meteoric rise to success came at the same time as her successful application to the Crafts Council Index and by *Crafts* magazine's decision to feature her work on the cover. The exposure was complete when her pieces were also displayed at the Crafts Council shop at the V&A. She says the sum of these events brought her so much work from all over the world, including a gallery from as far afield as Norfolk Island in the Pacific Ocean. She describes it as a 'truly creative era when I was fully stretched to complete commissions and orders. I had to employ two people on an occasional basis to help with repetitive tasks such as beading and the making of waistcoats'.

By 1980 she had more than found her feet and started preparations for leaving Fosseway Workshops. She bought

the small eighteenth century townhouse in the centre of Charlbury in Oxfordshire which, till five years ago, was both her home and studio. Now the whole house is her studio since purchasing a second property with her physicist partner. This new delightful house and garden, also eighteenth century, is only a few minutes walk away. Her first home still most clearly reflects her passion for collecting. The whole house is adorned with 1930s china, discerningly selected and displayed in or on furniture of the same period. The patterns and colours are subtly reiterated by her own painted stencils on dados and floorboards. Every room also stores and displays her work together with her vast collection of magazines and books. Everywhere you look are trunks and boxes and wardrobes full of ornate and richly decorated bags, cushions, and clothes. The room at the back, once a coalhouse, is the light and airy workroom whose walls are covered with what she describes as 'mood boards'. Visually interpreted these are 'ideas in the making' comprised of machine samples, photographs and fabric swatches. A sturdy worktable in the middle occupies the largest space flanked by a substantial desk at the side for paper work.

This is the story of someone who, in her Foundation Year

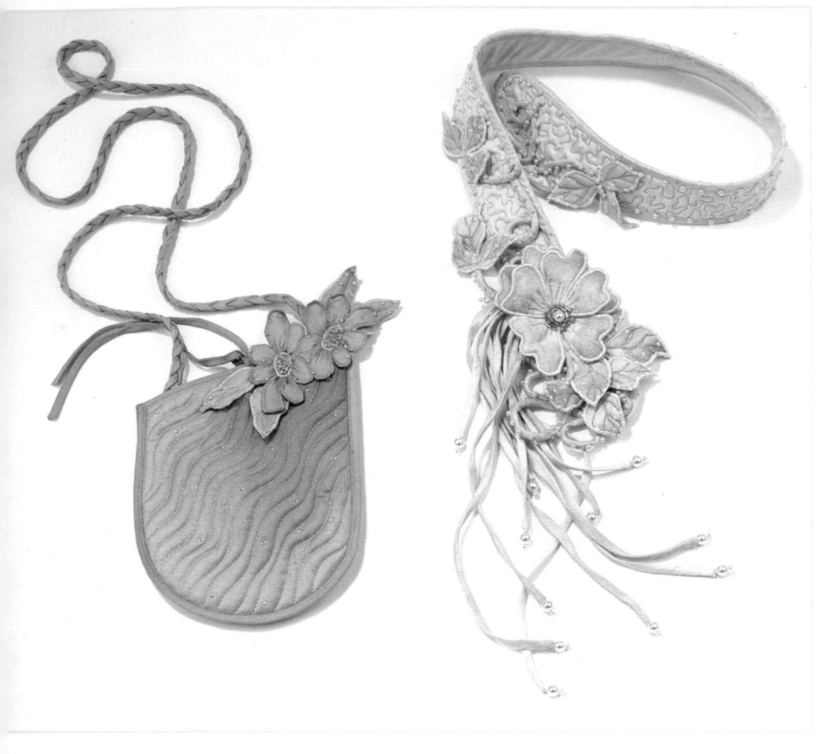

Opposite top left: *Small Quilted Bag,* 1980, with raised flowers. Silk spray-dyed and quilted and matching silk twisted strap. Private collection. Photo: David Hankey. *Belt* 1990. Spray dyed, quilted, sequins, rouleaux with pearls. Private collection. Photo: David Hankey

Opposite top right: *Bag.* Pink hand-dyed quilted surface with three appliqué flowers. Matching strap in twisted *rouleaux.* Typical of a large range made and sold in galleries worldwide in the 1980s and recalling the artist's love of Art Deco. Photo: Michael Wicks

Opposite bottom left: *Reticule,* 2003. Black silk ground quilted with lurex thread with sprinkling of sequins Photo: Michael Wicks

Opposite bottom right: *Guilded Rose Bag,* 2003. Vase shaped comprising three dimensional applied fabric leaves flowing up from the base finishing at the top with a flourish of ruched flowers. Photo: Michael Wicks

Above and right: *Silk Organza Cape,* 2004. Edged with two- and three-dimensional appliqué - manipulated roses in metallic organza seen both on and off the model. Photo: Michael Wicks

at art school, was reluctant to be persuaded to specialise in textiles for her Dip AD, instead choosing Fine Art/Painting. It proved to be a short lived journey taking only a year or two before turning around and completely immersing herself in fabric and thread. She says that 'the wonderful world of embroidery has even enabled me to forge friendships and to go abroad'. To the observer it is also obvious that, together with her immense capacity for hard work, she has been able to develop and focus on a lifestyle totally compatible with her personality and talent.

Not only surrounded by her work and the many objects that she has collected but also by the countless plants she has raised. She says that her next wish would be to combine these interests in a 'garden residency'; surely a project worthy of anticipation.

Footnote

47 Rouleau *is a hollow tube of fabric with edges turned in; particularly fashionable in shoulder straps of dresses of the 1930s and 1940s. Rouleaux first appeared in 19th century fashion trimmings*

48 *Michael Haynes 1941- Founder, together with Judy Brittain, of Fosseway House Workshops and 401½ Workshops 403 Wandsworth Road London SW8 still owned and run by M.H.*

49 *Bill Gibb 1943-1988 Revolutionised British fashion in the 1970s and 1980s. Named Designer of the Year by Vogue in 1969. Sixtieth Anniversary exhibition Aberdeen Art Gallery 2004*

Photo: Keith Paisley

PADDY KILLER

1949	Born Halifax W. Yorkshire 10 February
1967 – 71	Birmingham Polytechnic
1971 – 73	Embroidery Designer: Bellville Sassoon, London
1973 – 74	Embroidery Designer: Marie-Paule, Montreal
1974 – 81	Set up business in Canada
1975	Commission for University Hospital London Ontario Canada
1981	Returned to Britain
1982 – 88	Part-time lecturer, Sunderland Polytechnic
1983 –	Exhibits widely: '62 Group; overseas including Japan, Israel and USA; numerous individual exhibitions
1983	Rachel B Kay Shuttleworth Prize Winner Gawthorpe Hall, Burnley
1984	Solo show Calouste-Gulbenkian Gallery, Newcastle upon Tyne
1984 – 90	Part-time lecturer, Cumbria College of Art & Design
1985	Part-time lecturer Cleveland College of Art & Design and Newcastle College Solo show Woodhorn Church Museum, Ashington Solo show Cleveland Crafts Centre Touring Newcastle Playhouse Gallery Joined '62 Group
1986	Solo show Van Mildert Gallery University of Durham
1988	*Hats by Paddy Killer*: Cleveland Crafts Centre, Middlesbrough Northern Arts Award to launch *Dressed to Kill* *Embroidery/World of Embroidery* Autumn issue *Madeira* New issue 4
1988 – 90	Part-time lecturer Monkwearmouth College
1989	ZSK Project: Deutsches Textil Museum, Krefeld, Germany
1990	Northern Arts Award Winners: Touring Exhibition Northern Electric Visual Arts Award Visiting lecturer Glasgow School of Art *Ornamental Handwerken* Zonders Grenzen February issue
1993	British Council Travel Award to Australia
1995	Northern Arts Major Award to develop new work to be shown as part of *Living at Belsay*, Belsay Hall, Northumberland, during the Year of the Visual Arts
1996	*Tunnel Vision*: a Land-Art commission for Sustrans C2C cycle path Air U.K. commission for their 1997 calendar Participant and initiator of The Book of Hours Community Project with Gateshead Arts & Libraries
1997	*Paddy Killer* – New Work. Bankfield Museum, Halifax Solo show *In Arkadia* Myles Meehan Gallery, Darlington Arts Centre later touring to Collins Gallery, Glasgow and Upfront Gallery Penrith; Inverness Art Gallery& Museum; Belsay Hall, Northumberland; Ranger's House, Greenwich; Corrymella Scott Gallery, Newcastle upon Tyne
1997	National Lottery Commission to make the *TaleCoat* for storyteller Taffy Thomas
1999	Short listed for Artist of the Millennium by the BBC
2000	Site-specific commission for East Hartford Community Centre, Northumberland
2002	*Cat & Mouse: From Canada to Computers*; Paddy Killer, a retrospective, The Beacon Museum & Art Gallery, Whitehaven, Cumbria
2003	*Sex & the Seaside* commission for Kirklees MBC

Works are in numerous public and private collections including Tyne & Wear Museums, Darlington Borough Council, Embroiderers' Guild, Calderdale Borough Council, Bankfield Museum Halifax, Hereford City Museums, Churchill House Museum, Rachel B.Kay-Shuttleworth Collections, Gawthorpe Hall, English Heritage Belsay Hall Northumberland
Her work is included in numerous books and magazines
Profiles appear *Designer Textiles* by Fiona Adamczewski 1986 David & Charles; *Fairytale Quilts and Embroidery* by Gail Harker 1992 Merehurst

www.paddykillerart.co.uk

Right: *Tiles Shawl.* One of a series of shawls. Drawing and painting on silk organza. 180cm x 40cm (71in. x 16in.)

Paddy Killer

To be in the presence of this small, energetic, enterprising artist fills one with admiration. Her work is more than good drawing and master craftsmanship. It tells a story sometimes classical, sometimes biographical, even autobiographical, often humorous and always well researched; every work clever in its careful selection of imagery and motifs. The diversity of her subjects, coupled with a prolific output, surely places her firmly in the ranks of the best late twentieth century textile artists.

This remarkable work has come at a personal price for she does say 'life has been hard'. If you ask her what are the high points she may well say 'when I sell something or get a commission, then I know I can feed the cats'. Walter and Wilfred, two handsome Persian brothers are no ordinary four-footed companions but masters of the house – every corner of it! Endearing, clever, naughty they really compete for attention over Paddy's other companion, the computer.

On her fiftieth birthday, never having had a computer, she ordered one to arrive on the day. A knowledgeable friend stood by and made her unpack and assemble everything herself so that, from that day on, she would know what plugged into what. Five years on she has a phenomenal array of equipment at her finger tips. Now upgraded to a Mac G4, has a 23in. cinema display, an A3 and A4 printer, a portable scanner, a portable 15in. Powerbook, ADSL Broadband, a digital camera, Harmon Kardon Sound Sticks, an A5 Wacom Tablet, an iPOD and a 40 GB Pocket drive, she could be deemed to have everything – for the office. Complete fluency in handling the equipment enables her to manipulate her drawings with speed and accuracy. For instance, Paddy will make a drawing. She will scan it using Photoshop. She can then add layers and work on the reverse for printing. She enlarges the drawing and prints out selected areas. These are then placed under the fabrics for tracing outlines with pencil on the light-table. Drawing comes next with technical

Opposite page: *Watch the Tiger,* 1983. Appliqué and machine embroidery on satin, organdie and cotton-velvet. Collection of Tyne & Wear Museums. 55cm x 50cm (22in. x 20in.)

Above left: *The Mirror* 1986 Painting, appliqué and machine embroidery on satin. Private collection. 150cm x 125cm (59in. x 49in.)

Above right: *One Peugeot, Two Persians & Paddy,* 1994. Drawing, painting, marbling and machine embroidery on Honan silk with painted frame. 71cm x 50cm (28in. x 20in.)

Below left: *Who will wear the Crown,* 1991. Drawing, painting and machine embroidery on satin and cotton velvet. Collection of Tyne & Wear Museums

Below right: Counterpane for *Dido & Aeneas* 1992. Drawing, painting and machine embroidery on Honan silk and cotton velvet. Private collection. 250cm x 250cm (98in. x 98in.)

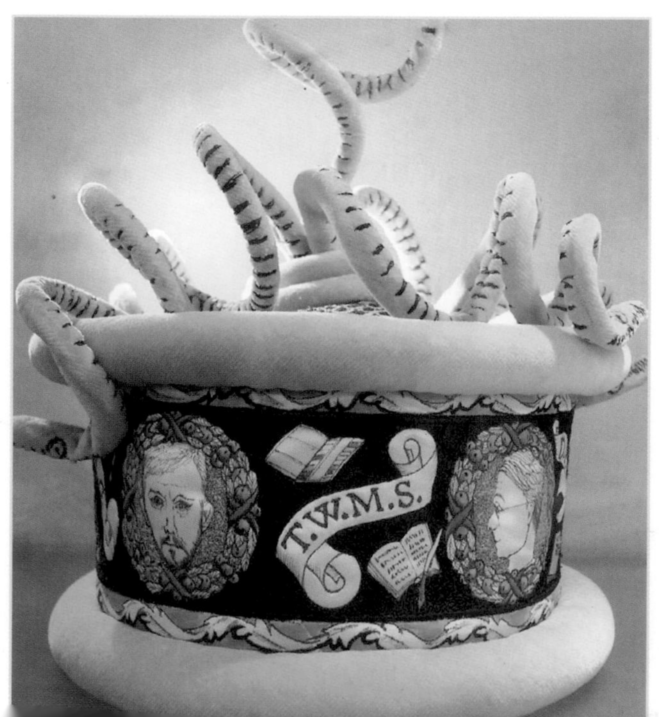

drawing pens, then painting with fabric paint (*Setacolor Transparent* or *Marabou* or *Setasilk* silk paints), finally proceeding to bonding and/or machine stitching.

Sometimes she will sketch from a digital camera image. At other times her inspiration will start with words or observed textures and colours or fabrics. She then moves to the possible ideas. 'I feel people are looking for proper art – I am trying to make meaningful images that communicate. I don't want to follow the fashion of making everything so intellectual that it leaves the viewer with no visual communication and without an artefact'.

Until she had a computer she did not know she was dyslexic. She always wondered why she was not good at reading. 'Now I buy novels on CD. I haven't bought a book for a very long time; I use the internet for research and for downloading plays from Radio 7'.

Sometimes though she has to resort to a book, as in her *Dido and Aeneas* piece. Great leather tomes, belonging to her great, great uncle Abraham, have come down to her and she finds these a great source of inspiration. 'All my life I've been surrounded by things that have come to me'. The walls and shelves of her tiny living room are filled with objects of interest such as the lampshade handmade by

Opposite page above right: *The Pillars of Art* 1994. Drawing, painting and machine embroidery on Honan silk. Site-specific commission for Bankfield Museum, Halifax. 235cm x 140cm (92in. x 55in.).

Opposite page below left: Drawing for *Chi fu Cheng Counterpane,* 1994. Ink & water colour on paper. 59 x 42cm (23 x 16in.)

Opposite page below right: *Sir Charles Monck* (detail) 1996. Made for *Living at Belsay*, Visual Arts Year 1996. Drawing, bonding and painting on Honan & organza silks Collection of The Garden Station, Northumberland. 80cm x 90cm (31in. x 35in.)

Left: *Dionysus* 1997. One of a pair of Hangings for *In Arkadia* solo touring exhibition. Drawing, bonding and painting on antung and organza silks. 273cm x 106cm (107in x 42in.)

Below: *Balmy Knight* 1996. Drawing and machine embroidery on antung silk.
Rachel B. Kay-Shuttleworth Collection, Gawthorpe Hall.

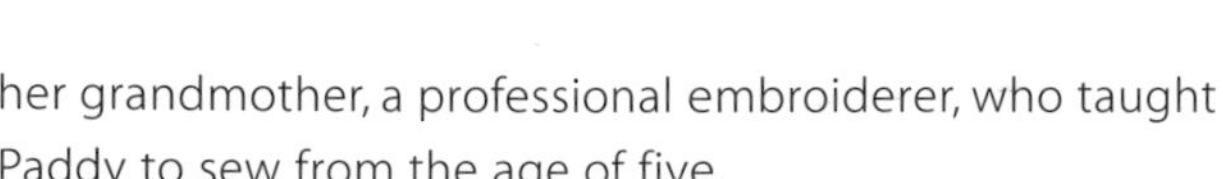

her grandmother, a professional embroiderer, who taught Paddy to sew from the age of five.

She has created an ornate space filling it with modern Chinese lacquer furniture and a Chinese carpet from John Lewis 'her second home'! These she purchased following a commission to make a counterpane for a client who was half Chinese; the interest in things Chinese was triggered.

In stark contrast is her well-lit, simple work room within a small Newcastle Edwardian terraced house. Viewing photo-

graphs of almost everything she has made, it becomes obvious that a résumé of the value of the work of this productive artist is a daunting responsibility.

Through her non-stop narrative, in the accent of her native Halifax, one is drawn to searching for the ground from which this talent and motivation spring. On the one hand there is a sense of the bereft; a loneliness without which her dedicated work may never have sprung. Her mother was rarely kind to her and her father, to whom she was close, died when she was only sixteen removing any emotional security available to her. However, though having only become a father at the late age of fifty, he had had the wisdom to sow the seeds of inspiration by taking Paddy to galleries and taught her to paint in oils, albeit by numbers.

A nine-year spell in Canada seems to have contained a years high point of happiness and success whilst working for the haute-couturier Marie-Paul in Montreal. Marriage too in this first decade of work was unsuccessfully sampled.

On the other hand a return to England in 1981 gave her a sense of a powerful new focus and direction for her work.

Opposite page above: *Revels,* 1997. *In Arkadia* solo touring exhibition. Drawing and machine embroidery on antung silk. Private collection. 285cmx107cm (112in. x 42in.)

Opposite page below left: *TaleCoat,* 1998. National Lottery Commission and Northern Arts commission for storyteller Taffy Thomas. Drawing, painting and machine embroidery on Honan silk and cotton velvet. Photo: Keith Paisley

Opposite page below right: *TaleCoat* (detail), 1998. National Lottery Commission and Northern Arts granted commission for storyteller Taffy Thomas. Drawing, painting and machine embroidery on Honan silk and cotton velvet. Photo: Keith Paisley

Left: *Marye the Quene* (detail). Work in progress. Drawing, painting and machine embroidery on Honan silk. Commission for Hampshire County Council

Below: *Sex and the Seaside,* 2004. Drawing, painting, and machine embroidery on Honan silk. Commissioned by Kirklees Council. 100cm x 260cm (30in x 102in.)

She joined the '62 Group[32] which she says she loves. 'It is a special community of like minded people'. She could also renew the bond, built throughout school days, with her art teacher Vicky Watling, whom she now views in the role of an older sister. Memories of the joy of art both at school and college created the resolve to make a successful living from her own work. Paddy recounts the story of deliberately cheating in her school physics exam in order to fail thus avoiding her mother's wish for a scientific career.

The textiles course at Birmingham was a common course for the first two terms after which Paddy chose to specialise in embroidery. She recalls that college was exciting because of a wonderful drawing tutor Claire Spencer and she felt that 'embroidery was all about drawing'. Visiting tutors of note included Constance Parker[18] and Zandra Rhodes[50].

She has made counterpanes, pillows, hats, waistcoats, hangings and countless panels. Many works are to commission whilst scores have been purchased from a great number

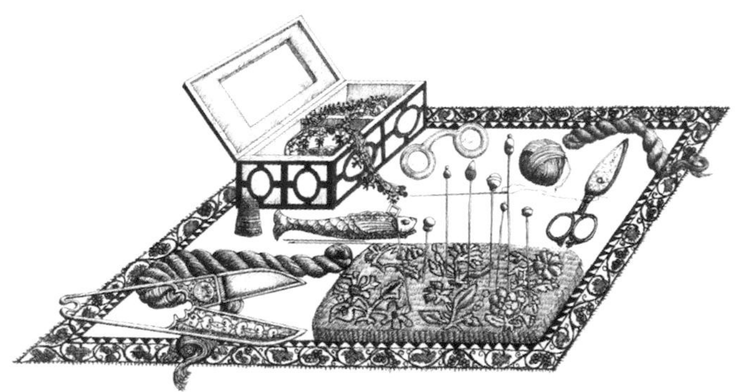

Above: *Wunderkammer,* 2003. Drawing, painting and machine embroidery on Honan silk and cotton velvet. Collection of Hampshire County Council.
112cm x 65cm x 5cm (44in. x 26in. x 2in.)

Below left: *Elizabethan Needlework Tools,* 1994. Ink on paper. Illustration for *The Embroiderer's Story* by Thomasina Beck

Below right: *William Lawson Pillows,* 1996. Ink on paper. Illustration for *Gardening with Silk and Gold* by Thomasina Beck

Opposite above: *Rocque's Counterpane,* 1994. Ink on paper. Illustration for *Gardening with Silk and Gold* by Thomasina Beck

Opposite below: *Cat & Mouse,* 2002. Ink on paper. Drawing for the retrospective exhibition in Whitehaven. Private collection

of exhibitions. She has produced numerous illustrations for which she says she is so much better paid than for the equivalent time as an embroiderer; She hopes that her impressive website will continue to bring her this spread of commissions.

For Paddy 'there is no difference between a piece of canvas and a piece of silk. Anything you can do on paper you can do on fabric – with the addition of texture'.

One of the aspects of her work that makes it so especially personal is her sense of poking fun, sometimes quite wickedly. While working on a portrait of Mary Tudor she turned round wistfully to announce that she plans 'to portray her with black finger nails because she put lots of people to death'.

Paddy's work is memorable in that it can reach the innermost of a personality. A good example is Wunderkammer, a folding triptych depicting the life of William Cavendish, 5th Duke of Portland, whose home was Welbeck Abbey near Worksop. An extraordinary man who had miles of tunnels built under the estate in order to live in lavish style beneath ground. Paddy's response was to depict him, how else, but as a mole. Incidentally, the Harley Gallery, where the work was first shown in a '62 Group[32] exhibition of the same theme entitled 'In Place', is in the building that was once the pumping station for the house.

'Sex and the Seaside', another recent commission, with the same depth of research, is for Kirklees Borough Council. This time characters from 1950s holiday postcards from the archive of the publishers Bamforth & Co. are the subject for her individual style of contemporary mirth and social comment. Transposed too is the location. Northern British resorts are now exchanged for sunny Benidorm, the new Blackpool. Disparate characters mix in a way not conceivable at home. Politicians, TV stars, sportsman; all selected to show how Bamforth's characters might have tackled the twenty first century's obsessions with celebrity, the media, sex, spin et al.

Paddy is certainly opening our eyes and making us smile.

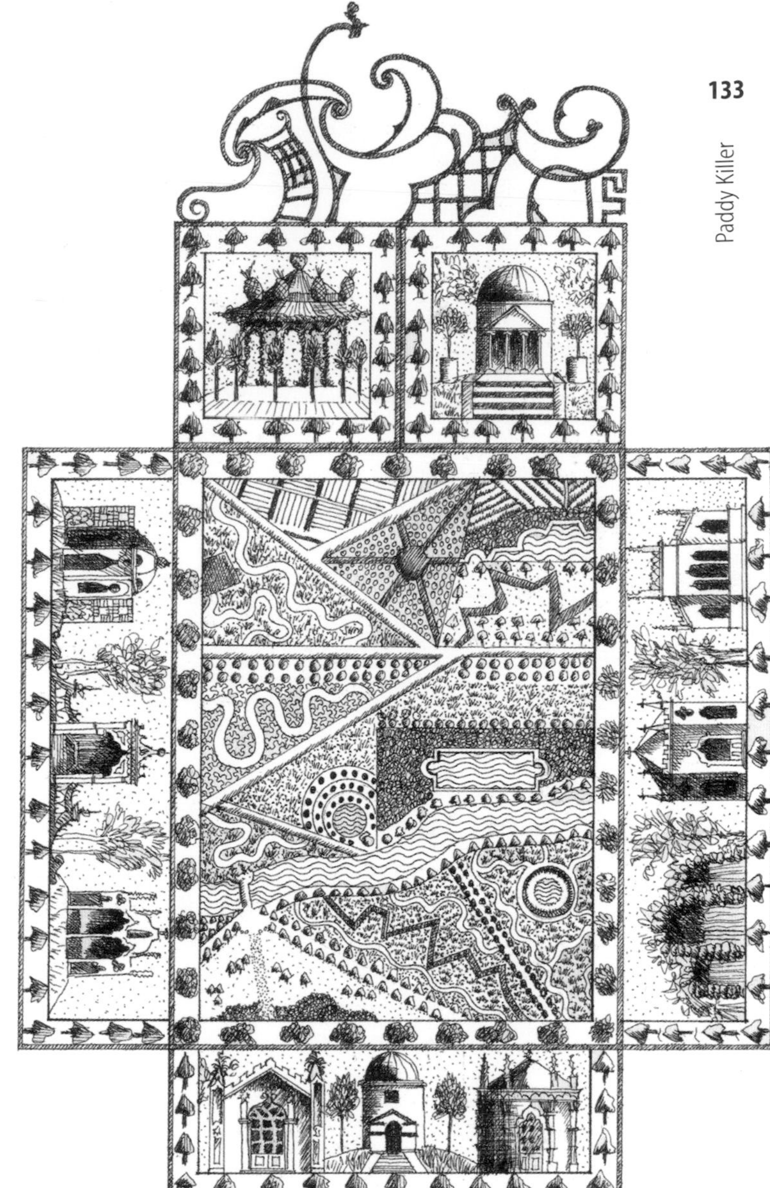

Footnote

50 *Zandra Rhodes 1940- Fashion and textiles designer*

Photo: David Hankey

JEANETTE APPLETON

1949	Born Essex 17 August
1967	Foundation Course St. Alban's School of Art
1970	Married
1974	Daughter Zoë born
1978	Divorced
1979	Loughborough School of Art & Nottingham University. Certificate in Embroidery
1980 – 94	Part-time lecturer at North Hertfordshire College
1987 – 1989	Post Graduate Diploma Textile Art Goldsmiths' College School of Art London Prize winner Hertfordshire Open Art Exhibition
1991 –	Visiting lecturer Universities and groups in Britain and abroad
1993	Joined '62 Group, Feltmakers Association, New Fibre Art Group Prize winner Hertfordshire Open Art Exhibition Four artist show *Felt Works – Work in Felt* Bankfield Museum Halifax Touring Norway. Finland
1993 – 4	Part-time lecturer Public Art/Design Chelsea School of Art & Design London
1994 –	Work exhibited widely with '62 Group. Embroiderers' Guild. Knitting & Stitching Shows
1995	Commission for Nant Mill Visitors Centre Clywd Wales
1995 – 6 1997 – 8	BA Hons. Fine Art Middlesex University London
1996-97	Research year *Nomadism* Japan. Australia. New Zealand. Fiji. USA
1997	Ethnographic Felt research trip to Denmark. Russia. Mongolia
1997 & 98	Award Personal Development Eastern Arts Board
1998	Membership Contemporary Applied Arts London Group show UK & USA artists NSA Gallery Durban South Africa Exhibitor/Lecturer Norwegian Felt Makers Symposium Bode Norway Profile *World of Embroidery* March issue
1999	Group show *Attraktion Filz* Galerie Handwerk Munich Germany ETN and GTG Invitation to lecture/exhibit National Picture Gallery Tbilisi, Republic of Georgia
2000	Four person show *Felt Crossing Borders* I Kragero Norway Eight artist show *Textile Works* Artmonsky Arts Gallery London Group show *Filt ar 2000* Galleri Bryggen Bergen Norway *Art Textiles II* Selected group show Bury St. Edmunds Gallery Membership Society of Designer Craftsmen
2001	Solo show *Nomad:Nomas* Margaret Harvey Gallery University of Hertfordshire. Author Nomad: Nomos catalogue. University of Hertfordshire Galleries. Author *Nomad: Nomos* World of Embroidery July/August issue Four person show *Felt without Borders 11* Tower Gallery Aars Denmark
2002	Four artists *Felt Crossing Borders III* Mitsuhashi Gallery Kyoto Japan
2003	Four artists *Felt Crossing Borders IV* Bankfield Museum Halifax
2003 – 2005	*Through the Surface* mentor project collaboration Japanese/UK catalogue, Surrey Institute of Art & Design
2004	Participant Eleventh International Triennial of Tapestry Lodz Poland

Work is featured in Public Collections including Contemporary Felt Collection Museum of Felt, France. Embroiderers' Guild of Victoria Australia & UK. Hertfordshire County Art Collection. K.P.M.G. Peat Marwick Ltd.Private Collections Britain,. Germany, Denmark, Norway, New Zealand, Australia, USA, Japan.

Right: Detail of *Sown and Unsown Land,* 2000. Heat transfer printing on the surface of stitched felt. 90cm x 264cm (35in x 104in)

Jeanette Appleton

Words that most readily come to mind when describing Jeanette's stitched works on felt are those that evoke harmony and poetic beauty. Subjects for these lovely hangings are founded on an innate sense of discovery, particularly when expressing the concepts of shape and colour. Being by nature a very gentle, modest and unassuming person, it is clearly a surprise to her that her talent as both an artist and a craftsman has attracted widespread appreciation.

The journey to these lyrical works has been in slow thoughtful steps. For Jeanette, failing her 11+ exam remains with her as being one significant fact responsible for her indirect artistic beginnings, coupled with her sense of rather low future expectations. When she left secondary school she didn't really know what course was appropriate or where a training in art might take her. She applied for a Foundation Course at the suggestion of an enthusiastic art teacher because she had done well at drawing for 'O' level art. She was the first pupil from her school to go to art school and the headmistress, never believing she would succeed at interview and, in an effort to prepare her for what she believed had to be inevitable disappointment, said 'don't worry if you don't get in'. But get in she did and enjoyed everything, but feels she excelled at nothing. Without the pre-requisite 'O' levels at this stage there was no chance of progressing to a Dip.AD course. She had tried an industrial fashion course and another in graphics and 'still didn't really know what I was doing or what I wanted to do.' Marrying a fellow student in 1970, she felt she could opt out and happily follow the trend of the time, which was to marry, have children and not necessarily expect to work. Indeed the birth of a daughter a few years later had the reverse effect. She became more focussed and saw time being a precious commodity allowing her to return to study; initially with a 'sandwich' course at Loughborough School of Art. Then, twelve years from the time of

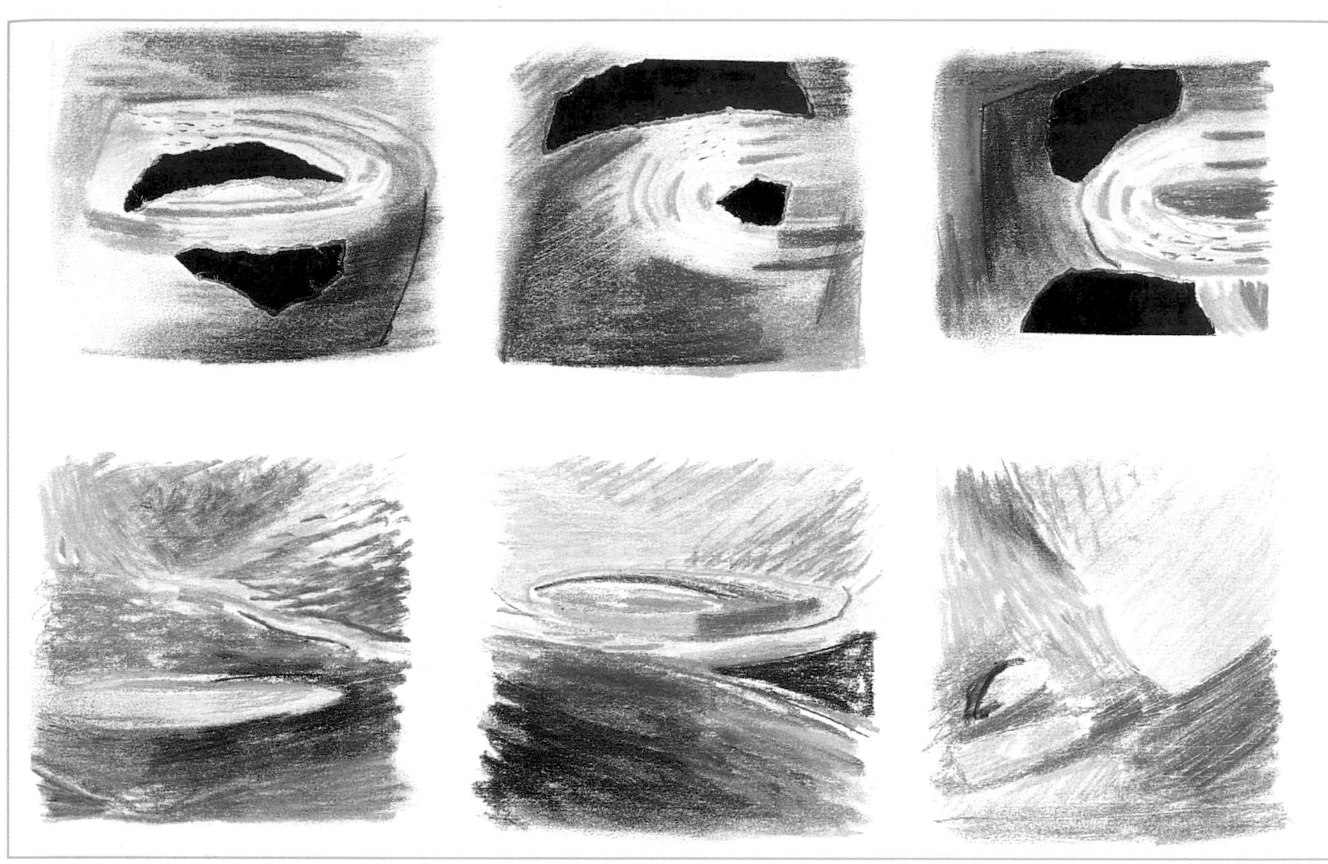

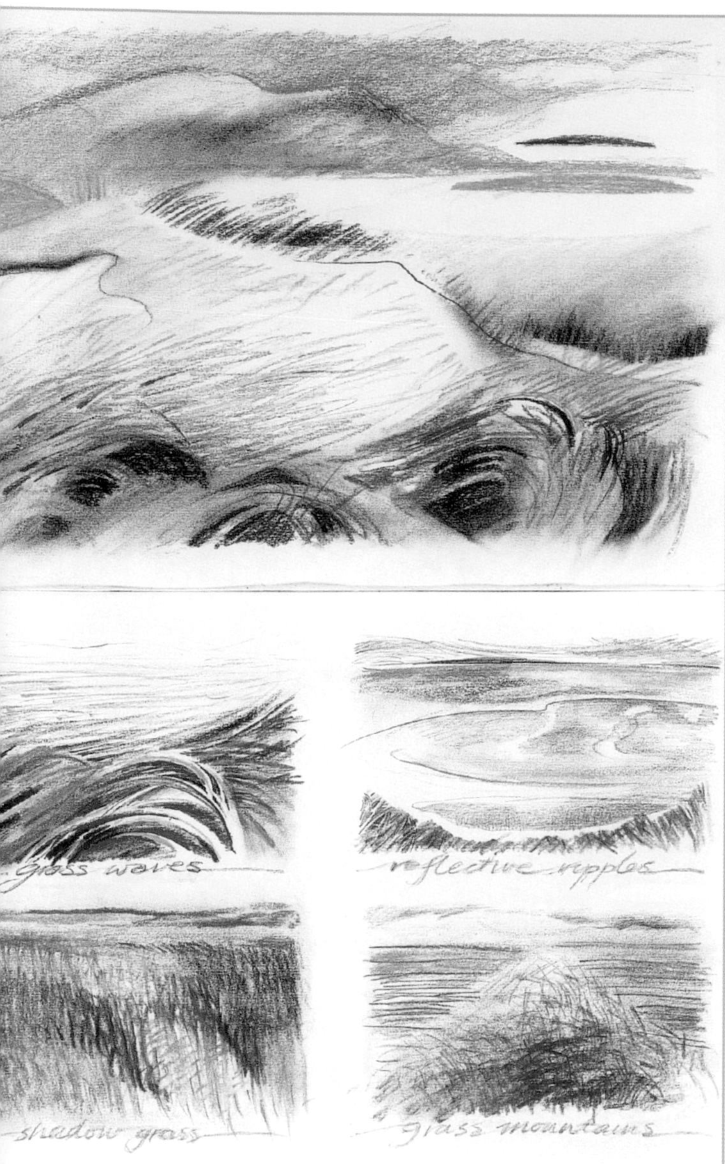

Opposite page top: *Six Sketchbook Pages,* Island Series, 1998-9. Pastel – typical of all drawings inspired by travel which are always made with great immediacy

Left: *Series of Drawings for Island Series,* 1998-9. Pastels

Opposite page bottom: *Islands V,* 1998-9. Personal felting process combining hand dyed merino wool and rayon. 82cm x 115cm (32in. x 45in.)

her initial one year foray into art school, her potential recognised, she was accepted into the one year Post Graduate Diploma at Goldsmiths' College, without first being a graduate! 'People seem to see a potential in me before I see it myself'. Her story continues to be remarkable because she appears to gain qualifications to fit the assignment, whether it be teaching in higher education or exhibiting at national or international level, but only when the need arose. This could be summed up in her own words when she says 'I seemed to work backwards in attaining my qualifications not achieving a BA Hons. till I was fifty. Through experience I have seen each time what I needed and then got qualified.'

The really influential turning point was the London year referred to above. At this time she valued drawing, was good at it and 'loved the skills of representation'. She says she was aware of still lacking the imagination she was seeking. She had always drawn uncreatively right up to and including her first college year. As a child her mother had taken her for walks along the same route every day encouraging her to keep a nature diary of images and collected objects. The reason for this was that her father worked at night and a quiet house in the daytime was important. For this reason also, quiet in-house pursuits were also planned. In tune with early post-war years and the need for thrift and self-sufficiency her tailoress mother encouraged the idea of making everything from knitting constructing clothes. Jeanette recalls with a smile how 'there was always a need to keep everything – even saving every rubber band; and that can take over your life – can even lead to a state of denial! It took me a long time to change that'. Simple childhood holidays were also visually documented and on one occasion she can recall making repeated visits to watch someone who was sketching nearby. Clearly the need to perceive and record has been with her since an early age.

'To draw you have to stand still. Drawing is capturing - extracting - quite different from photography. I went to Goldsmiths' to do embroidery but instead I learned to use my imagination. I had to make marks with many techniques and I had to create a mood within the drawing.' The most significant material discovery was felt, which for the past fifteen years has been the centre of her life. Apart from learning to how to make it she discovered the Horniman Museum close by where she saw her first piece of felt in the form of a yurt. This opened up a new set of issues relating to home and ownership and helped her to relate to her own, now insecure, domestic life. Of these two combined experiences she says, 'Felt made me nomadic. It blended seamlessly with my earliest introduction to wool when as a child I stepped out of bed onto a soft, hand-made wool rug'. Fifteen years ago felt was not widely considered to be a medium for art – it was either industrial or nomadic. The catalyst for her development was an invitation in 1992 to join a government funded project for a week in Eastern Germany designed to give impetus to the regeneration of small industry for local artisans.

Ten foreign artists responded. Jeanette maintains that everyone but her was an experienced felt maker but that she was the only person working in a sketchbook. She learned much technically from those coming from around the world and it enabled her to make lasting contacts with a feltmaker from each of three countries: Norway, Denmark and Japan. 'We all had the common aims of wool – the rest was the difference – it was also about discovering my difference.' The difference is plain to see. Inspired by travel her subjects become visual poetry. 'I love travelling – I turn a corner and there is a new surprise'. Sketches are made with great immediacy resulting in final works of particular atmosphere and mood achieved by a personal felting process. Chiffon, which she hand-embroiders, shrinks when felted onto the wool ground leaving the rayon or cotton stitches in their original size and therefore loose on the surface. Machine stitching in the same situation condenses. The process starts when she dyes the merino wool which is

Opposite top: *Islands 1*,1998-9. Personal felting process combining hand-dyed merino wool and rayon. Embroiderers' Guild collection

Opposite bottom: *Sown and Unsown Land,* 2000. Heat transfer printing on the surface of stitched felt. 90cm x 264cm (35in. x 104in.)

Left: *Emerging,* 1999. Felting with hand dyed merino wool with various natural and synthetic fibres, fabrics and threads Private collection 250cm x 79cm (98in. x 31in.)

then carded[51] ,pulled apart and layered with one colour upon the other. Hot soapy water is applied and the layers are then rubbed together. As the surface shrinks colours on the lower layers begin to show through giving unexpected colour mixes. Sometimes separate areas of felt are made and then applied by stitch. These can also be worked in by hand or machine-sewn lines creating a feeling of embossing or etching. By this method images can seem as if they are emerging from beneath rather than being applied.

A great part of the last fifteen years has been devoted to regular teaching commitments, which she feels has been a compatible balance. Travelling extensively to these assignments both overseas as well as at home has been fundamental to her inspiration. She describes arriving in Georgia by helicopter and watching the way the clouds parted to reveal the patterns of the village below. The sense of being encapsulated in space for her was very akin to a nomadic dwelling, which encloses a small area within a vast expanse. Felt enables her to take students through the basic concepts of making a mark through to colour and eventually to composition of the whole; a marvellous medium for heightening awareness of the design process.

Acceleration of her own journey to creativity started with the unexpected surprise of being accepted for a place at art school and at the same time winning the art prize in that last term of secondary school. So too the arrival of her daughter, far from removing artistic motivation, helped her to structure her life – highlighting the preciousness of time. To these special landmarks she can add the more transitory moments – memories that also last a lifetime such as witnessing felt being 'rolled' by two horsemen in Outer Mongolia; a poignant contrast to the comparatively small scale of her own methods, tools and materials – soap, water, hands and an old Bernina sewing machine.

These she can carry with her as any nomad might for she now plans to live in Spain for six months of each year. Teaching will now be freelance and fitted around a more

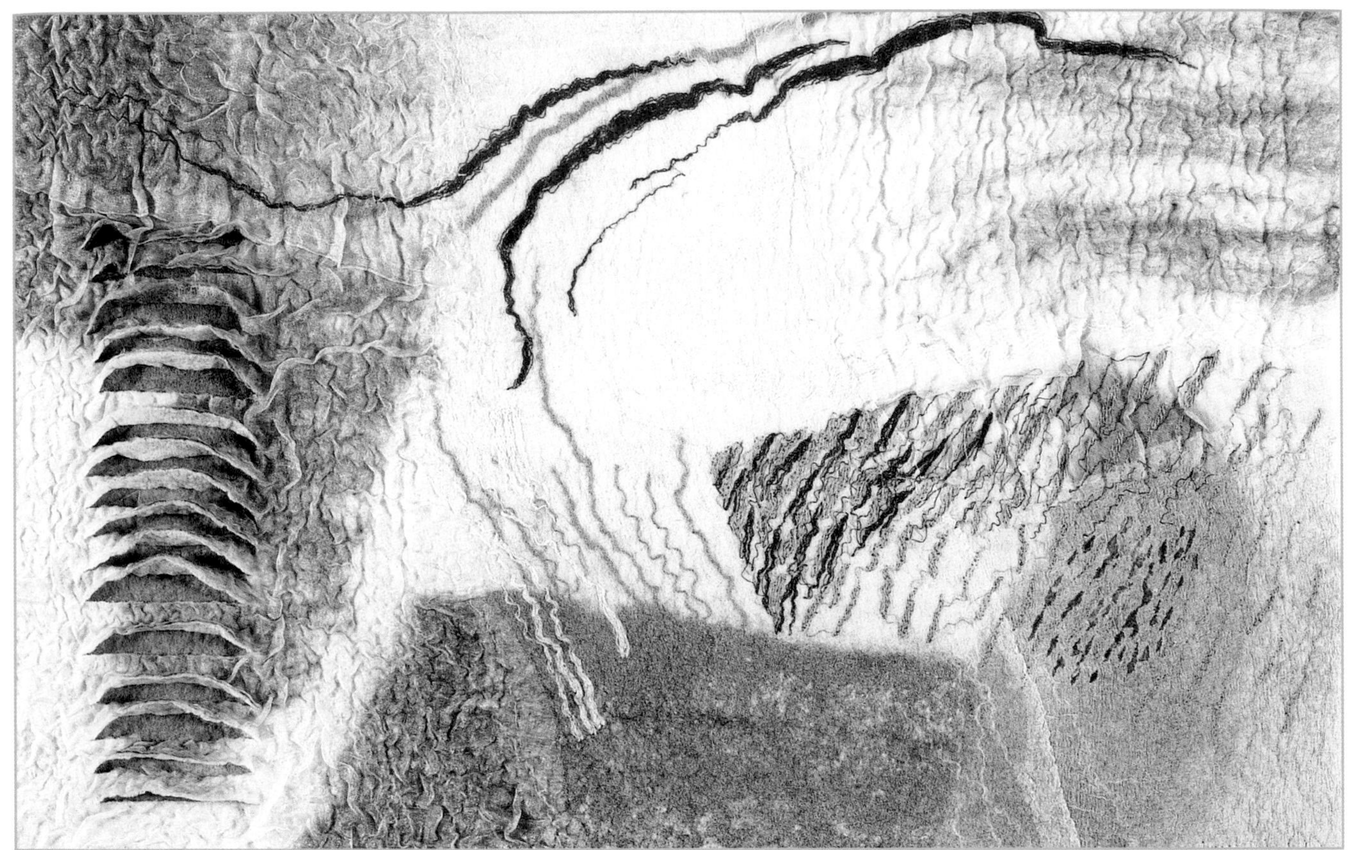

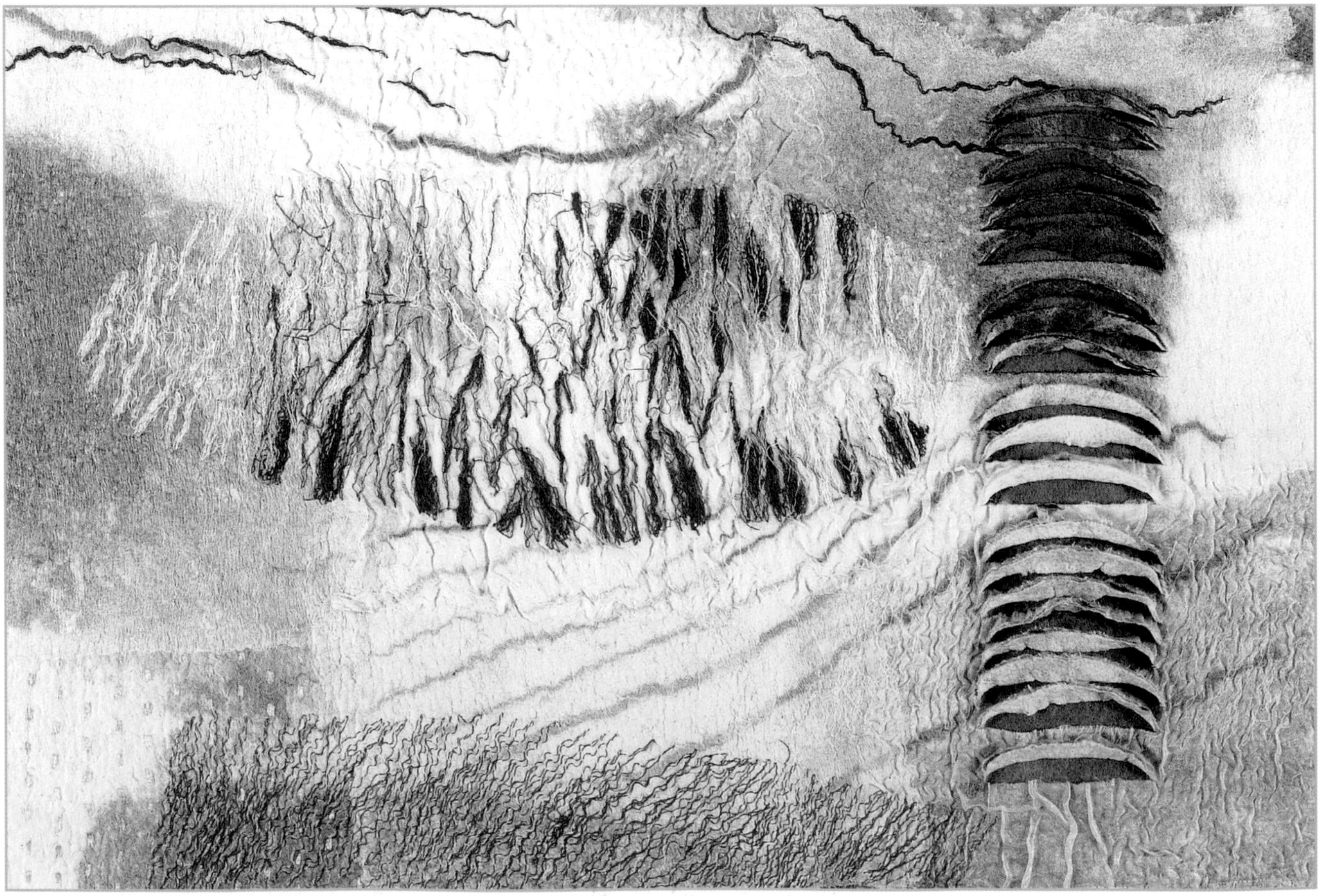

sustained pattern of making her art. Her lyrical works have emerged in thoughtful steps; none more so than now with a move to working in concentrated units of time. Her strength of purpose can only lead to the emergence of even greater work than that achieved to date.

Footnote

51 *Carding is the technique by which the unspun fibres of wool are passed between fine wire tines fixed to rollers or hand held boards. This removes impurities and leaves a fine film of wool with the fibres lying in one direction*

All Photos: David Hankey

Opposite top: *Veiled Land: Coded Site,* 2000. Felting with hand dyed merino wool with various natural and synthetic fibres, fabrics and threads and machine stitching 47cm x 68cm (18in. x 27in.)

Opposite bottom: *Veiled Land: Coded Site II,* 2000. Felting with hand dyed merino wool with various natural and synthetic fibres, fabrics and threads and machine stitching. 47cm x 68cm (18in. x 27in.)

Above: *Georgia sketchbook,* 1999. Arriving by helicopter, the clouds parted to reveal the patterns of the village below

Below: *Cushion,* 2000. Felting with hand dyed merino wool with various natural and synthetic fibres, fabrics and threads Private collection 43cm (17in.) square

Photo: Keith Tidball

PAULINE BURBIDGE

1950	Born Dorset 8 May
1968	Pre-Diploma Yeovil Technical College
1969	Diploma course London College of Fashion
1973	Dip.AD Fashion/Textiles St Martins College of Art London.
1978	New Craftsman's Grant Crafts Council London
1979	Solo show *New Work* Foyles Art Gallery London Living in London
1981	Author *Making Patchwork for Pleasure & Profit* John Gifford Ltd UK. Moved to Nottingham from Brighton
1982	John Ruskin Award Selected for Crafts Council Index
1983	Solo show *New Patchwork Quilt* Midland Group Nottingham Award of Excellence Quilt National USA
1986 – 87	Crafts Council committee 'Setting up Grant'
1989	Solo show Ruskin Craft Gallery Sheffield Crafts Council Committee
1991	Solo show *The Works* Gallery Philadelphia USA
1993	Co-selector for *Contemporary American Quilts* Crafts Council exhibition. Mainstream Design Conference St Johns Newfoundland Tutor/Speaker. Two person show with sculptor Charles Poulsen Joining Forces Angel Row Gallery Nottingham and touring UK Marriage to Charles Poulsen
1994 –	Annual *Open studio* exhibition Allanton Scottish Borders
1995	Split Rock Arts Program University of Minnesota USA Summer School
1995 – 2002	Annual workshops in own studio
1996	Scottish Arts Council grant Quilt Surface Design Symposium Columbus Ohio USA Summer School
1997	Quilt week Yokohama Japan Teacher Lecturer Exhibitor
1998	Mixed show *Take 4 New Perspectives on the British Art Quilt* Whitworth Art Gallery
2000	Solo show European Patchwork Meeting Saint-Marie-Aux-Mines Alsace France *British Contemporary Quilt Exhibition* Matsuzakaya Department Stores, Nagoya/Tokyo/Osaka Japan Curated by Michele Walker Author *Quilt Studio* The Quilt Digest Press USA
2001	Included *The Nineties Collection* The Quilters' Guild of the British Isles
2002	Profile lecture Victoria & Albert Museum Two person show with sculptor Charles Poulsen *Matterart* Shire Pottery Gallery Alnwick, Scotland
2004 – 05	Solo show *Quiltworks* UK touring exhibition Shipley Art Gallery. Knitting & Stitching Shows. Canterbury Royal Musuem & Art Gallery. Collins Gallery Glasgow. Bankfield Museum Halifax

Lectures widely. Represented in key publications. Work has been purchased by many private collectors. Public collections include Aberdeen Art Gallery. National Museums of Scotland Edinburgh. Museum of Costume & Textiles Nottingham. The Glasgow Museums. The Whitworth Art Gallery Manchester. The Victoria & Albert Museum London. The Shipley Art Gallery Gateshead. The Ruskin Gallery Sheffield. The James Collection International Quilt Study Centre University of Nebraska USA. John M Walsh III New Jersey USA.
Participation in group exhibitions are numerous both at home and overseas

Right: *Water Force,* 2004. Paper collage. 40cm (16in.) square.
Photo: Keith Tidball

Pauline Burbidge

There are many reasons for suggesting that Pauline Burbidge deserves a special place in the history of British textiles. Most significantly she has produced, and is still producing, the most beautiful 'quilts' in respect of both design and workmanship. She uses the word quilts because her wall hangings, whether in patchwork or appliqué, are always completed with some type of quilting stitch that joins the layers of fabric and wadding together and the fact that she was inspired by traditional patchwork quilts, their images, texture and scale.

At the outset of her career thirty years ago she resisted compromising the development of her own work by too big a teaching commitment. She bravely chose to survive largely on making, exhibiting and selling; allowing teaching to interject only at carefully scheduled times and in well spaced intervals. Though these teaching commitments were small in terms of contact time she places great value on the numerous invitations she received to give workshops. Not only did these give her a great deal of pleasure but provided the reason to formalise her many processes of designing and making. She shared her design and technical knowledge generously finally committing it to print in her book 'Quilt Studio'. Now, no longer even giving the popular workshops at her studio, she justifies this by saying 'everything is well tried and in the book'. At one time she would be visiting as many as seven different colleges but sometimes for as little as one or two days a year which she found very exciting and remarks 'over that twenty years my work went along with the teaching'.

It has been a great privilege to witness the discipline and integrity of Pauline's work from the time she was awarded one of the much coveted Crafts Council 'Setting up Grants' twenty five years ago, to the present. When asked what she would consider as being a high point in her work to date she replied 'in career terms, the success

Design for "Pyramid in Disguise" and "Stripey Step"
Pauline Burbidge © 1985

Use one colour from last + add 2 new ones in next

'Pyramid in disguise'
Pauline Burbidge
© 1985

Opposite page: *Pyramid in Disguise,* 1985. Silk. Private collection. 168cm x 158cm (66in. x 62in.). Photo: John Coles

Left: Detail. *Pyramid in Disguise.* Photo: John Cole

Top: Designs for *Pyramid in Disguise,* 1985. Pencil drawing on left and coloured pencils on right. Photo: Keith Tidball

Above: Quilting Plan and Drawing for *Pyramid in Disguise,* 1985. Photo: Keith Tidball

Above: *Aberdeen Study IV,* 2001. Collection Aberdeen Art Gallery. 202cm (80in.) square. Photo: Keith Tidball

Left: Detail. *Aberdeen Study.* Photo: Keith Tidball

Opposite above: *Pittenweem Quilt,* 2002. Free form fabric collage with stitching and quilting based on images of Pittenweem. Harbour reflections 150cm (59in.) square. Photo: Keith Tidball

Opposite below: Detail. *Pittenweem Quilt*. Photo: Keith Tidball

getting that grant, even today it is still in my mind'.

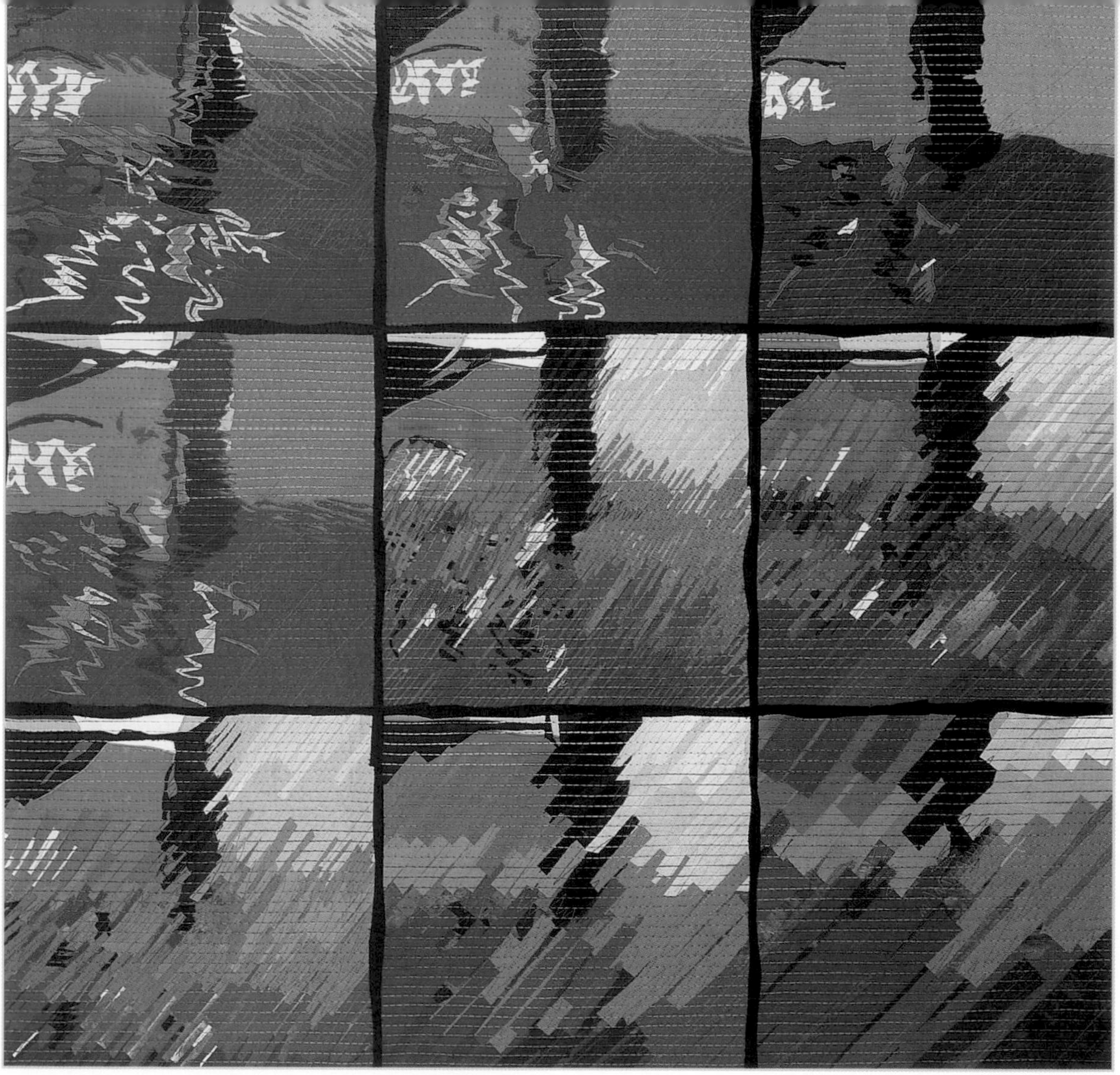

The early works are exclusively geometric and inspired by traditional patchwork. The patchworked shapes were assembled in block-style with a precision based on pattern cutting skills learnt as a student. The character is one of bold plain colour contrasts, often with the addition of black, achieved by straight, machined seams. Separate units once assembled were visually softened by the machine or hand quilting that followed. She says that the technical proficiency gained in these early years of 1975 to mid 1980's have given her the total confidence with fabric that she enjoys today. 'For me I needed to have followed this discipline though I do remember consciously trying to free up – in the end geometry was driving me mad'. Fortunately at this stage the general mood of traditionally constructed patchwork quilts, particularly in America, was gradually breaking down in favour of a less formal style. Encouraged by this Pauline moved from meticulously prepared graph-paper drawings, often based on decorative box lids, book jackets

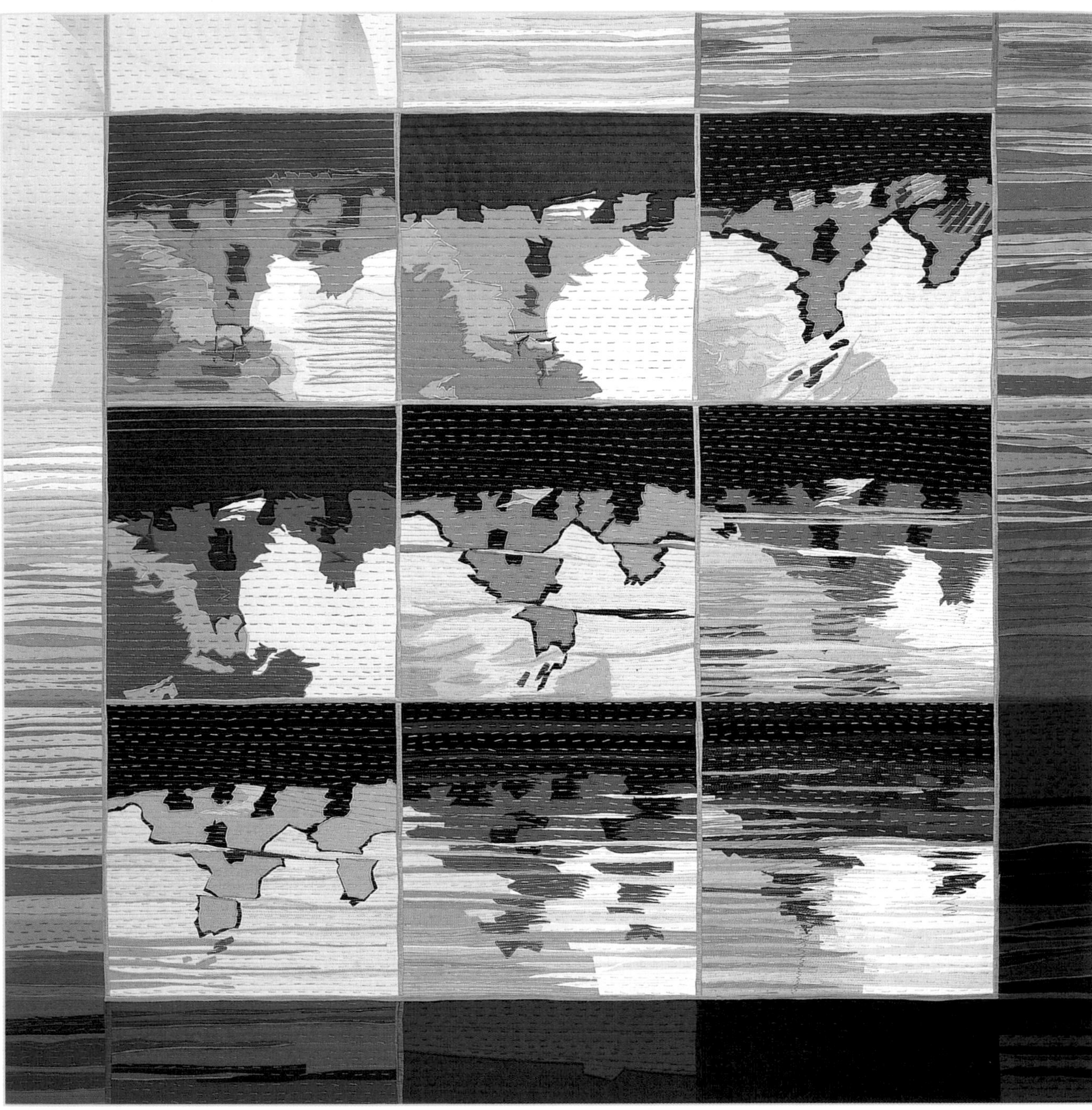

and other bits that had caught her attention in second hand markets, to much freer representations of subjects around her. As a consequence her technique moved from patchwork to appliqué and the shapes moved from hard edged to organic. Observational drawing of figurative subjects and still-lives developed sequentially, and in series, and ever more critically, with no loss to the continuing highest standards of craftsmanship.

Looking back at her childhood it is clear that although she did not come from an art or craft background, a sister, when studying art as a main subject in preparation for infant teaching, was always happy for Pauline to join in on her sketching trips.

It is also significant to note that by the age of ten, art was proving to be a strong attraction. With an eye on 'the brilliant and wonderful art department' in the nearby Sherborne secondary school, coupled with her view that the art department in the grammar school was not comparable, she planned to fail her 11+ exam. She got her way and in time the art master was helping her with the admission application to the Foundation year at Yeovil Technical College.

Brought up on a working farm in Dorset, the youngest of four girls, life was very happily one of outdoor play, of

Opposite page: *Eyemouth House Reflections,* 2002.
Private collection 152cm (60in.) square. Photo: Keith Tidball

Top: Sketchbook drawings of Hector Falls 2003.
Photo: Keith Tidball

Above: *Waterfall II,* 2003. Drawing in gouache 38cm (15in.) square. Photo: Keith Tidball

Right: Drawing of Waterfall, 2003. Photo: Keith Tidball

gathering and stacking of produce and of cooking. A very 'hands-on' way of life. Her mother did sew and possessed an old Singer machine and made their clothes. Pauline tells the story that, lest her mother should try to direct the making of a certain gingham top, she hid under her parents' bed to cut it out her way; she confesses with a laugh that she still recalls that it did not even go over her head. She also recalls the pleasure of being allowed to use the sewing machine on paper thereby creating regular perforations to make their own 'stamps'.

Five years at art school was to see a gradual increase in the study of Textiles and Fashion. A year spent at the London College of Fashion proved not to contain the creative element she was seeking and again, with her own special brand of self-determination, took her portfolio to St Martin's School of Art and was accepted. Confessing now that she remembers 'finding that fashion was not quite for me', she contented herself with life drawing and the chance to meet and socialise with painters and a world of fine art.

She left college with many skills but above all with the will to work hard and to the highest standards. Though her success is due to her own efforts she highlights the importance of being supported by the establishment. In addition there is no doubt, when spending time with her at her home and studio, that her marriage to Charles Poulsen[52] is fundamental to her output. It is a very significant and perfectly balanced partnership of personal and professional support. She admits that being an artist is a lonely business. Each provides mutual support in the daily running of a business and of being self employed – everything; including making decisions as to whether to go for this project or that. They have built together an environment that is totally suited to their individual needs in a working space.

A converted mill in a village some eight miles west of Berwick-upon-Tweed gives them numerous outbuildings and a complete sense of identity. They feel they could have chosen to live anywhere provided the shape and nature of the space was suitable – even an industrial building. They stopped work for a year in order to work on the buildings and create a habitable space. Today it is a remarkable place each room being an extension of their art either in colour, pattern or sculptural relief; some for living, some for different aspects of work and some for display.

In an upstairs room set aside for finished work it is possible to grasp a sense of the magnitude of what has been achieved. She is still hugely motivated and moving forward. The latest series, based around the theme of water, begun before she moved from Nottingham in 1993 but stimulated by a recent opportunity to spend a month in America, is closely linked to what she has seen. Large black and white appliqué hangings of great sensitivity emerge from the experience of having made pencil drawings, bold brush gouache drawings and digital photographs. The gestural, almost calligraphic approach of these marks on paper, enable her to eliminate all but the critical personal selection of shapes and movements.

This work is clearly a high point. For her these are when the current work is going well. She admits to sometimes being too serious 'it takes you over and you have to make an effort to do other things'. To get away from work is difficult, as with many artists, she lives amongst it. She and Charles do not go on holiday unless it is work related. They love to beach comb but admit to not doing enough of that. Regular relaxation is joining the two-hour Morris dancing session in the village hall 'it is such a nice relief to be told what to do'.

She clearly loves to do what she is doing – her own work – and though continually asking herself what she wants from life, the answer changes from year to year. At the moment it

Below: *Boatday/Contemplation,* 2004. Quilt Fine cottons, silks, fabric paint, stitching and quilting. Reflected images of a person with reeds and grass, in a still water pond near the artist's home.112cm (44in.) square

Opposite page: Detail. *Boatday/Contemplation,* 2004. Photo: Keith Tidball

Below: Paper Collage Study *Boatday II* 2003. One method used as starting points for quilts – some of which develop into finished works 38cm (15in.)square. Photo: Keith Tidball

Top right: Quilting Plan *Boatday/Contemplation*, 2003. This shows the plan for all the large stitches that cover the piece thereby adding to the image as well as quilting the three or more layers of cloth together 15cm (6in.) square Photo: Keith Tidball

Below right: Top Stitching Plan for *Boatday/Contemplation* 2003. For work on the top cloth 15cm (6in.) square. Photo: Keith Tidball

Opposite top: *Under the Waterfall*, 2004. 'I could walk underneath and behind the waterfall at Watkins Glen in upstate New York. It was very exciting and I began working from my digital photographs and then on returning home I let the fabric take over.' 112cm square (44in.). Photo: Keith Tidball

Opposite below: Detail of *Under the Waterfall*, 2004. Photo: Keith Tidball

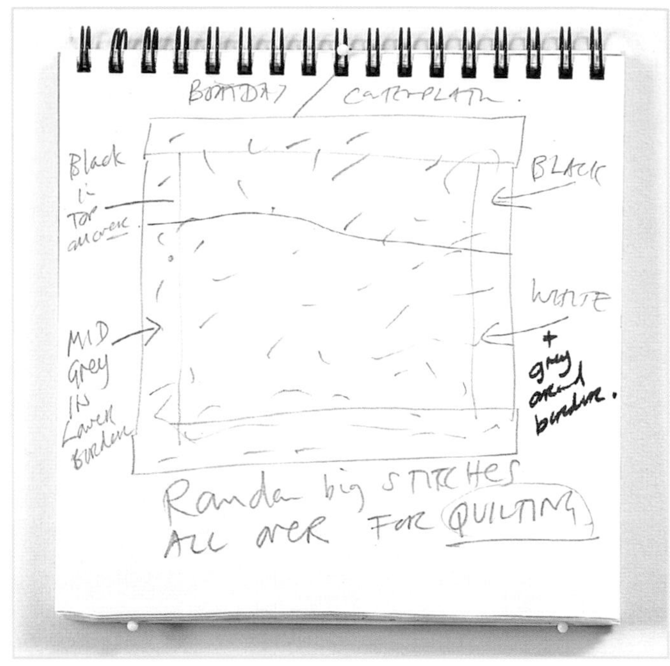

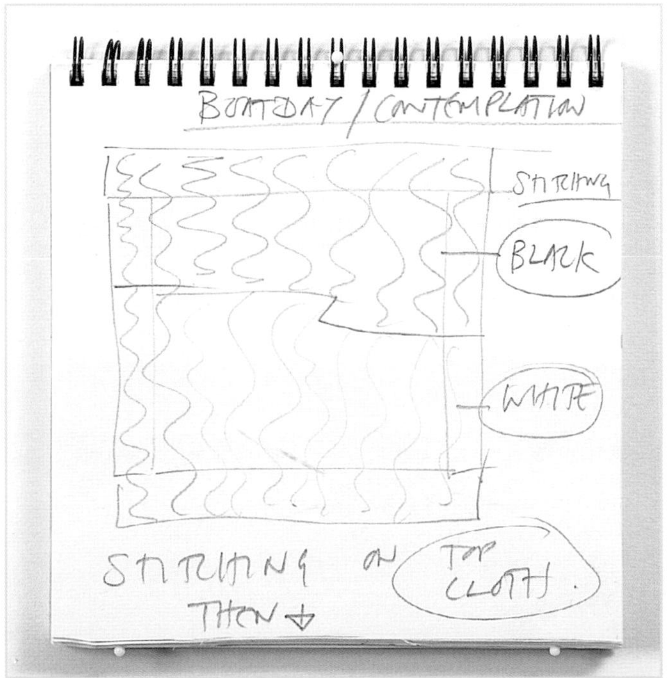

is a serious focus on producing a large body of work to tour in 2004. As this begins to be assembled it is here that one is able to absorb what is so personal to this output. The outcome of a disciplined commitment through observation, design, technical perfection, sustained over three decades, yields work of integrity and lyrical beauty.

In spite of the nearness of the solo exhibition she positively sparkles when recounting what is next. Standing in a corner of the display room is her latest acquisition – a Grace Quilting Machine – which is really a quilting table frame that will hold her own small old Bernina 707. The big excitement is that she wants to experiment with what she is calling 'quilt drawings'; a move away from being a person working in flat shapes to someone working in lines. The underlying plan and hope is that it will give her the chance to produce less expensive and practical/usable works. Apart from the early years, when her work was constructed from repeating and regular shapes and templates, she has not

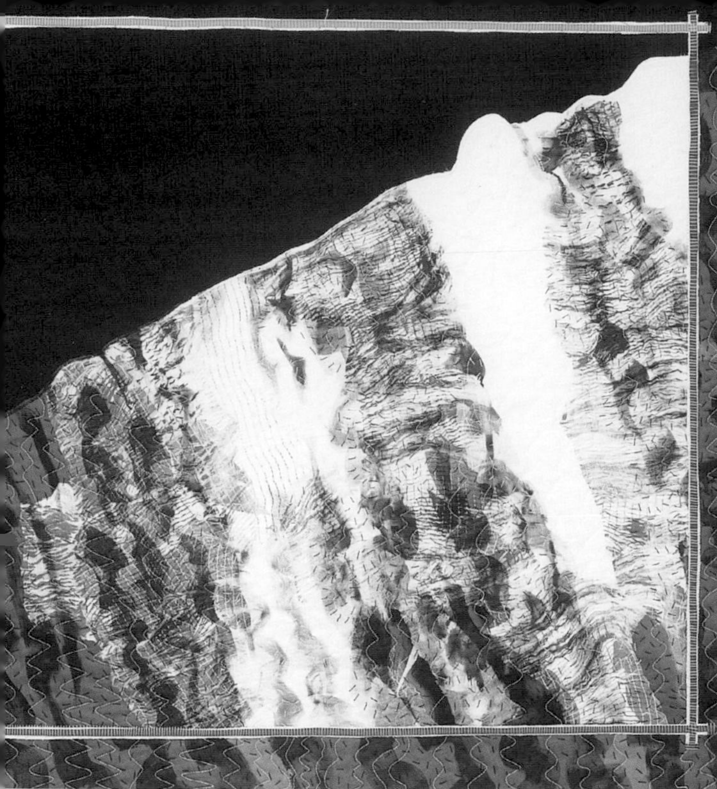

been able to benefit from employing additional hands. Looking around her design and making room it is obvious that she has very little desire or need for sophisticated equipment. Recently however she has acquired a computerised Bernina Artista 180 in order to have a 9mm wide zig zag. A spin-off facility is that now she can enjoy producing very splendid machine stitched labels with her name and titles of works for the reverse of every finished piece – a final mark of absolute professionalism.

The three ordinary techniques of Patchwork, Appliqué and Quilting[53] have, in the hands of this quiet and gentle personality, taken on a new identity.

Footnotes

52 *Charles Poulsen 1952-. Sculptor working mainly in lead sheet for buildings and garden sculpture*

53 *Quilting: stitching by hand or machine to attach three or more layers of fabric together. Appliqué: applying pieces of fabric to another by means of stitch. Patchwork: areas of fabric seamed together with turnings*

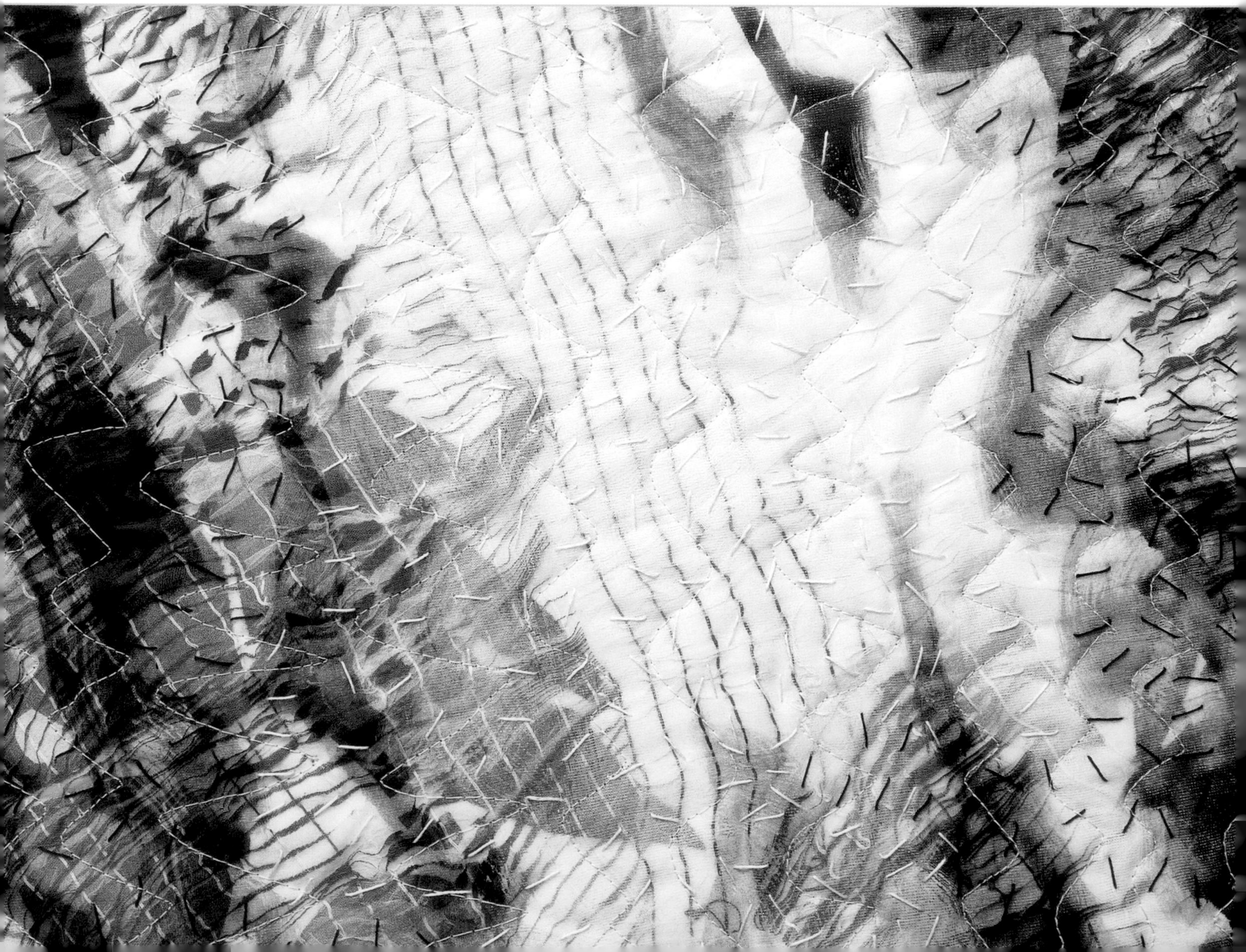

Photo: Peter Clark

KAREN NICOL

1952	Born N. Yorkshire 27 May
1969 – 73	Foundation and BA Hons. Embroidery Manchester School of Art
1973 – 75	MA Textiles Royal College of Art
1979 – 99	Embroidery and Knitwear Consultant Designer and production outlet for German Fashion House Cissule Uta Raasch Dusseldorf
1981	Married Peter Clark
1983	Birth of daughter Katy
1987	Birth of daughter Grace
1990 – 2004	Design and production of embroidered horsehair for furnishing textiles for John Boyd Textiles. Clients include: Zimmer Rhode, Clarence House, Brunswig Fils. Seating for Washington Museum. Dining chairs for George Bush and King Gustav of Sweden. Upholstery for Thai Royal family. Chairs for King of Norway. Senior Lecturer Mixed Media Textiles Royal College of Art
1996 – 2004	Designs and production of mixed media/embroidered for couture fashion pieces for Bruce Oldfield
1997 – 2004	Designs and production of mixed media/embroidered fashion pieces for Clements Ribeiro
1998	Designs and production of mixed media/embroidered fashion pieces for couture for Chanel
1998 – 2004	Designs and production of mixed media/embroidered fashion pieces for John Rocha
1999 – 2002	Designs and production of mixed media/embroidered fashion pieces for Markus Lupfer
1999 – 2004	Designs and production of mixed media/embroidered fashion pieces for Matthew Williamson Ranges of embroidery, brand, print and bead suede, leather and sheepskin designs and production for Preston Knight (Maxfield Parrish)
2002	Four design groups for Givenchy design collection
2002 – 03	Designs and production of mixed media/embroidered fashion pieces for Michiko Koshino
2002 – 04	Designs and production of mixed media/embroidered fashion pieces for Julian Macdonald and for Betty Jackson
2004	Designs and production of mixed media/embroidered fashion pieces for Chloe, and for Tracey Boyd

Other clients include: Antonio Beradi, Whistles, Browns, Tracy Mulligan, Lulu Guiness, Marks & Spencer, Courtaulds, Jaeger, Harvey Nicholls, Harrods, Anne Tyrrell, Liberty, Mario Testino, Grey Advertising, Mulberry, Scott Henshall, Cashmere Studio

www.karennicol.com

Right: *Arthur,* 2004. Spectacle lenses with opticians marks set in organza for Karen Nicol

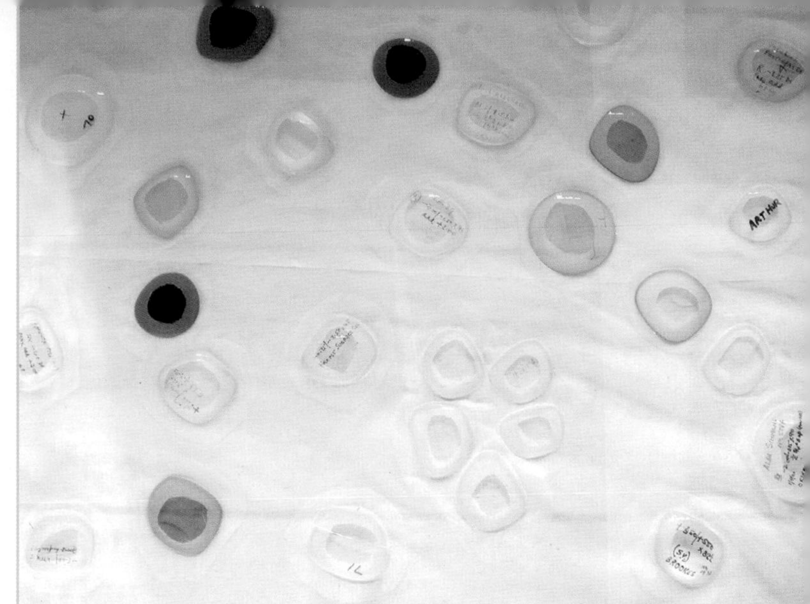

Karen Nicol

Karen's name is unlikely to be widely known in the embroidery world. She chose instead to work without authorship with many established dress and interior designers of whom many are names, not just familiar, but famous. For the past twenty five years she has been the anonymous hand behind the design of embellishment of so many fashion items and objects of interior decoration. Both trusted and revered by her impressive client list she is charged with considerable freedom. In the case of Clements Ribeiro for instance 'they give me the silhouettes, the style of the collection, the theme, and then I can experiment'. For example their current collection for spring summer 2005 is to be inspired by Maharaja jewellery – the clothes will be simple and Karen's task will be to richly accessorise by means of embroidery and beads. She clearly loves her work and not only accepts the daunting schedule but is comfortable with it. Her work pattern is governed by two main elements per year around which the rest fits. The first is to respond to two fashion collections per year, February and September, and the second is her two day teaching commitment at the Royal College of Art. The fashion designer's brief will arrive in July for the September collection. She will then be designing for two months, which includes 'sampling'. It is clearly an exciting stage. When this starts she has to fit in about seventeen hours of embroidery per day for four to six weeks in order to complete embroidery on all the garments that will be required for the catwalk shows; sometimes on up to forty or fifty garments for a collection.

This means 5.30am starts and seven days a week. Two of these days are taken out for teaching which, for her, is an inspiration and a privilege and something she would not relinquish. She is senior tutor for Mixed Media Textiles and values the opportunity to work in this unique situation of guiding eight to nine students per year group, adding up to a total of no more than sixteen to twenty students over the two year period. In return for her

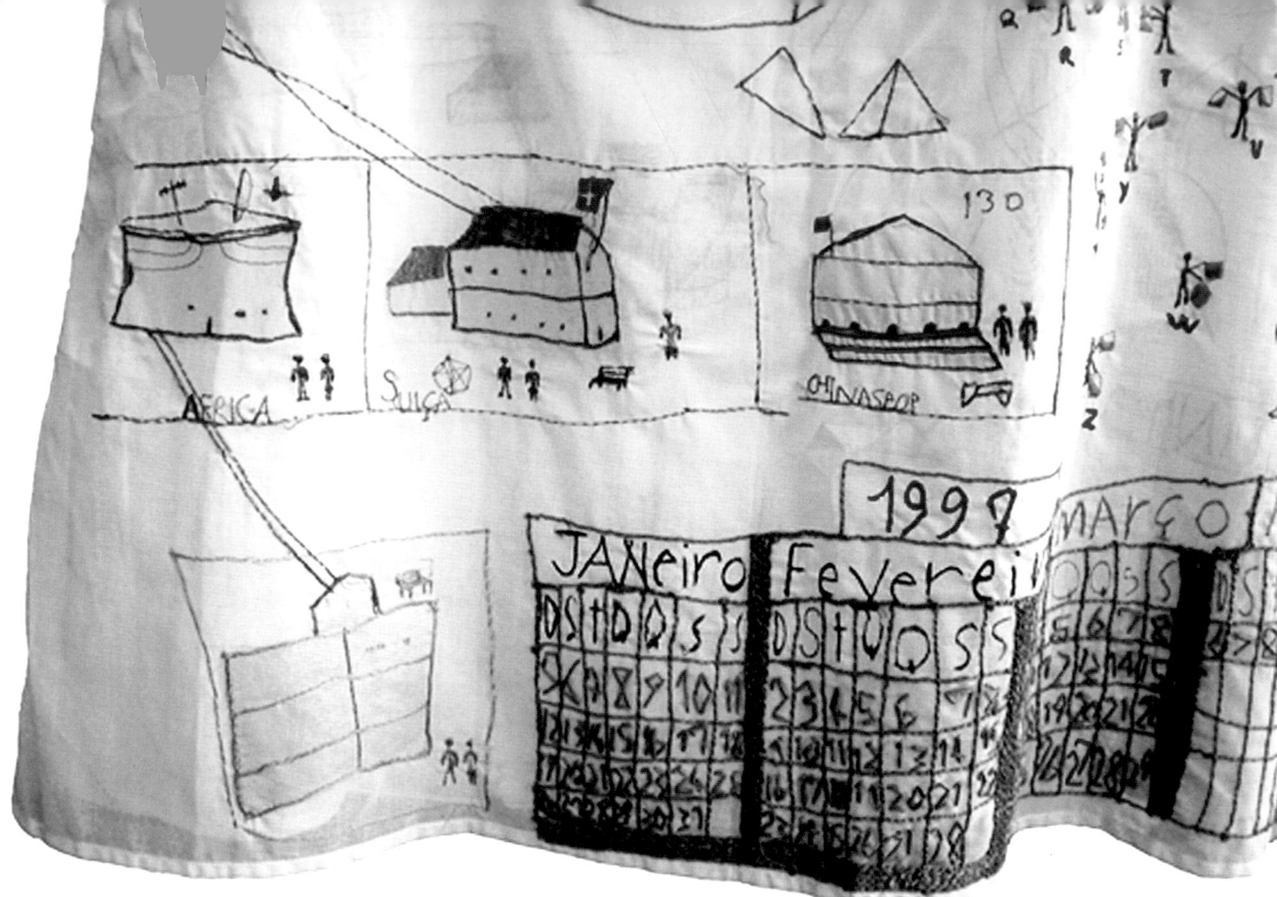

Above: *Bispo Calendar Dress,* 1987. Detail of dress inspired by Brazilian artist Bispo and designed for Clements Ribeiro

Opposite top left: Branded Sheepskin, 2003. Detail of free hand drawing on skins with hot metal for Maxfield Parrish/Preston Knight

Opposite top right: *Yellow Collar*, 2001. Designed for Bruce Oldfield. Three dimensional flowers in cashmere built into the collar

Opposite below left: *Rag Shawl,* 2002. Designed for Clements Ribeiro. Fabrics used to 'embroider' the flowers

Opposite below right: *Tartan Man.* Embroidered drawing inspired by *Art in Psychosis* exhibition for Clements Ribeiro

expertise and experience she finds the available technology and the library of profound importance.

She entered the embroidery scene with almost an inevitability. Her mother Kit Nicol was art school trained in embroidery and taught the subject in evening classes at Rotherham College of Art. Her sister Lyn, older by some three years, preceded her in taking the BA Hons degree in embroidery at Manchester Polytechnic. When Karen enrolled for her Foundation year she was determined that her BA subject would be anything but embroidery – Fine Art instead, she thought. However once embarked on the exploratory units of the first year there was no question in her mind that Embroidery was her overriding passion.

School years, which included the last four at a boarding school in Harrogate, seem to have contributed little to her artistic interests or ambitions. However, influences from home were fundamental. Her mother, now eighty, was the key to her profound early interest in sewing and cloth. At the age of thirteen she was told 'you can have as much fabric as you want but from now on you make your own clothes.' I was terrible – I used cellotape, staples, anything that fixed a hem or a seam, to hasten the realisation of my ideas'.

She had to wait till college to meet her next significant mentor. She speaks of Judy Barry[54] as being a great influence. 'She was so wonderful, so passionate about everything visual and really opened my eyes.'

It takes more than the influence of others to succeed in a niche business. Behind this quietly spoken modest exterior must lie enormous energy, determination and vision.

Before leaving Manchester Karen had developed an ambition. Unlike her peers who sometimes saw an embroidery career as a balance of teaching with making embroidery she, on the other hand, had a clear plan to make a business out of embroidery.

First she had to negotiate her way around the MA course at the Royal College. Due to the absence of embroidery as a subject she tried her hand at print, weave and knit. Desperately looking to make a surface on which she could

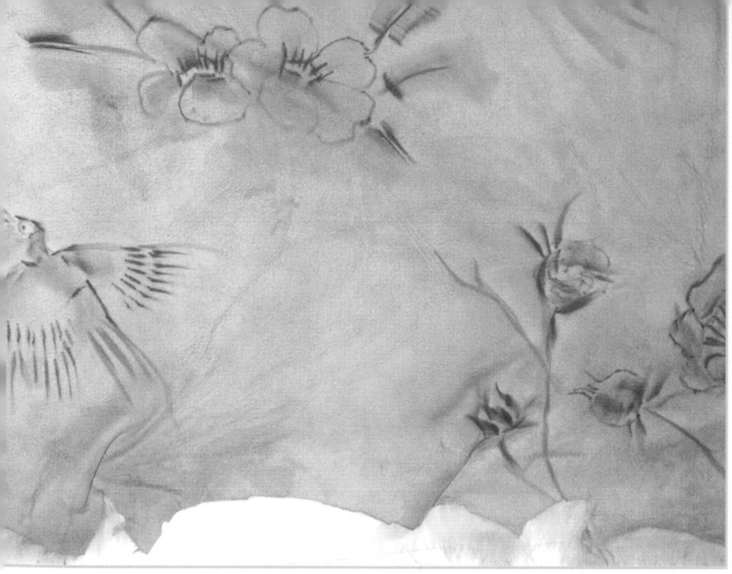

embroider she taught herself to use a knitting machine with the help of the handbook. Though having to go to Goldsmiths' College to access the Irish and Cornely embroidery machines that she needed, she was eventually realising her dream to produce embroidered knitted garments.

By the late 1970s she had developed enough work to fill a suitcase and set off for Paris. She went into shops she liked the look of and, here and there, they bought one or two. She had the good sense to label them with care explaining the individuality and source 'lest an American buyer might think the embroidery was applied by "a kit".' The breakthrough came when Uta Raasch, the German fashion designer saw one, bought one, read the label and flew to London the next day. This became a working partnership for the next fourteen years. 'She gave me the time to learn and to set up the business'.

The demands of the business now, and certainly over the last many years, have meant that work and living have to be in one and the same place. The main workroom, along with an adjacent one for her artist husband Peter Clark[55], is in the well-lit basement of a charming Victorian house in a leafy enclosed garden in the congenial setting of East Molesey, Surrey. This proximity to each others work brings mutual artistic support – each the absolutely honest creative critic of the other.

The house is, of necessity, simply furnished in order that project 'rushes' can spread to every available space. Collected treasures are therefore not obvious until their joint specialist passion for flea markets, of which they are experts, becomes evident. For Karen this special resource of pleasure is stowed in two high stacks of transparent boxes, one upon the other, crammed full. Lids lifted one by one; reveal highly discerningly collected small objects of ornament. Categories include diamante, buckles, beads, clasps, hatpins and so much more. Peter's enthusiasm lies in a specialist eye for amassing printed paper suitable for constructing his wonderful perceptive humorous collages. Old ledgers, maps, print of every type and the marks of many a hand, line the shelves.

The sewing work room is big enough to house three ancient Irish machines, a Cornely machine, a large central work table with two further machines, up to four assistants

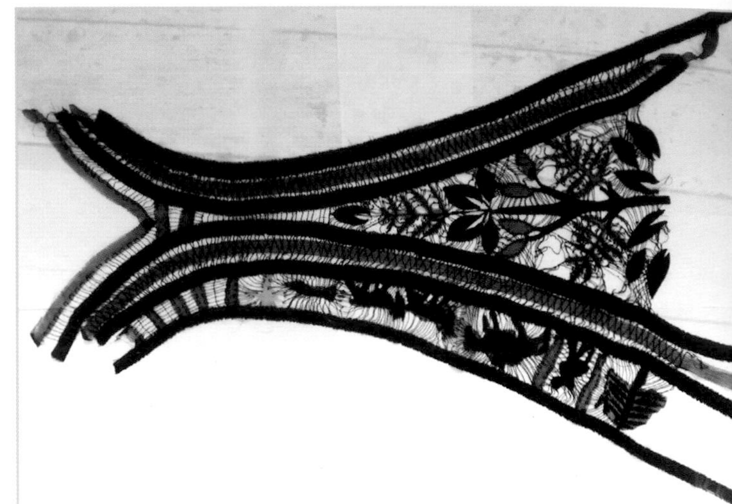

Above left: *Crow,* 2004. Detail of embroidery for Karen Nicol

Above right: *Woodland Lace,* 2004. Torn chiffon and thread. Black embroidered lace for Karen Nicol

Below left and right: Hair Accessories – Blue, Pink. 2003. Raffia and millinery ribbon flowers for Hankyu, Japan

Opposite page top: Tulle Skirt, 2003. Leather and lace embroidery designed for John Rocha

Opposite page below: Layered chiffon feather skirt, 2004, designed for John Rocha

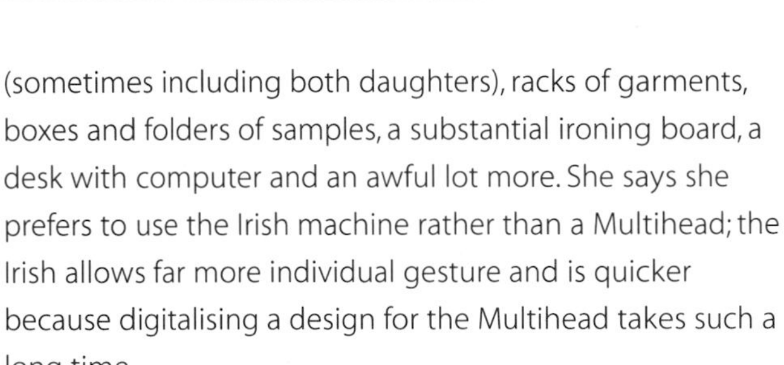

(sometimes including both daughters), racks of garments, boxes and folders of samples, a substantial ironing board, a desk with computer and an awful lot more. She says she prefers to use the Irish machine rather than a Multihead; the Irish allows far more individual gesture and is quicker because digitalising a design for the Multihead takes such a long time.

Karen is aware that during this last year the nature of part of her type of business is changing. The quicker simpler embroidery that they regularly undertook in repeats of around a thousand a year are now being produced in India or China. Instead she is only retaining requests to do the production on the orders of the heavily worked garments; something that may take a day and a half to embellish. Financially this is more difficult to reconcile. The work has become couture for a ready to wear market needing ready to wear prices. If the true price for an item taking a day and a half to embroider were to be realistically charged, this part, when multiplied by seven by the time it gets to a shop, would be unaffordable.

Undaunted, and with her warm smile, she will explain the pleasure of receiving parts of garments from John Rocha. 'They have everything beautifully made in Italy. It is much cheaper for them if we work on a made up garment and then send it back to them'.

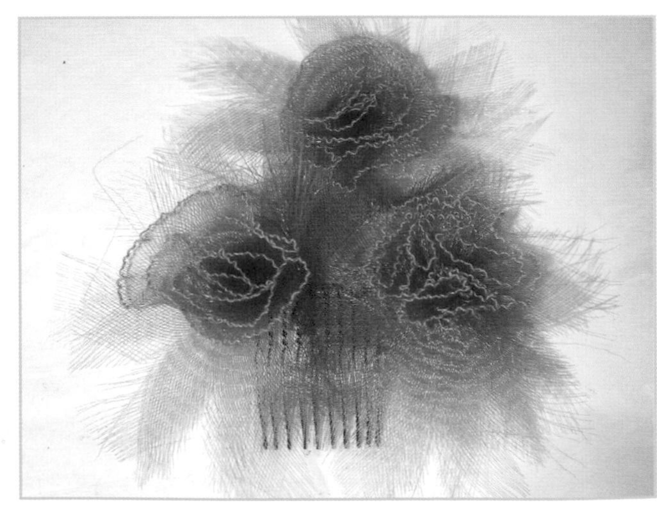

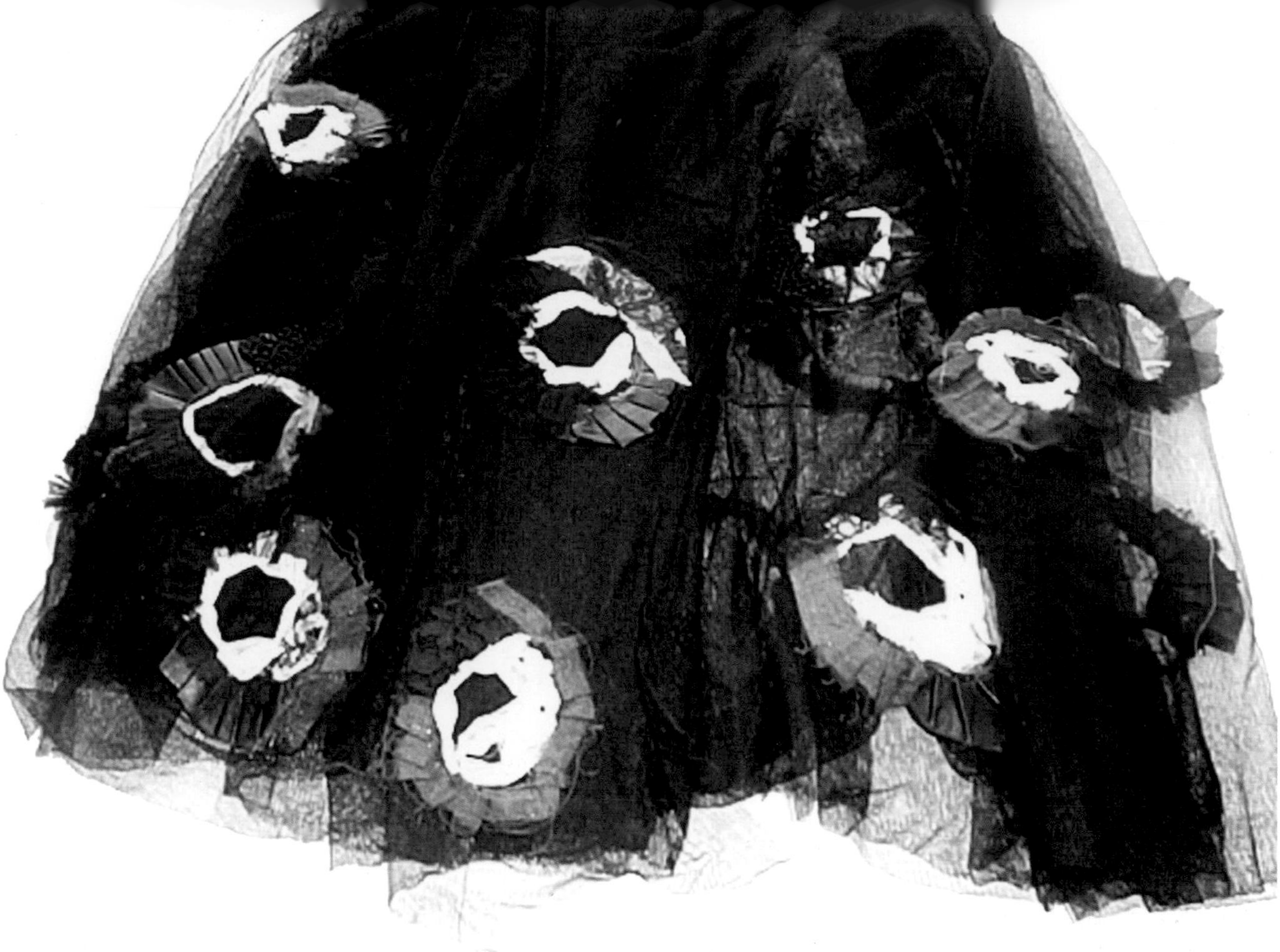

F.I.E. PATPARGA
DELHI-92

Opposite above: *Maharaja Crown,* 2004. Indian tobacco paper embroidered into hat designed for Clements Ribeiro

Opposite below: *Maharaja Jewels* x 2, 2004. Poker chips and pearls, jewellery designed for Clements Ribeiro

Above: *Rose Dress,* 2004. Chiffon rag flowers on a lace dress

Above right: *Peony,* 2003. Paint and appliqué on suede

Right: *Rice Sack* embroidered with mother of pearl sequins. Karen Nicol

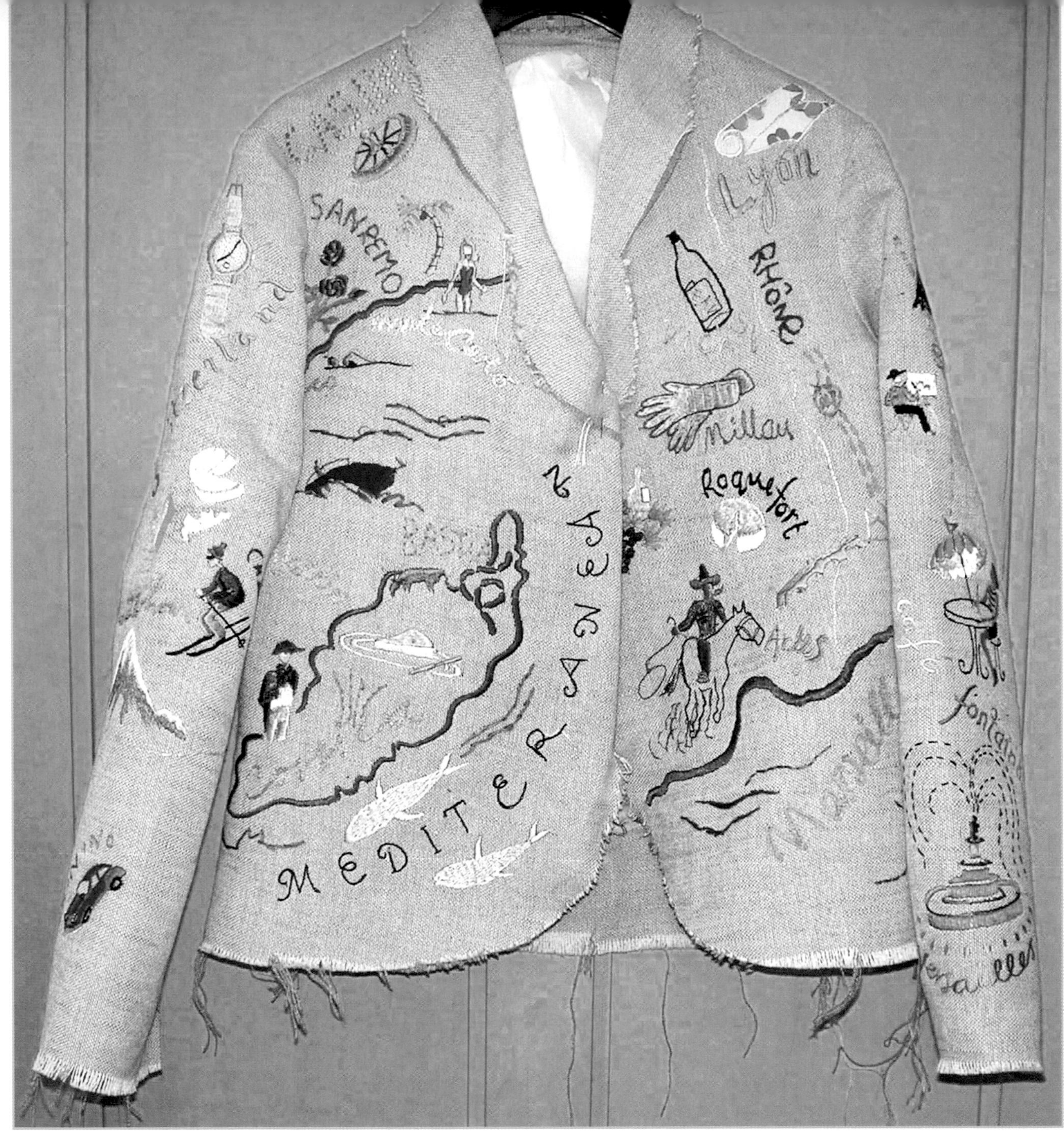

Above: *Riviera Jacket,* 2003. Embroidered linen jacket designed for Clements Ribeiro

Opposite top left: *Stocking,* 2004. Embroidered knitted stocking. Karen Nicol

Opposite right: *Textile Accounts,* 2004. Embroidered paper. Karen Nicol

Opposite below right: *Tulle Leather Throw,* 2003. Furnishing fabric. Karen Nicol

Aside from this changing world of the Collections, her work for the couture world remains steady. Her collaboration with Bruce Oldfield, for instance, sees her responsible for the whole of the embroidery element, which can be a royal wedding dress or ball gown.

Steady too has been her output for interiors; in particular for John Boyd Textiles on whose remarkable fabric she embroiders. This cotton/silk warp with a horsehair weft is much in demand by clients, including foreign royal families, for upholstery. It is a durable yet sympathetic surface for endless forms of stitchery.

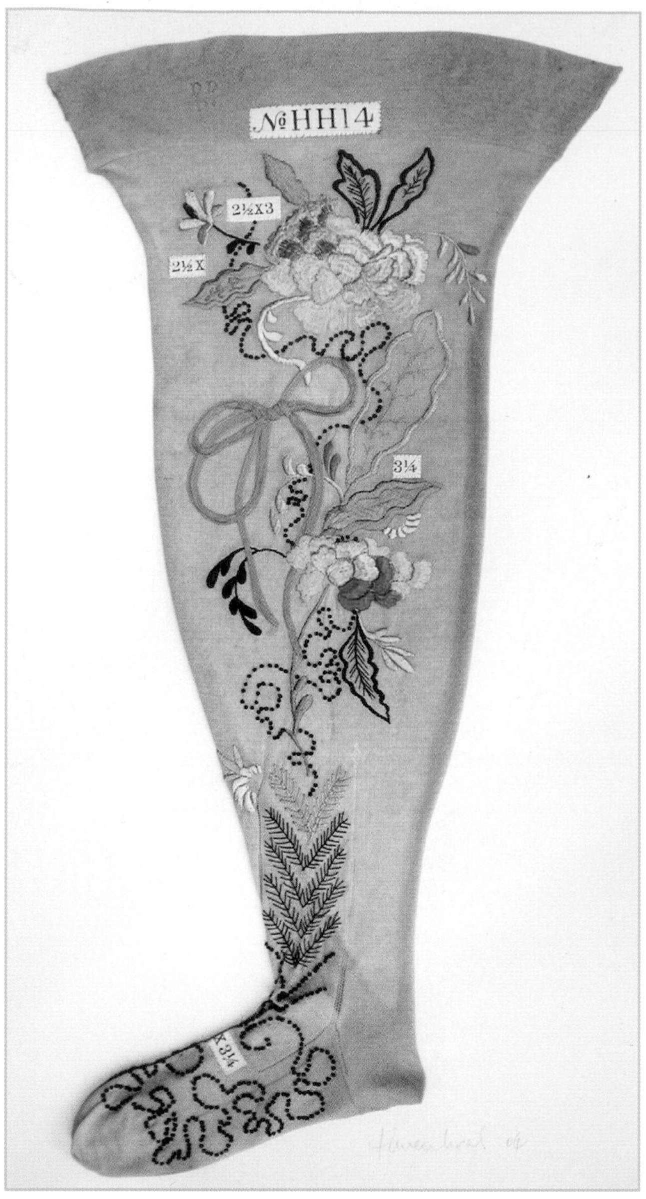

When asked how she can possibly keep this punishing pace of work year after year she admits that she is coming to the point of considering a change of direction. 'I am trying to find my niche and where I fit in the art world'. She has been offered an opportunity to make and show her own uncommissioned work in an exhibition in April 2005 at the Charlotte Street Gallery. She sees this as a chance to demonstrate her 'love for the diversity of embroidery', saying: 'For this show I can do what I like!' What a remarkable extension to her existing four-part output this promises to be.

Footnotes

54 *Judy Barry see page 60*

55 *Peter Clark 1944-. Illustrator and artist. Works exhibited with Rebecca Hossak Gallery and Charlotte Street Gallery London*

Photo: Mark Watson

JANE POULTON

1957	Born Manchester 23 November
1981 – 82	Foundation Course Manchester Polytechnic/Metropolitan University
1982 – 85	BAHons Textiles Manchester Polytechnic/Metropolitan University
1985 – 86	MA Textiles Manchester Polytechnic/Metropolitan University
1987	Joined the '62 Group
1988	Crafts Council Index
	Solo show *The Heat Of The Moment* Anna Bornholt Gallery London
	Solo show *Surface and Symbol* STOV Gallery Amsterdam
1989 –	Visiting Lecturer Manchester Metropolitan University
1989 – 2000	Advisor to N.W.Arts Board-Visual and Combined Arts
1990 & 91	Group shows *Images* The Association of Illustrators London
1992 –	Book jacket designs for Macmillan Books
1994 – 95	*Signs Of Life* Commission North British Housing Association
	Children's Library Panel for Bury Metropolitan Borough Council
1995 –	Group shows CCA Galleries London
1995 – 96	Design *Centenary* Commission North British Housing Association
1995 – 97	External Examiner HND Design: Multi Media Textiles Stockport College
	Design gateway/railings Flame Memorial Park Bury Metropolitan Borough Council
1996	Two person show Brewery Arts Centre Cirencester
1996 – 97	Artworks, identity logo and site furniture Bowlee Park Middleton Lancs Rochdale Metropolitan Borough Council
1997	Identity logo and letter forms for a social housing development in Winterburn Park Liverpool
	International Artists' Workshop Montenegro
	Riverside Housing Association/Brock Carmichael Associates
1998/99/01/02	Locum for Course Leaders – Embroidery and Contemporary Crafts Manchester Metropolitan University
1998 – 2002	Town Centre Artist Stockport Metropolitan Borough Council
	Public Art design proposals, consultation and implementation working with the Historic Areas Regeneration Team
2000	Moves to Filey
1986 – 2004	Group shows include Stov Gallery Amsterdam. Morley Gallery London, Stafford Art Gallery, Dixon Bate Gallery Manchester, Contemporary Textile Gallery London, Crafts Council Gallery London, Commonwealth Institute London, Collins Gallery Glasgow, The Scottish Gallery Edinburgh, Hankyu Store Osaka, Mitsukoshi Store Tokyo, Victoria & Albert Museum, Bankfield Museum Halifax, Yew Tree Gallery Gloucestershire, Whitworth Art Gallery Manchester, Bury Art Gallery Lancashire, Castlefield Gallery Manchester, Primavera Cambridge, Pendle Heritage Centre Barrowford, Shire Hall Gallery Stafford, Tib Lane Gallery Manchester, Pannett Gallery Whitby, Elm House/Folly Gallery Lancaster, Scarborough Art Gallery

Work in Public Collections include Victoria & Albert Museum. Whitworth Gallery. Embroiderers' Guild. Equitable Life Assurance Company. Macmillan Books. Stafford Art Gallery & Museum. Royal ExchangeTheatre Manchester. Heathrow Sterling Hotel London. Rachael Kay Shuttleworth Collection Gawthorpe Hall.
Work in numerous Private Collections in Australia. Japan. Canada. Britain and Europe

Right: *Gift,* 2001. Work on paper mixed media including gold and silver leaf. 30cm (12in.) square. Photo: Mark Watson

Jane Poulton

Jane is someone who is known for her exquisite miniature embroidered pictures. These have been created in tandem with a very personal style of drawing and painting, so closely interactive, each with the other, that it is often not clear as to which came first.

Subjects are always intuitive; those that are stitched have always involved recognisable motifs such as animals or landscape detail. 'I try to avoid obvious meaning in the work'. Whether an image on paper or one intimately embellished on cloth, they evoke a form of visual poetry. In her speculative pieces the almost isolated collections of shapes are founded on thoughts, emotions and personal stories rather than on direct observation. She says 'My iconography is used in a symbolic way that is why I least like working to commission'.

Several commissioned projects however, of two distinctly different types, have been successfully undertaken, bringing about a different satisfaction to that of personally conceived works. For example, drawings produced for illustration. Working for Macmillan Books she created an extensive series of drawings for their Picador Travel Classics which clearly resulted in artistic fulfilment. She recounts that 'It is very satisfying to feel that one's work is going into peoples' homes – homes that might not consider buying, or might not be able to afford, original art work'. The painting entitled *Coast Walk* ,when seen by the publisher, led directly to the first book jacket commission.

Public art too has involved her inclusion in schemes for several borough councils. Though making demands on her for observational drawing, the main temptation for participation can perhaps be sighted in the 1995 *Centenary* project of the North British Housing Association where the combined element of social history and research were of paramount interest to her. The most delicate pen and wash images, of the tools that would have been used by the

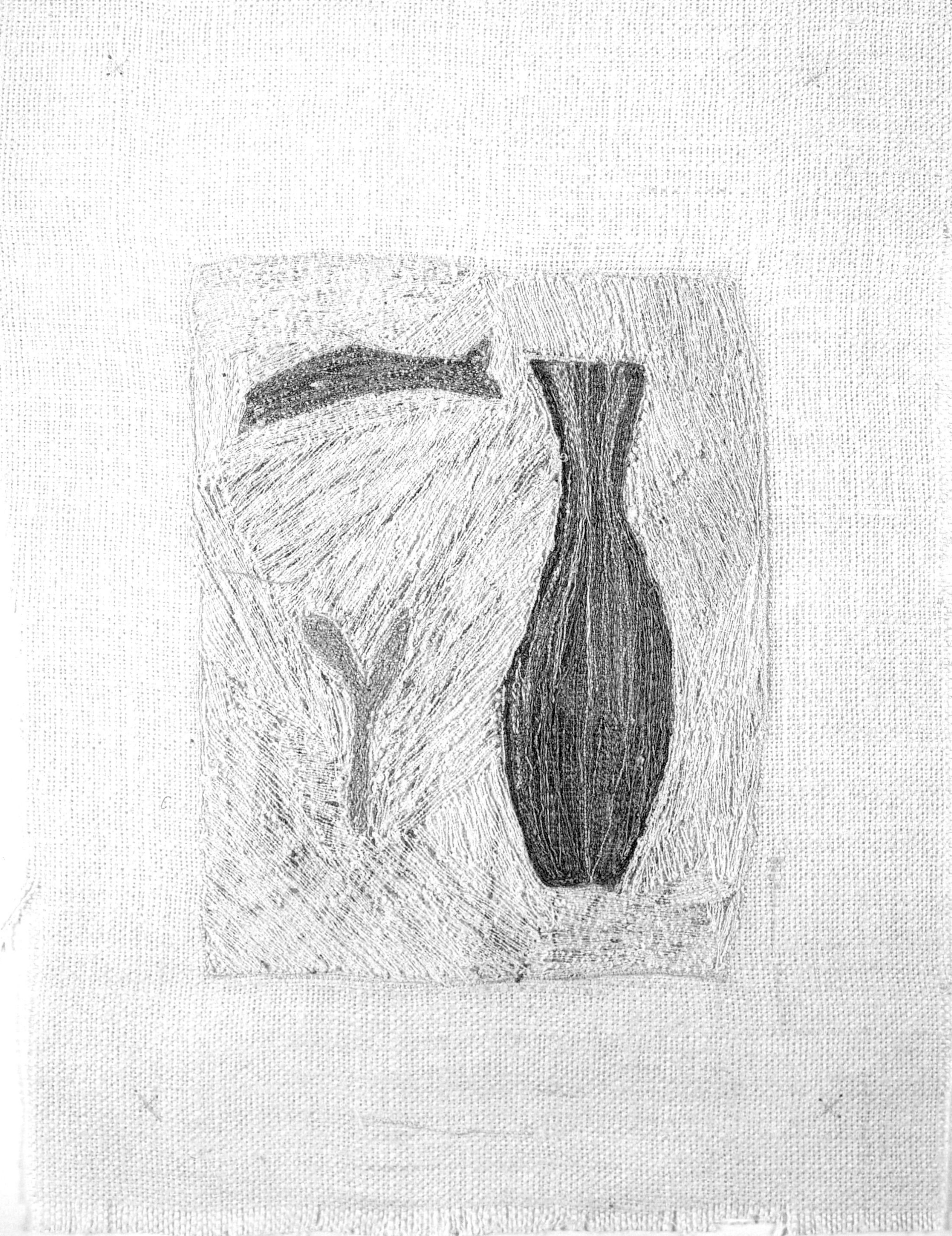

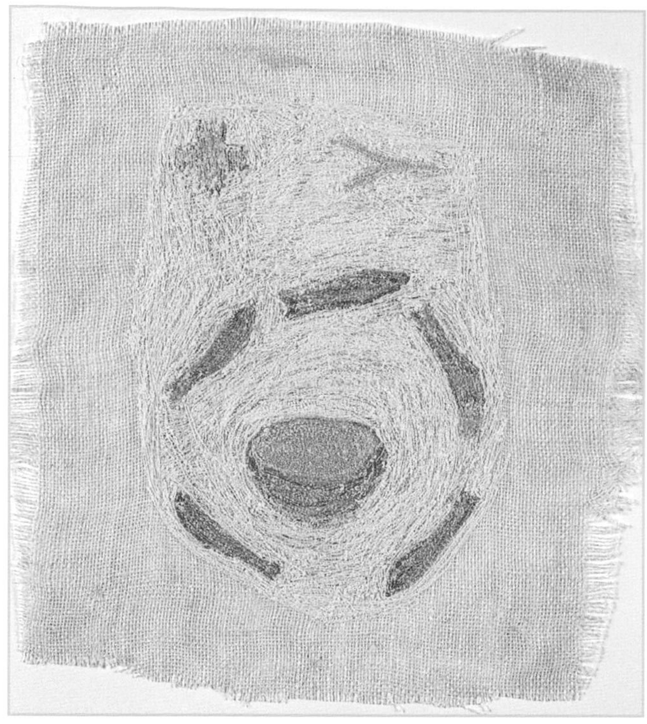

Opposite page: *Fish Flask and Seedling,* 1985. Machine stitched 18.5cm x 24cm (7in. x 9in.). Photo: Mark Watson

Left: *Five Fish and Bowl,* 1985. Machine stitched 20cm x 21cm (8in. x 8¼ in.). Photo: Mark Watson

Below: *Lucky for Some,* 1986. Machine stitched. 20.5cm x 22cm (8in. x 8¼ in.). Photo: Mark Watson

tradesmen who inhabited the 1895 site, provided the basis for collaboration with the sculptor who would carve the images in relief in Portland stone. Easily recognisable separate images for both this, and the earlier *Signs of Life* project, are typical of her style of drawing of plants, birds, signs and symbols, all evoking imaginative thoughts and aspirations. Whilst commissioned work is always grounded on intensive factual research, her personal works on paper or fabric are always exploratory and spontaneous. Nevertheless they can be seen to unmistakeably evolve from the same stable.

By nature she is a very private person. An only child, whose father died when she was only four years old, she was brought up by her mother, a nursing sister, with considerable help from an aunt. Also in the sequence was a short spell at boarding school which, through its lack of art, delayed the day when she could embark on a subject that would eventually be her life. Not until she reached her secondary school was she able to take refuge in the art room'. The emphasis was on traditional drawing and this, combined with the influence of her aunt's interest in dressmaking, provided her with the idea that art was for her. However, an early marriage to a childhood sweetheart and a stint of clerical work in an office kept admission to art school on hold for several years.

Having got to college some six years after leaving school her student years were clearly very decisive. She talks of 'throwing herself into the course' and of the great contribution made by the staff in the shaping of her work. By the second year she recalls having 'developed her own handwriting'.

It is not insignificant to note that these five full time years of study were not only in one college but in the same area in which she grew up. Familiarity with location may well have been a strong contributor to her development as an artist for she moved forward rapidly to considerable acclaim.

However, recently, with an even greater urge for space and time, she chose to throw off everything with which she was acquainted and move to far flung Filey on the north east coast of Yorkshire. This radical change of location in her mid-forties even meant partially parting company from a good friend and partner. 'I had had enough of city life. I needed new pastures in which to work. In Manchester I felt well known for what I did and it was important to go somewhere no one knew me and I could develop new ways of working'.

This cross roads of her life could be seen to be offering the new direction to anonymity that she so positively seeks and yet it would appear that many of the signs on the old road remain pointing towards socially connected projects.

"Blow, Wind, blow!"

Opposite top: *Blow Wind Blow* 1988. Machine stitched. Private collection. 17cm x 23cm (7in. x 9in.). Photo: David Hankey

Opposite below left: *Big Sky* 1988. Machine stitched. Private collection 22cm x 12cm ($8^1/_2$ in. x 5in.) Photo: David Hankey

Opposite right: *See You See Me* 1992. Machine stitched. 18cm x 16cm (7in. x 6in.). Photo: Mark Watson

Above: *And Then What?* 1990. Machine stitched. 17cm x 21.5cm (7in x 8in). Photo: Mark Watson

Above right: *Letting the Days Go By* 1988. Machine stitched. 18cm x 38cm (7in. x 15in.). Photo: Mark Watson

Below: *Not all Wormes wear Brown* 1989. 24cm x 10cm ($9^1/_2$ in. x 4in.). Photo: Mark Watson

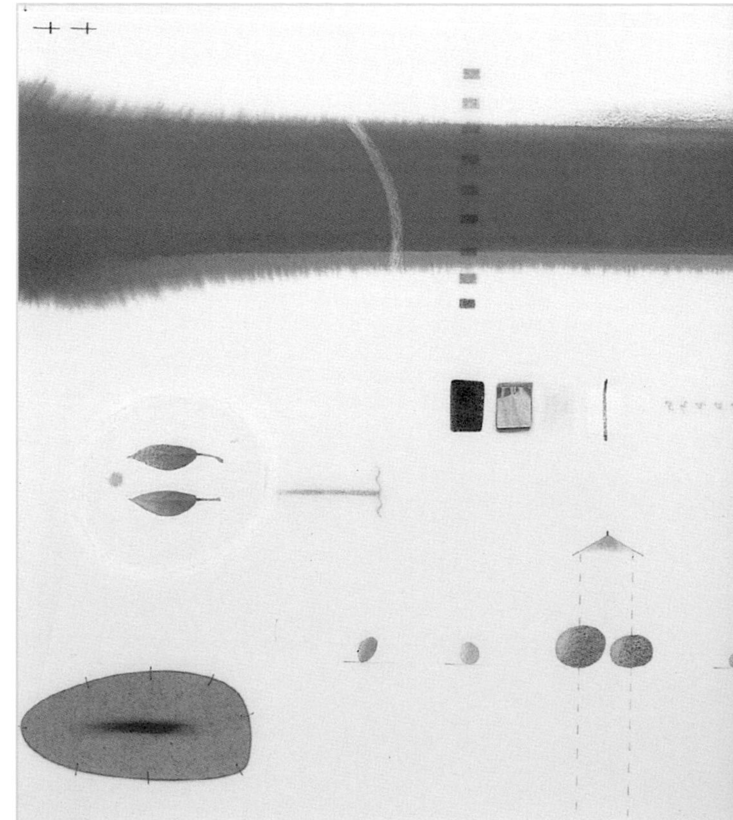

Opposite top: *Bananas, Orange and Fish,* 1984. Work on paper. 38.5cm x 39cm (15in. x 15½ in.). Photo: Mark Watson

Opposite bottom left: *East,* 1986. Work on paper. 19cm x 26cm (7½ in. x 10in.). Photo: Mark Watson

Opposite bottom right: *Coast Walk,* 1992. The painting that led to the first book jacket commission with Macmillan Books for *The Road to Oxiana* by Robert Byron. 28.5cm (11in.) square.

Above: *Heat of the Moment* 1988.
Works on paper. 20 cm (8in.) square. Photo: Mark Watson

Left: *Red Garden,* 2001. Work on paper mixed media. 30cm (12in.) square. Photo: Mark Watson

This innate love of a collaborative result, as opposed to a singular production, is finding new expression with her research into Gansey production of fishing jumpers for Filey Museum. The skill of the knitters together with their social reminiscences involve a lot of her time in building relationships prior to her new work with photography.

She is a recent recipient of Arts Council funding for the purchase of photographic equipment in order to learn to use the medium format photography for study of people in various social contexts. She says it is refreshing to work with others in the community.

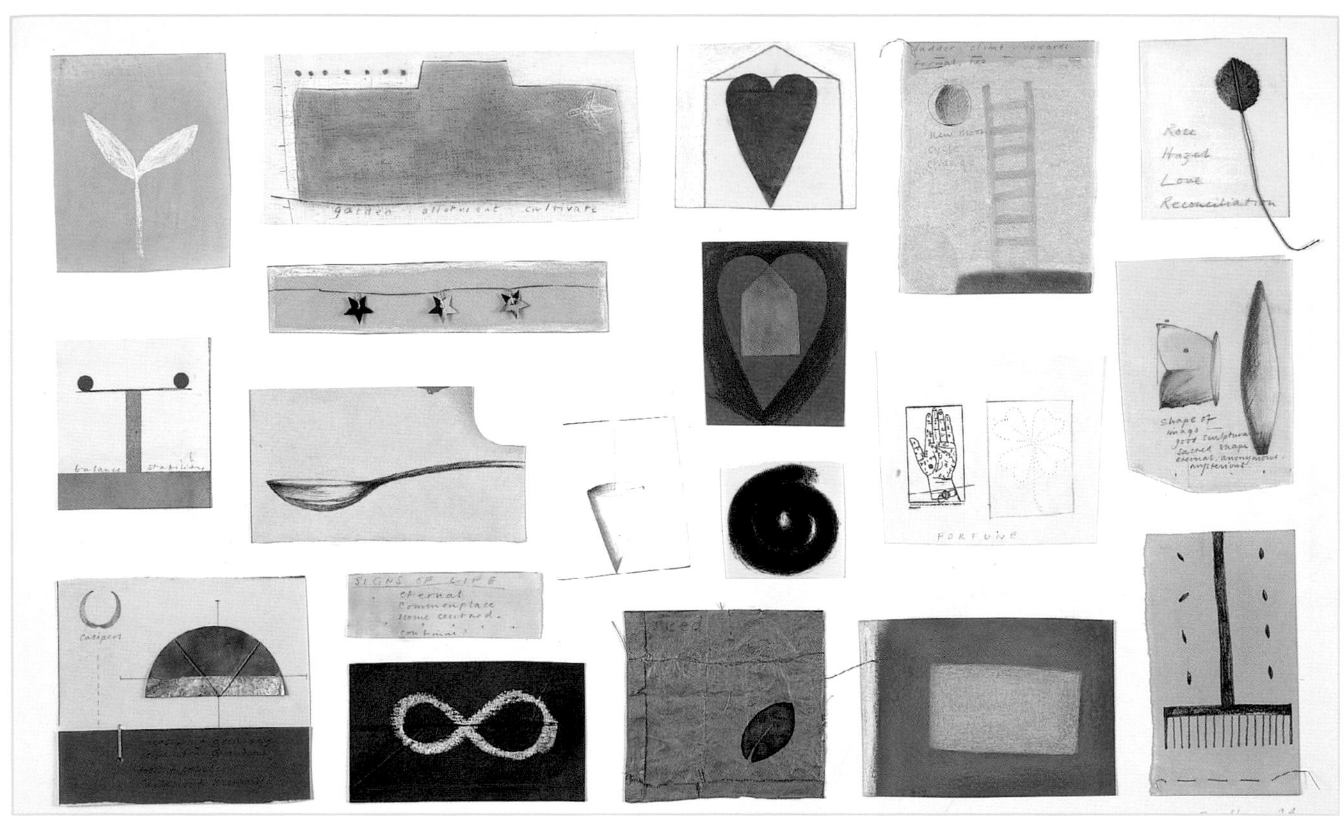
garden allotment cultivate
Rose
Hazel
Love
Reconciliation
SIGNS OF LIFE
eternal
commonplace
FORTUNE

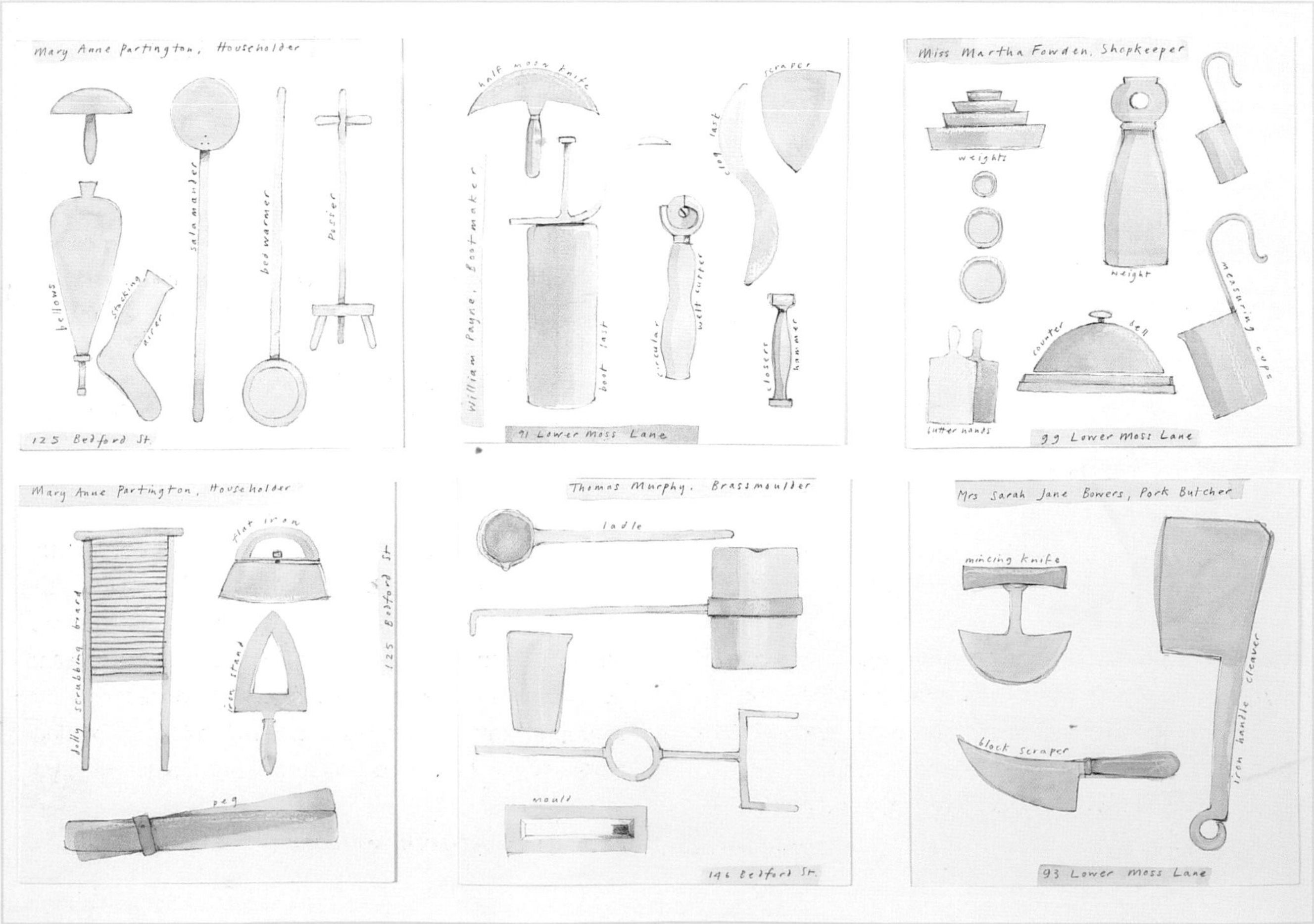

Mary Anne Partington, Householder
bellows
stocking airer
salamander
bedwarmer
posser
125 Bedford St.
William Payne, Bootmaker
half moon knife
scraper
boot last
circular
welt cutter
closers hammer
91 Lower Moss Lane
Miss Martha Fowden, Shopkeeper
weights
weight
counter bell
measuring cups
butter hands
99 Lower Moss Lane
Mary Anne Partington, Householder
flat iron
dolly scrubbing board
iron stand
125 Bedford St
peg
Thomas Murphy. Brassmoulder
ladle
mould
146 Bedford St.
Mrs Sarah Jane Bowers, Pork Butcher
mincing knife
block scraper
iron handle cleaver
93 Lower Moss Lane

Rarely seeking holidays, travelling only if invited, she is content with a great deal of her own company, the company of her old metal Bernina 801 and her brand new Bronica camera.

High points in her creativity have clearly been when the Victoria & Albert Museum purchased *Flame Tree Golden Seed* or indeed when anyone bought her pictures from the numerous shows in which she took part. Always carried out in her inimitable style of single images, connected only by implication, these intimate, reflective and meditative works culminate in something akin to visual verse. Each is executed with an enviable technical precision produced by completely covering a surface with straight machine stitching in mercerised cotton usually on a linen union ground cloth. Early works are recognisable for their duller finish having been sewn with Sylko; later pieces were made using Madeira Tanne 50s thread giving a more lustrous finish.

The content within the work of this artist and poet has not, to date, radically changed. What has changed is the way it is expressed. It remains to be seen whether the desire to remain anonymous can balance comfortably with her clearly stated need to make contact with others. Jane's aspirations for new directions of creativity can be now eagerly awaited. If generated by the same inspiration that produced more than a hundred embroidered gems they will add to her existing body of work thereby contributing richly to British heritage.

Opposite top: Preparatory sketches for *Signs of Life,* 1994-5. Mixed media. Commission for North British Housing Association. Photo: Mark Watson

Opposite below: Preparatory Drawings for *Centenary,* 1995-96. Pen and wash. Commission for North British Housing Association. Photo: Mark Watson

Above: *Flame Tree, Golden Seed,* 1989. Mercerised cotton on linen ground cloth Collection Victoria & Albert Museum. 20cm x 13cm (8in. x 5in.)

Photo: Paul Knight

CLAIRE JOHNSON KNIGHT

1960 Born Cheshire 30 June
1976 – 78 Northwich School of Art
1977 London Examinations Board Prize for selected design for reproduction
1978 – 81 Manchester Polytechnic/Metropolitan University BA Hons Embroidery
1981 – 82 Year exhibiting and voluntary teaching in primary school
1982 – 83 PGCE Manchester Polytechnic/Metropolitan University
1981 Received Rachel Kay Shuttleworth Trophy
Joined '62 Group as student. Exhibiting regularly to date includes: Winchester College of Art Gallery. Seven Dials Gallery London. Victoria Art Gallery Bath. Swansea University Gallery. Contemporary Textiles Gallery London. Leicestershire Art Gallery & Museum. Woodlands Art Gallery Greenwich London. Walsall City Art Gallery. Turnpike Gallery Leigh. Collins Art Gallery Glasgow. Commonwealth Institute London. Bankfield Museum and Art Gallery Halifax. Royal Museum and Art Gallery Truro. Bury Museum and Art Gallery Lancashire. Braintree Museum and Art Gallery Essex. Quarry Bank Mill Styal Cheshire. The Shire Hall Gallery Stafford. Maidstone Museum and Art Gallery. City Art Gallery Edinburgh. Retrospective at Knitting and Stitching shows London, Dublin, Harrogate. Harley Gallery Welbeck Worksop
Included in *Degree Shows* by Diana Springall Autumn issue Embroidery
1983- Teaching Malbank School Sixth form College Textiles/Art to AS levels
1986 Group show *Stitched Textiles for Interiors* RIBA London
Group show *Threads* Exhibition for Children Suffolk Craft Society
1986 Author *Figures of Fun* Autumn issue *Embroidery*
1992 Group show *Threads of Inspiration* The Merchant Adventures Hall York
1993 Group show Bankfield Museum Halifax Yorkshire
1994 Group show *Open Arts* Chester City Museum
1995 Group show The Black Swan Guild Somerset
1996 Group show *The Work to Wear*
1997 Married Paul Knight
1998 Daughter Charlotte born
Group show of international artists *The Textile Road* UNESCO Paris
2002 Group show *Angels* Cajoba Gallery Birkenhead
2003 Teacher-training Mentor on Malbank School site for PGCE in association with Chester College and Liverpool University

Work purchased for numerous public and private collections both in the UK and abroad including the Embroiderers' Guild.

Work profiled in *Twelve British Embroiderers*, by Diana Springall, 1984 Gakken Tokyo
Work featured in *Needlework School* 1982 Constance Howard, New Burlington Books. *Making Bags & Purses* 1991 Gisela Banbury/Angela Dewar, Blandford. *The Art of Appliqué* 1991 Juliet Bawden Mitchell Beazley. *A Complete Guide to Creative Embroidery* Jan Beaney/Jean Littlejohn Century 1991 and Batsford 1997

Right: *The Garden,* detail, 2003. Embroidered panel. Small pieces of machine embroidery on silk felt applied to form low relief. 26cm (10in.) square

Claire Johnson Knight

Claire's modest and gentle personality hides the sheer size of her artistic ability and achievement. Her work stems from observational drawing evolving, through a process of metamorphosis, to become either three dimensional soft padded pieces or richly machine-decorated panels or objects.

Credit for initially identifying this exceptional talent must go to the art-trained deputy head of her secondary school. Contrary to the general trend for their pupils to continue to sixth form college, she arranged for Claire to do her art 'A'level at the local art school. Commencing this specialism from the age of sixteen provided more than a head start. She was also in place to move seamlessly into her Foundation year. She remembers being a little too 'workaholic' for some tutors. Nevertheless, one lunchtime, some of them said 'We are getting in the car and going to Manchester to see the Degree show – embroidery is what you are going to do next'. For her part she says 'That was it. I knew that that was what I wanted to do. It was the most amazing exhibition I had ever seen – absolutely fantastic and wonderful'. Also at this time she is indebted to them for her successful nomination for the London Examinations Board annual prize.

With that level of support, acceptance on the BA course was inevitable. With her passion for the subject undiminished, she responded positively to the team of tutors. She does remember possibly being the keenest student working every available hour. She recalls the great support given by the full-time tutors Judy Barry[54], Isabel Dibden Wright[56] and Anne Morrell[57]. She admired Isabel's patchwork with its meticulous approach 'I loved the way she stuffed things and the fact that every little thread end had to be cut off neatly'. Of Anne,head of the embroidery school, she remembers strict discipline and in particular one remark that has stayed with her to this day 'five minutes may be all you've got but it is five minutes

Opposite and above: Development of sketchbook pages into designs for embroidery

Below: The first eight pages of a typical sketch book skilfully and artistically torn to reveal glimpses of the page ahead 1992. 20cm x 26cm (8in. x 10in.)

when you could put something down'. It is obvious to see, when reviewing Claire's achievement both as a teacher and artist, that she has lived by this philosophy to this day. Responding to the question 'When do you do all this?' the answer will be 'In little bits and pieces; in little spare moments at work; in the evenings; at the week ends; in the holidays'. This fits around the responsibility of a small daughter, a home to run and the challenge of undergoing the surgery involved in overcoming Raynaud's disease which, for years, had affected the use of her hands. She acknowledges that none of these little spare moments would occur without the support of her husband, her mother, the other two grandparents and not least her very far-sighted headmaster at Malbank School. It is significant to note that she has actually been teaching in the same school for two decades. She loves teaching in this well-established art department where her dedicated, all-round input is clearly valued. Here she can enjoy the books and the chance to interact with the children in a large number of ways using materials of many kinds.

At first glance her textiles appear to fall into two categories of style but on second glance it is obvious that they are intimately connected by the same eye and hand that created the on going glorious sketchbooks. In the first ten years of

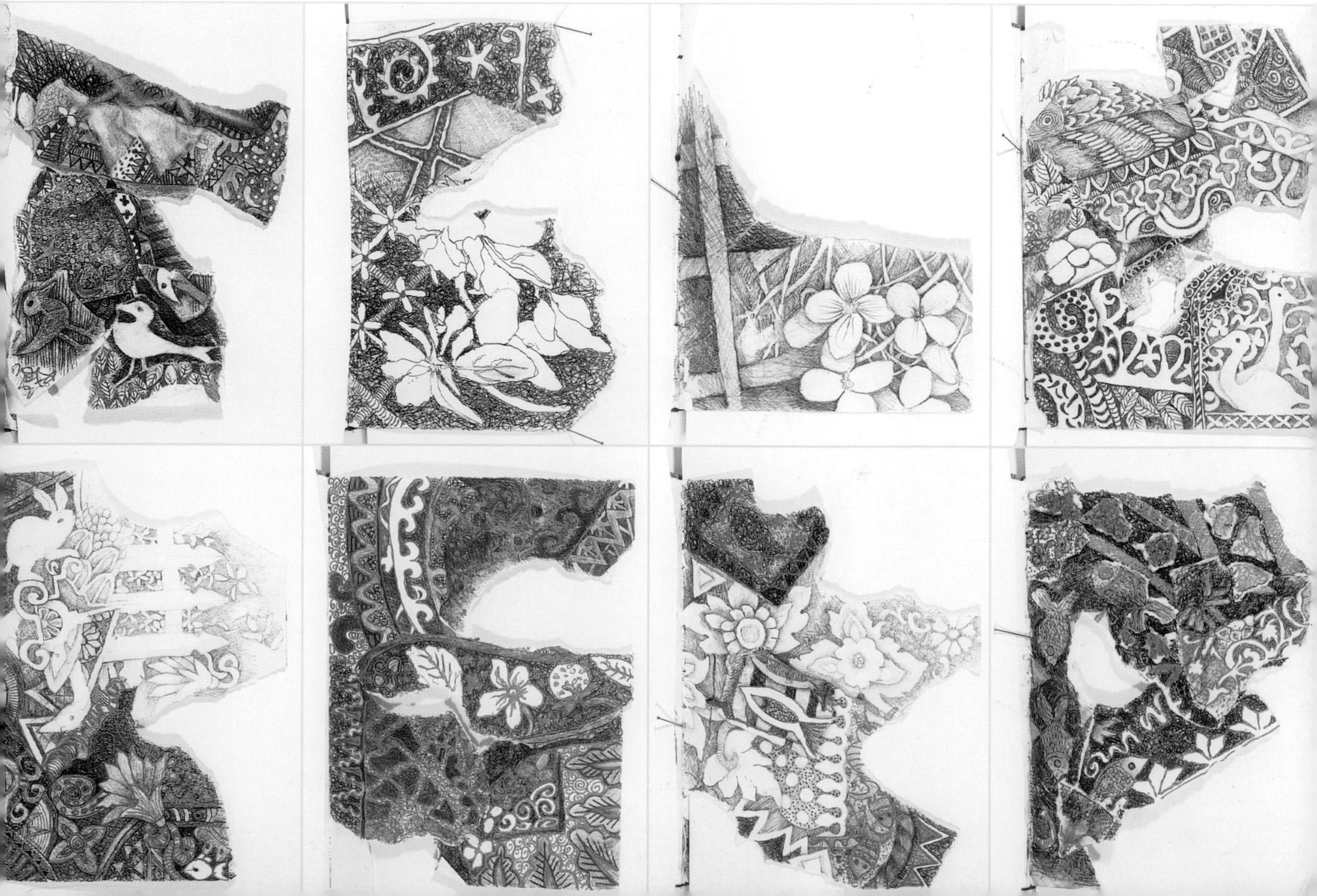

Opposite page: *Poppy and Max,* 2003. Embroidered panel. Small pieces of machine embroidery on silk felt applied to form low relief. 31cm x 41cm (12in. x 16in.)

Above top: Embroidered Bag, 2003. Machine embroidery 17cm x 25cm (7in. x 10in.) overall. *Wall Piece* Machine embroidery 17 x 22cm (7 x 9in.)

Above: Embroidered Shoes, 2003, length 16cm (6in.)

Right: Assortment of torn fragments of drawings, typical of any that might be used for assembling a finished design, 2003

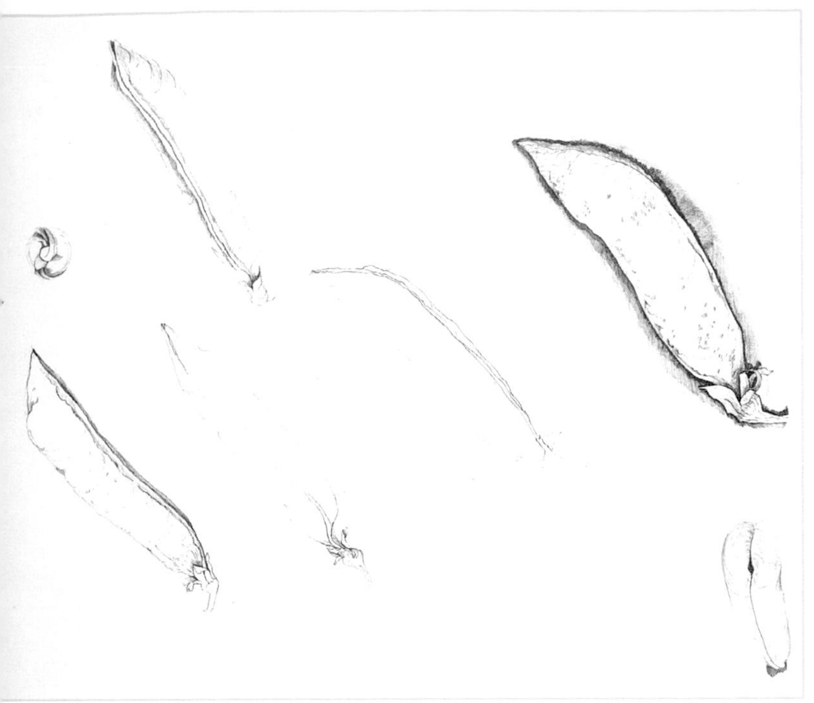

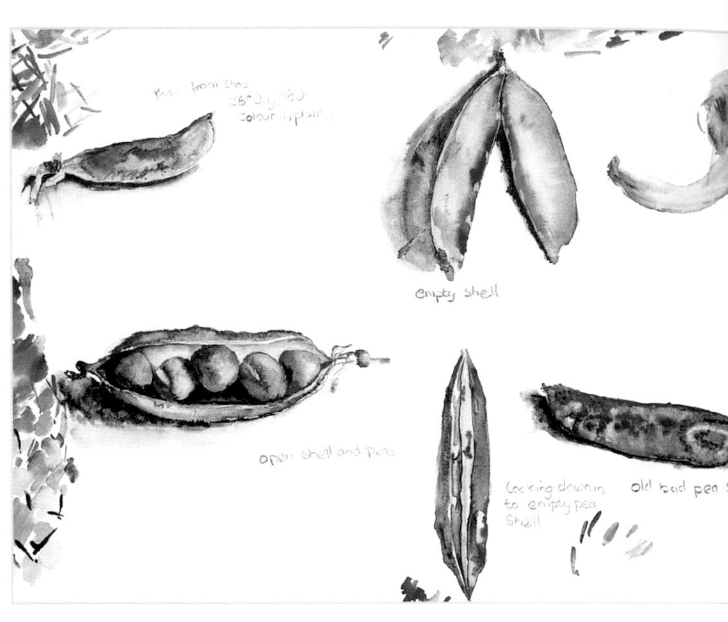

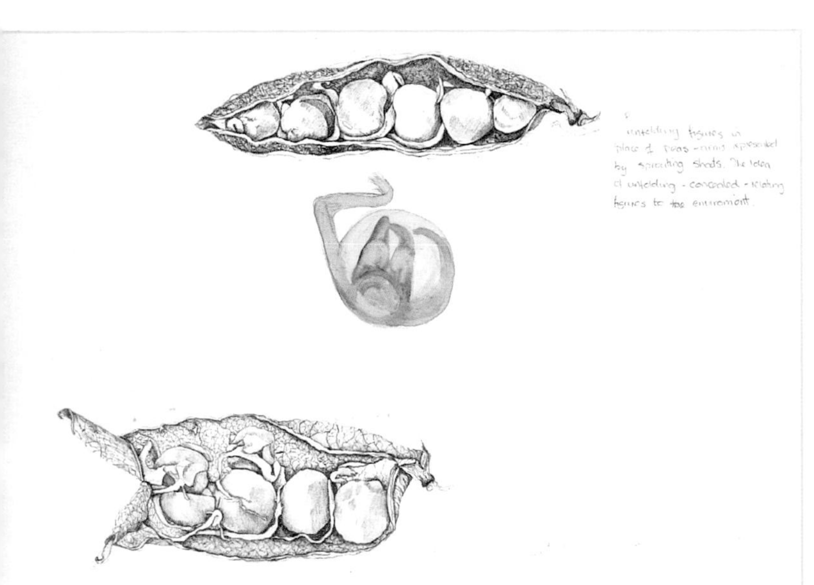

work they could be described as soft sculpture either in low relief or three dimensional; padded, delicately coloured, with little or no stitched embellishment and often resembling small people. In this last ten years they are still in low relief, or three dimensional, but are rarely obviously figurative or descriptive; instead they are intricately machine stitched combining soft colour with metallic lustre akin to ornate filigree jewellery. Everything is due to her drawing ability; without drawing there would probably be nothing. It was John Renshaw[58] who she credits with 'opening up for me a whole new way of drawing'.

She comes from an artistic family. Her grandfather was an artist, trained at Manchester School of Art, and a contemporary of Lowry[59]. Her mother too paints; her very accomplished watercolour landscapes and flower paintings can be seen hanging on the walls of the family home in Northwich where Claire, from the age of four, was raised with her brother. Also good at sewing and dressmaking she created a household where materials were always around. Both parents were very supportive of Claire's talent giving her a Bernina Minimatic sewing machine for her twenty first birthday. In addition she now has a Bernina 1020 heavy duty domestic model. Her late father, a chemical engineer with Shell Company, also

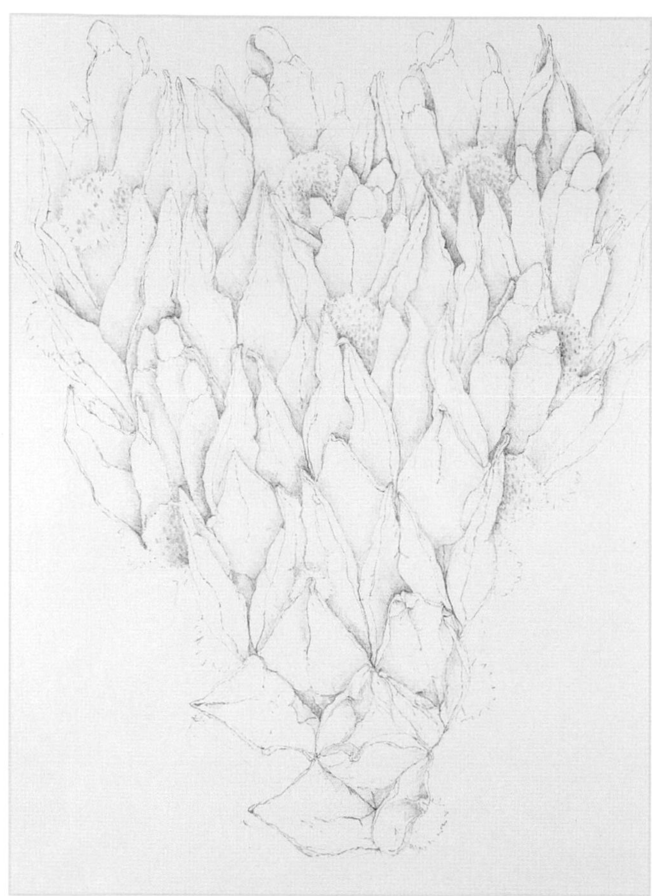

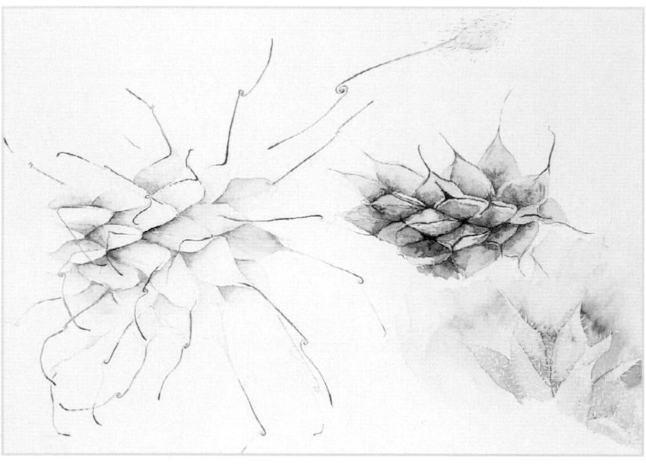

arranged for Claire to receive a student bursary from them. The amount was paid annually but based retrospectively according to her end of year assessment grade; an added incentive, if one were needed, to work hard.

Claire herself likes to create her own environment for work. She is happiest working alone at home, on the edge of the countryside in Weaverham in Cheshire, or in her schoolroom. She is not comfortable producing her own things in a group situation, nor does she really like looking at what her peers are doing.

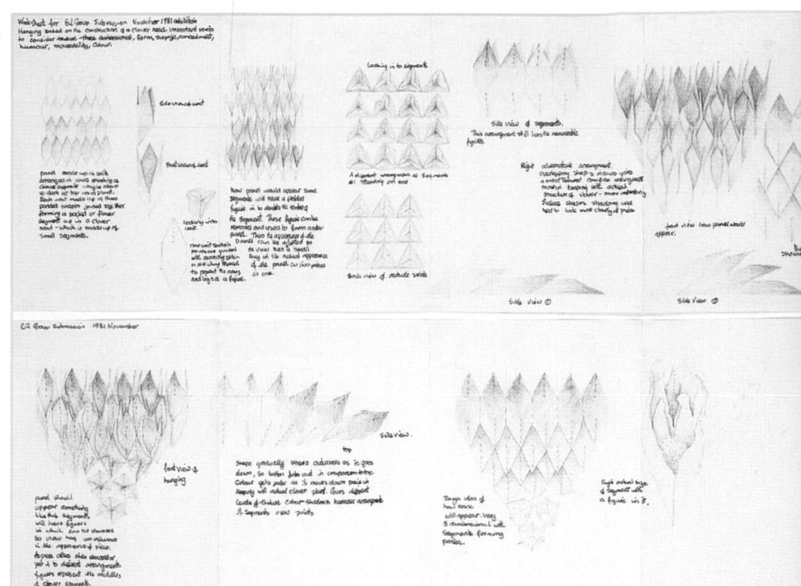

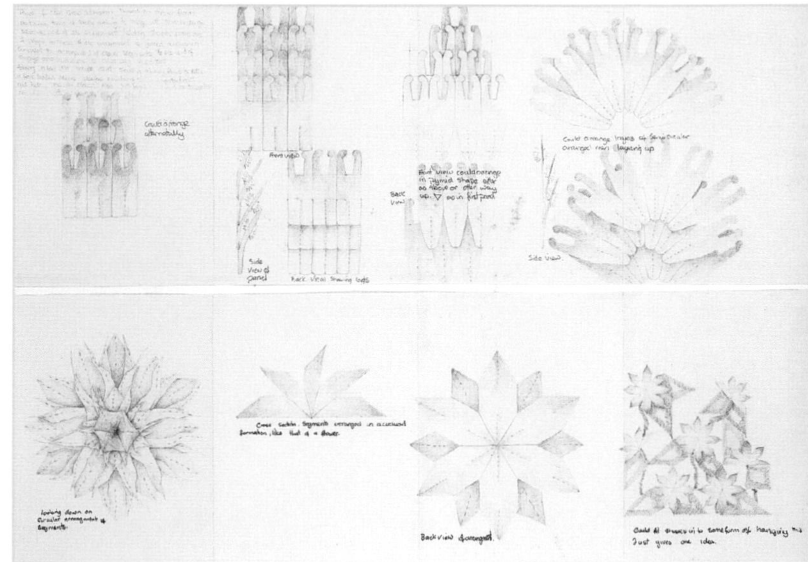

Top left: *Clover Head* – further study – pencil/crayon

Below left: *Clover Head* – study magnified to view in detail

Top right: Work sheets assembled to show development of Clover as repeating pattern

Below right: Further work sheets showing final development towards three-dimensional textile sculpture

Development of a theme from first observational drawings to finished artefact 1981

Opposite top left: *Pea Pod.* Pencil drawing

Opposite top right: *Pea Pod.* Water colour

Opposite below left: *Pea Pod.* Pencil and water colour showing metamorphic move to human form

Opposite below right: *Clover Head* – first study – pencil/crayon

Opposite: *Clover Men.* Hand dyed soft cotton fabric padded. Fine wool pom-pom heads. Private collection. 74cm x 104cm (29in. x 41in.)

Above: *Child's Clock Book,* 1983. Hand dyed soft cotton, padded, and decoratively stitched. 18cm (7in.) diameter

The appreciation of her work by others has always provided an incentive to make more. Significant moments are clearly those when people buy her work. Almost everything she makes sells either because it is fun or because it is exquisite or both and always because the originality of the idea has been carried out with impeccable craftsmanship. She cites the time that Jan Beaney[33] said 'I am going to buy all your little bags so that when you go home you will have to make some more'. She has also always enjoyed the challenge of a commission.

Her machine embroidery of recent years is most often worked on a ground of silk felt[60] that she makes herself; she likes the idea of having made the whole thing.

Every piece can only fill the viewer with a sense of admiration and wonderment at an almost fairytale vision carried out in fabric and thread. This seemingly effortless imagination is inspired in part by what she sees around her; it is a visual storytelling from an artist from whom there will clearly be a lot more to come.

Footnotes

56 *Isabel Dibden Wright 1952- Profile* Twelve British Embroiderers *Gakken Tokyo 1984. Author* Making your own Patchwork & Quilting *1994 New Holland. 1976 Senior Lecturer in Embroidery Manchester Metropolitan University formerly Manchester Polytechnic. External examiner BA.Hons 1991-95 Glasgow School of Art and 2002 University of Central England, Birmingham and Opus School of Textile Arts London. Work in public and private collections in the U.K. & overseas. Recent commissions include collection of pieces for Leicester Royal Infirmary's new Osborne Building. Former Chairman and Vice-Chairman of the '62 Group exhibiting 1975-1991. Founder member of Quilt Art exhibiting 1985-1991. Member of the British Quilt Study Group 1998-. Included in The Quilter's Guild slide Index.*

57 *Anne Butler Morrell 1939- Leading figure in the world of embroidery. First artist to promote the abstract use of stitch. Profile* Twelve British Embroiderers *1984 Gakken Tokyo. 1965-68 Lecturer Goldsmiths' College. 1968-92 Lecturer/Senior Lecturer/Principal Lecturer Manchester Regional College of Art Manchester Polytechnic/Manchester Metropolitan University. 1992 Appointed Professor of Embroidery. Work in numerous public and private collections. World renowned consultant in particular Calico Museum Ahmedabad India. Author of ten books most notable* Encyclopaedia of Embroidery Stitches *B T Batsford 1994 and by Arco USA ISBN 0 7134 3317 5.* Techniques of Indian Embroidery *B T Batsford 1994 and by Interweave USA ISBN 0 7134 6410 0.* Contemporary Embroidery *Cassell 1994 ISBN 0 289 80105 2.*

58 *John Renshaw 1946- A practising artist with associated research interests situated at an interface between pedagogy and aspects of Fine Art practice, particularly drawing. 1975-81 Lecturer, Art and Design Foundation Course Stockport College. 1978-88 Visiting lecturer in Drawing and Visual Studies. Manchester Metropolitan University, Faculty of Art and Design, Department of Textiles and Fashion. 1981-86 Tutor in charge of Foundation studies Cheshire School of Art & Design Northwich. 1981-87 Lectures/workshops for Embroiderers' Guild and Cheshire Textile Group. 1986 - 87 Department of Education and Science Teacher Fellowship in Art Education ,Chester College and Cheshire Education Services. 1987 – Tutor in charge of Painting and Drawing. Currently Undergraduate Programme Leader for BA Hons Fine Art University College Chester. Author of numerous Seminar and Conference Papers that include* On the issue of Teaching Drawing and Painting *1995 and* The Original Creative Principle *2002 for National Society for Education in Art and Design . Works exhibited UK, Hong Kong, Canada, USA.*

59 *L.S.Lowry 1887-1976 Painter of industrial and slumscapes in his native Manchester. Known for his matchstick figures. Lived as a recluse. Elected to RA in 1962.*

60 *Silk felt is made from carded cocoon strippings for paper making. The process involves teasing out the fibres and placing them in little patches on a J-cloth. At this point other elements can be added followed by a second layer of felt to hold pieces in place. The cloth is then rolled up, together with the silk contents, and steeped in hot water for 30 seconds. This is then wrung out, ironed with a hot iron and left to dry at which point it is ready to receive drawing, sewing etc.*

Photo: Mike Keegan

NICOLA HENLEY

1960	Born Bristol 13 December
1979 – 80	Italy *au pair*
1980 – 81	Foundation Course in Art Bristol Polytechnic
1981 – 84	Goldsmiths' College School of Art London First Class BAHons. Fine Art/Textiles
1983	Revisits Italy
1984	Marries
	Birth of son Max
1984 –	Exhibiting regularly Contemporary Applied Arts London. The Scottish Gallery Edinburgh. Primavera Cambridge. The Guinness Gallery Dublin. Galerie Pousse Tokyo Japan. Hibernia Florida USA
1986	Two person show Courcoux and Courcoux Gallery Salisbury
	Crafts Council Setting Up Grant
1987	Birth of daughter Erin
1988	Contemporary British Crafts Mixed show National Museum of Modem Art Kyoto Japan
	South West Arts Project Award
1989	Solo show Cirencester Workshops Cirencester Gloucestershire
	Solo show Contemporary Applied Arts London
	Solo show Bristol Old Vic Coopers Gallery Bristol
1990	Solo show Galerie Pousse Tokyo Japan
	Travel Award to Japan British Council
	Solo show Oxford Gallery Oxford
1991 –	Living and working in Ireland
1992	Solo show Galerie Pousse Tokyo Japan
1993	Birth of daughter Georgia
1994	Leader Grant Co. Clare Ireland
	H.Q. Gallery Craft Council of Ireland Dublin
	Crafts Council Shop Victoria & Albert Museum London
1996	Marriage ends
1997	Solo show H-1-P-O-TESI Barcelona Spain
	Travel Award to Madrid Arts Council of Ireland
1998	Solo show Galerie Pousse Tokyo Japan
	Travel Award to Japan Department of Cultural Affairs Ireland
1999	Solo show Primavera Cambridge
2000	Two person show Guinness Gallery Dublin Ireland
2002	Solo show Mrua Gallery Co. Clare Ireland
2004	Commission for Two Hangings Cunard liner Queen Victoria

Work in collections of Microsoft Ireland Dublin. British Rail St Pancras Office London. British Crafts Council London. Irish Crafts Council. Embroiderers' Guild. The Rockshop Co. Clare Ireland. Museum of Modem Art Kyoto Japan. Galerie Pousse Tokyo Japan.
Private Collections worldwide
Lectures widely in Britain, Ireland, Australia, Japan

Right: *Gull Movements Fanore,* 1997. Private collection, Japan. 97cm x 143cm (38in. x 56in.)

Nicola Henley

The confident yet sensitive works of art, on cloth, depicting the space inhabited by birds, give little indication of an early, slow journey towards the development of a personal art form. Working on calico, with a range of print techniques combined with stitching, Nicola, for over twenty years, has become known for her skies with birds.

As is often the case in life, it was chance that brought together the various experiences that eventually gave powerful direction to her content and technique.

By her own admission, textiles and more specifically embroidery, were not a consideration for her choice of subject at art school. From the time she was at school she knew that art was what she wanted to do; so a Foundation course was not a problem. Following that, and still unsure where her strengths lay and not wishing to restrict herself too early, she looked, without success, for a course offering different media. Settling instead for a course in Fine Art Textiles, she says 'I had very confined views of what embroidery was and I had to get over those prejudices'. Only through her deep interest in the history of textiles, she remembers that 'the more I looked the more respect I had for it'.

Whilst that aspect of understanding was increasing, her acceptance of the current thinking on this subject at Goldsmiths' College was much harder to accept; one based around freedom and independent structure rather than continuous projects but she says 'at least it made me soul-search and try and find out what is me'.

Before embarking on her Foundation Course at Bristol Polytechnic she had spent a year as an au pair in Florence. This immersion into the history of the Italian Early Renaissance, and with it the formulation of a particular love of fresco painting, was to have a profound and lasting influence. The rough, multi-surfaced, stylised, flat imagery is still vividly with her today. On the whole the scenes that attracted her were large and had little perspective. The full

impact of what she was absorbing lay dormant till well into the second year of her course. Participation in various four-week units of different materials and techniques was a college prerequisite; print, being one of these. This was another area of study that Nicola viewed with prejudice, and one that she felt had to be put off at all costs – 'too big, too flat and with no room for small secrets.' The connection of print with frescoes was yet to be made. First she had to discover discharge printing[61]. That discovery led to the realisation that a fabric surface could be created, as opposed to being selected, from the ready-made; for instance one that could bear great tactile resemblance to a wall of frescoes.

One college holiday, whilst returning to Italy and to Assisi and Venice in particular, she filled sketchbooks with aerial views, 'with landscapes and scenes without perspective'. Eventual subjects for prints on fabric now moved to those reflecting the Italian visits. However, growing subjectively in parallel was the preoccupation with birds; an idea that eventually was to take over as her central subject matter. These images, as if arriving from nowhere, in reality surely relate to the fact that her mother is a keen ornithologist and her father one of a syndicate of doctors who, at the time, shared the ownership of a hot air balloon. Whilst a student, Nicola joined in the flights. Images of earth below were of course aerial. Added to these experiences was a freak event

Opposite: *Crow Descent,* 1990. Private collection Japan. 96cm x 26cm (38in. x 10in.)

Top: Sketchbook studies of *Crows in Flight* – drawn in the field by the artist's house in Co. Clare

Above right: Sketchbook drawings from the cave paintings in southwest France, which were to influence much work of the 1990s

in her final year at college. She and her future husband were camping on an island off Cape Clear on the southern coast of Ireland when their tent was blown away by a ferocious storm. Seeking shelter at the world-renowned ornithological research station on the island inevitably resulted in her being made very aware of the surrounding bird-life on the island. Never having focussed on them before, as subject matter for her work, circumstances now provided her with a unique opportunity to fill her sketchbooks. She says that this was the first time she had really looked at birds. These early drawings were abstract marks depicting the progress of a bird which she describes as 'little dynamic bursts of energy'.

It is clear that the greater part of her art school years were ones of uncertainty; unsure of what she was doing; and wary of her lecturers. She felt she was getting nowhere in particular. She recalls that Michael Brennand-Wood[62], lecturing part time at the college at that period, helped her to progress and collate the variety of stimuli that to her still seemed disparate and with which she still felt confused.

Also of influence, though very different, was the work of Sally Freshwater[63], whose work is often reminiscent of birds in flight.

Fortunately by the third year the subject of birds and textile printing came together in a complete breakthrough of artistic endeavour culminating in the start of the passionate and perceptive work seen today. This final year also saw the birth of her first child.

The role of artist versus mother had now begun and twenty years later this skill of juggling work with children is still a necessary balance; the youngest of three is only eleven years old.

Also balancing in the equation is teaching. Nicola, having started on her art training without particular ambition or direction, except to try everything, certainly did not have teaching in mind. Now very much part of her success story, and giving her great satisfaction, leads her to say 'I could go completely in that direction but it is not my plan to do so.'

It all started characteristically gradually. Living in Bristol until

Opposite above: *Curlews,* 1994. Private collection. 82cm x 175cm (32in. x 69in.)

Opposite below: Drawings made on Valentia Island, Co.Kerry for curlew work

Above: Studies made at Fanore Beach, West Clare, for *Oyster Catchers*

Right: *Oyster Catchers at Fanore,* 1996. Private collection. 95cm x 140cm (37in. x 55in.)

1991 a need arose to educate her son in a Steiner school. Coupled with this was the longing to re-live the childhood memories of countless blissfully happy family holidays spent in Ireland. She says Ireland went very deep and she clearly remembers the atmosphere. Eventually the pull was strong enough to move from England to seek out a Steiner school in Ireland. Art within this specialist education is respected and features strongly. Nicola became interested in teaching at primary level when her children switched to the local state school and when she discovered the curriculum contained little or no formal teaching of art. Initially she volunteered to teach based on her own art skills and her experience of art education in the Steiner system. In 1995, determined to offer a wider art experience of value in the lives of all the children in her local school she, together with friends, started the Mountshannon Arts Festival based around visual arts and education. They began modestly in the friend's large house in Mountshannon with the aim of bringing music and art together. Not too difficult as Nicola is also accomplished at the piano.

An exhibition of Contemporary Art would be hung, not for sale, but to educate and encourage appreciation. So what began with a motivation to improve the quality of art appreciation for her own children now grew to a new dimension. She approached local schools to become involved in the Arts programme of the annual festival and, in time, Clare County Council formed a register of artists who were willing to teach art in schools throughout the County; this work she now continues throughout the year.

At the same time her ideas for collaboration with the Irish Museum of Modern Art in Dublin were received with enthusiasm. Not only did the little town of Mountshannon become the first ever beneficiary of loans of art from their 'Collection' but was the foundation for The National Programme linking the museum with other local authorities throughout Ireland. In the last two or three years this has further developed into a teaching commitment of a day per week in different schools.

So from tiny beginnings and early trust by the Irish Museum of Modern Art, she has found herself more integrated with the community. There is a sense of mission in her passionate need to add to the life of children. She feels that education through art 'is the only way to change the next generations' appreciation and access to art in Ireland.'

Increasingly sharing her artistic self in this way, she was recently selected to do a three months' residency with a

Opposite above: *Ringed Plovers Feeding,* 1996. Private collection. 120cm x 70cm (47in. x 28in.)

Opposite below: Sketchbook studies of Ringed Plovers on the West Coast of Co. Clare

Left: *Rook Waiting,* 1996. Private collection. 88cm x 63cm (35in. x 25in.)

Below: Sketch book studies of a dead rook found hanging on a fence as a scarecrow

Bottom left: Typical sketchbook pages showing movement of gulls at Fanore, West Coast of Ireland

Bottom right: *Gannet, Azure,* 1998. Private collection. 50cm (20in.) square

Left: Studies of Gannets off the coast of Co. Kerry

Below: Studies for the Heron made at Lough O'Grady behind the artist's house

Bottom: *Heron* 1998 Private collection 35cm x 124cm (14in. x 49in.)

Opposite: Detail of *Song Thrush Liberation* 1999 Private collection 76cm x 112cm (30in. x 44in.)

Dublin artist experienced in working with elderly people. Nicola is no stranger to ageing folk for her father, in his role as a doctor, also ran a home for the elderly. Success in the work that followed was almost assured. Teaching drawing at a local day centre for people of a great age was a rewarding and deeply appreciated project. Groups from different parts of County Clare would be brought in turn for ten-day cycles.

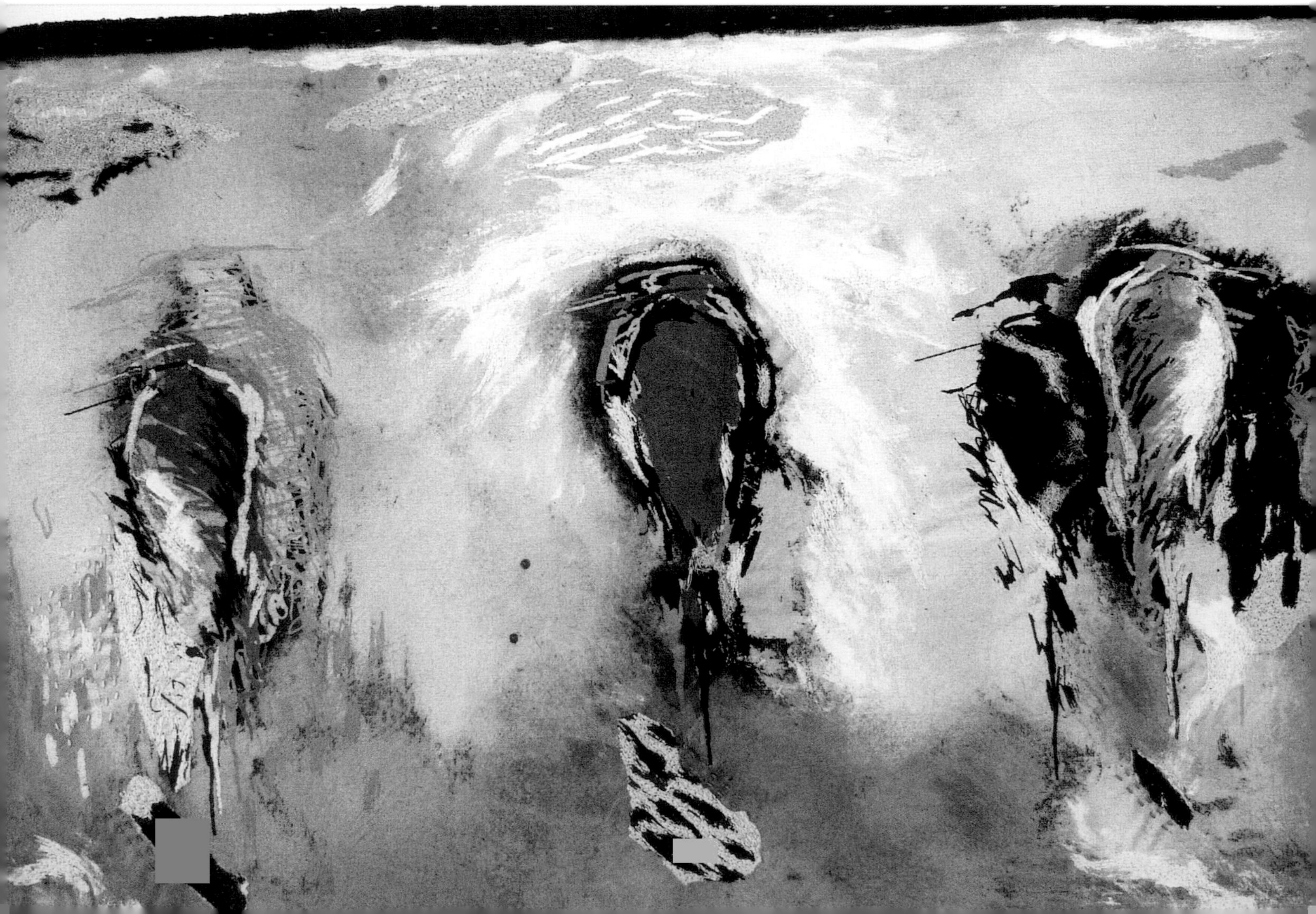

Top left: *Feeding Frenzy, Valencia,* 2003.
One of a triptych of hangings.
Private collection 103cm (40in.) square. Photo: David Hankey

Top right: *Feeding Frenzy, Valencia,* 2003. Second of a triptych of hangings Private collection 103cm (40in.) square Photo: David Hankey

Left: Detail *Feeding Frenzy, Valencia,* 2003. Photo: David Hankey

Opposite top left: *Gulls Adriatic*, detail, 2004. Cunard/P&O for S.S. Arcadia to be launched 2005.
240cm x 270cm (94in. x 106in.) Photo: Mike Keegan

Opposite top right: Detail: *Gulls Adriatic,* 2004. Photo: Mike Keegan

Opposite below: Detail: *Gulls Atlantic,* 2004. Cunard.
140cm x 270cm (55in. x 106in.) Photo: Mike Keegan

Most participants had never ever held a pencil to draw. The personal testimonies in the catalogue for the exhibition staged in Dublin moved many to tears and had the sponsors, National Irish Bank, stating that it was their most successful project of the year.

Her present studio, a converted barn adjoining the family home, large and square, has space for an old grand piano alongside a wall draped with the first of two panels commissioned for a new Cunard ship. At a little over two metres by a little under two metres a skyscape greets the eye, charged with light and inhabited by the rhythmic movement of birds. Cotton fabric is printed in all her personalised methods with tiny additions of small pieces of brown paper and handmade Japanese paper applied with the sparkle of machine stitching in gold. The large work-table supports the second piece, not yet complete, the result of five days solidly printing for up to twelve hours a day in succession. She describes her state of mind at the time as being emotional, at times euphoric and totally detached from everyday life. Now that she is experienced with the process she employs, she has precise control over the effects she seeks.

With her normally fragmented week she has to build up to a piece and plan to work with intensity and great single mindedness when consecutive days occur. A trusted old Jones sewing machine stands by, as do numerous silk screens not fully cleansed of their indigo body.

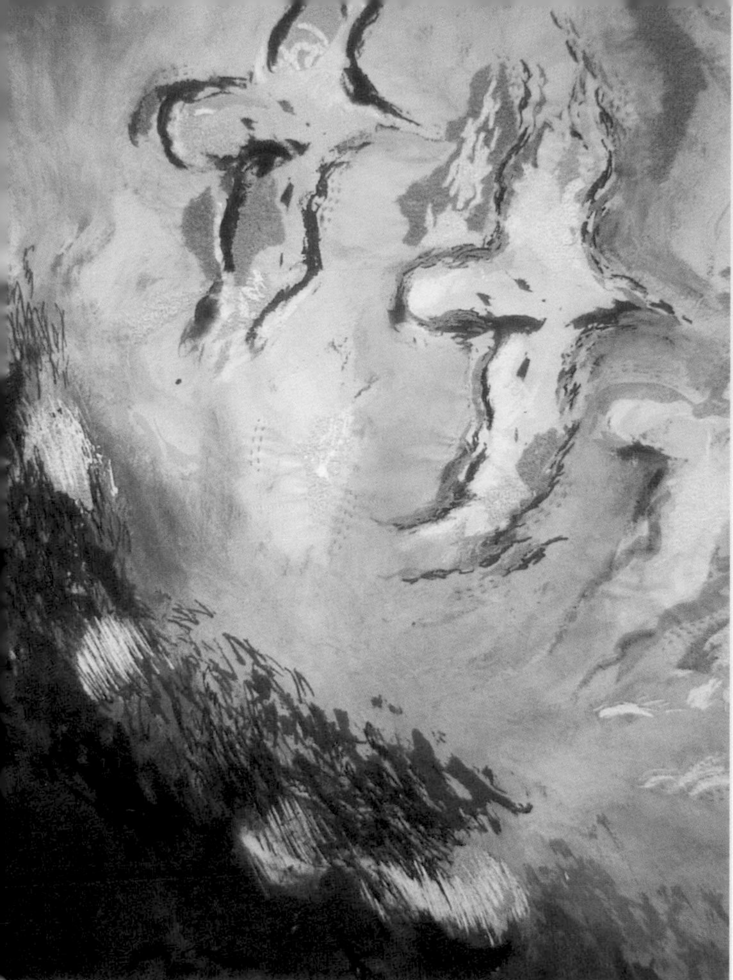

With her twelve year marriage over since 1996 she finds it financially necessary to teach the piano or be an accompanist one day a week at the Steiner School and in term time also teach art one day per week. This leaves her with three clear studio days on a regular basis. She values being free to make a body of work for a period of one to one and a half years with the plan to circulate it for show. Her list of exhibiting venues is impressive and she has been very successful. Rarely does she sell all the pieces exhibited at any one time, though this did happen once at Gallerie Pousse in Tokyo in 1990 when all twelve pieces sold.

A story of financial insecurity is evident in the lives of most textile artists. Nicola is no exception in saying that one is lucky to get £700 for a month's work and that is not every month. To that you add the shortfall created by those galleries who only pay after repeated reminders and in some cases do not even notify the artist when they have made a sale.

An outwardly tentative personality belies an inner determination to continue to produce glorious images with fabric and thread.

Footnotes

61 *Discharge Printing: The printpaste, formaldehyde based, when applied to a surface previously dyed with Direct dye replaces this original colour with the new pigment that has been added to the print paste. The new colour goes right into the cloth. Steam and heat are required to trigger the reaction. It makes it possible to apply light colours/neutral/white to a dark background giving a 'deeper' and more varied texture.*

62 *Michael Brennand-Wood 1952- Visual artist, curator, lecturer, arts consultant. 1979- occupies central position in research, origination and advocacy of Contemporary International Textiles. Prolific artist exhibiting in galleries and museums worldwide. Work is in numerous private, public and corporate collections. Commissions UK and abroad. 1987 won The Creative Concept Award. 1989 won The Fine Art Award Kyoto. 1990 RSA Art for Architecture Award. Extensive lecturing programme includes Senior Lecturer Goldsmiths' College London and many overseas countries. 1999 Major retrospective Bankfield Museum Halifax UK*

63 *Sally Freshwater 1958- Minimalist use of textiles often in large scale commissions for public places*

Photo: James Newell

ALICE KETTLE

1961	Born Winchester 21 October
1979 – 84	University of Reading BA Hons. Fine Art
1985 – 86	Goldsmiths' College School of Art Postgraduate Diploma in Textile Art
1986	Solo Show Oxford Gallery
1986 –	Exhibits widely in shared shows
1987	Solo show University College Chichester Solo show Painting and Textiles Oxford Gallery *Alice Kettle A Formal Image* Autumn issue *Embroidery*
1987 – 91	Tutor Goldsmiths' College School of Art
1988	Solo show *Alice Kettle Showcase* ICA London. Solo show Oxford Gallery Solo show Quay Art Centre Newport Isle of Wight Receives Taittinger Prize
1990	Solo show *My Eyes Your Hands* Brewery Arts Centre Kendal Solo show Scottish Gallery Edinburgh Alice Kettle September issue *Needle Arts* USA Marries Mathew Koumis
1991	Commission *The Saga of McGuiness Dog* Southem Arts Solo show Galerie Filambule Lausanne Switzerland Birth of daughter Poppy
1992	Commission *Overtures of Gold* Open University Faculty of Arts Solo show Salisbury Playhouse *Spotlight on Alice Kettle* Elizabeth Benn *Embroidery* Summer issue *Material Advances* one of four featured Margot Coatts *Crafts* Autumn Birth of daughter Tamsin
1993	Cosmopolitan Achievement
1994 – 95	Commission Six Panels *Glimpses of India* MV Oriana P&O Cruises
1994	Commission Altar Frontal Holy Sepulchre Chapel Winchester Cathedral *Alice in Winchester* Margot Coatts *Crafts* November issue
1995	Commission *Grandeur of the Seas* Royal Caribbean Cruise Lines *Eye of the Needle* The Textile Art of Alice Kettle Monograph Telos
1995 – 97	Commission *In Camera* High Court Lawnmarket Edinburgh
1996	Birth of daughter Maia
1997	*The Embroidery Art of Alice Kettle* – expanding the definition of handwork Ilze Aviks, *FiberArts* USA January issue Artist in Residence Canberra School of Art Australia
1997 – 2003	Responsible Graphic Design for several Telos books
1999	Kreinik Prize and Bernina Prize
1999 – 2000	Commission The National Library of Australia Canberra
1999 – 2001	Commission Three Altar Frontals for High Altar Gloucester Cathedral
2000	Commission *Chagall Column* Paul Foster
2001	Profile *Textile Fibre Forum Magazine* Australia March issue *The Textile Art of Alice Kettle* January issue *Australian Craft*
2002	Solo show Newbury Spring Festival
2003	Marriage to Mathew Koumis dissolved
2003 – 5	Commission School of Music and Drama Manchester University Commission Calderdale MBC Museums and Arts *Alice Kettle Mythscapes* April issue Selvedge *Journey through the Mythscapes* March issue Embroidery Review David Briers *Crafts* May/June issue
2004	Review *Mythscapes* July/August issue *Embroidery*
2004 – 6	Solo touring exhibition *Mythscapes* commencing Bankfield Museum Halifax

Her work is in public and private collections worldwide. Numerous lectures. Four music album covers.

Right: *Me and You,* detail, 2000. Machine embroidery. Private collection. 38cm x 30cm (15in. x 12in.). Photo: David Hankey

Alice Kettle

It is unlikely that anyone meeting Alice for the first time would associate her with the creation of monumental works of art. This gentle, caring, quiet personality, outwardly delicate in stature, hides the most powerful will to work. Twenty years of phenomenal artistic endeavour have resulted in magnificent machine embroidered panels and hangings for which, so deservedly, she is renowned today.

Significant to Alice's identity and character is to note that her father and his brother, though coming from a humble background, rose to the world of high academia through winning scholarships to Oxford and Cambridge Universities respectively. Her father, qualifying as a linguist, went on to teach at Winchester College for the rest of his life. Even more significant was his additional role as a housemaster. This meant that on marrying he, his wife and young family of three daughters, enjoyed the privilege of an exceptionally beautiful home. Alice was born there and remembers her childhood as being incredibly happy; one that was steeped in tradition, history and interesting things. Home, being part of a boys boarding school, was a protected and closed community involving the whole range of the arts from plays to concerts; 'a captivating and extraordinary environment'. Her own schooling, which she regards as excellent, was at the local state school.

Unquestionably the strength of this scholastic influence was later to influence Alice's choice of institution for the study of art. Most often those wishing to pursue a career in art would select an art school; instead she chose a fine art department within a university. This natural inclination was in harmony with a progressive course leader at her sixth form college who, through connections with Reading University, set the seal on choice.

Why art at all? one might ask.

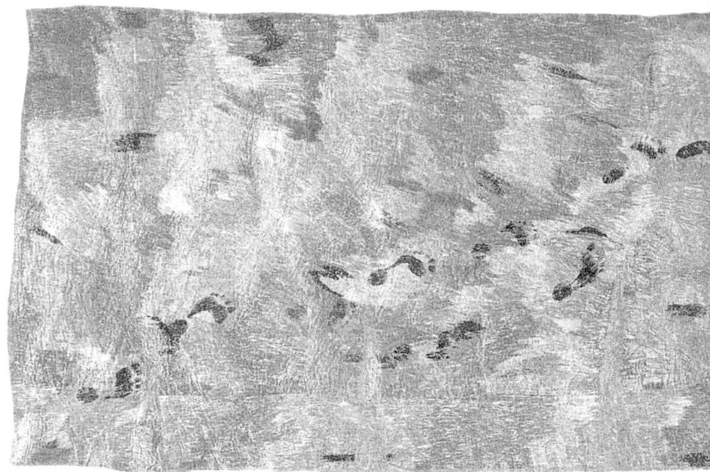

Left: *Blue Baskers,* 2000. Machine embroidery. Private collection. 16cm x 22cm (6in. x 9in.). Photo: David Hankey

Above: *Rite of Passage,* 2003. Machine embroidery. 250cm x 155cm (98in. x 61in.). Photo: James Newell

Below: *Lotus Eaters and Hermes, in memory of Evie,* 2003. Machine embroidery. 185cm x 280cm (72in. x 108in.). Photo: James Newell

Opposite above: Sketch for the *Odyssey,* 2003. Watercolour. Private collection. Photo: James Newell

Opposite below: *Odyssey,* 2003. Machine embroidery. 185cm x 380cm (72in. x 150in.). Photo: James Newell

Alice's mother was by nature artistic and expressed it in the way she ran the boys' boarding house. This one-time geography teacher now excelled at wonderful arrangements of flowers, at deciding on imaginative furnishings for the house and was particularly bold in her selection of carpets and wallpapers. 'My mother was quite apart from others in her ability to choose and was able to appreciate all she saw in the newly-arrived Habitat shops. Through her we were also selecting bravely. I can remember being allowed to have a silver wall in my bedroom.'

Her mother's breadth of artistic interest included taking the three girls to the Winchester School of Art's annual degree shows which, when one considers the 1960s and 70s, was quite an unusually enlightened choice for recreation.

In addition, she amassed an amazing dressing-up cupboard, gathering up strange garments from anywhere thus giving a huge feel for the appreciation of fabric.

There was also her sister's friendship with Terence Conran's[64] niece Lucy. 'A part of me wanted to do art and be like her'.

A further catalyst in the creative circle was a lady called Joyce Hitchcock who, through opening up a tiny but superb craft shop in Winchester, gathered like-minded people around her; people with style and creativity who could help. Alice was about twelve years old when her mother started to work there one day per week. She also wanted to be part of it, eventually working there herself till she was about twenty. Gaining this first exposure to contemporary craft of a high order, from knit to jewellery, she says, 'Hitchcocks gave me a glimpse of a world outside academia that I would never have seen and Joyce gave me great support which I still enjoy.'

Life at this stage seemed safe and assured. So from the nurture of 'genuine and caring socialist parents who thought about everybody' she sets forth on her fine art course full of confidence. She was just seventeen. Just one month later she was to suffer the first of her life's cruel blows. Returning from taking Alice back from an exeat her mother was killed in a car crash. This catastrophe of losing the mother she described as 'simply good at being lovely' she says, 'If I'm honest, I have struggled all my life with my mother's death'.

The four year BA.Hons. course was spread over five due to a year off somewhere in the middle on compassionate grounds. Fortunately the Reading days, spent in the Painting department, are described as very happy. One of a small group of students, she had joined the colour painting studio which was comprised of individual spaces within a studio/house. They enjoyed great freedom and personal responsibility in a largely unstructured course that included visits from many leading painters of the day. It was clearly a very formative period where she worked hard, was excited by the activity of paint and its potential of layering one colour upon another. She also enjoyed the small family atmosphere and friendship of the other students.

Still profoundly wounded, she took another year off during which time she joined an evening class that included members of the local branch of the Embroiderers' Guild[13] in Winchester. Not only does she speak of their kindness but through them her attention was drawn to the advertisement for the one-year Diploma course in Textiles at Goldsmiths' College School of Art.

A grant from her local authority enabled her to work full time on what was clearly to be the emergence of one of Britain's most significant artists. Twenty years on she speaks with clarity of the detail of the interview, what she wore, what work she took, the eagerness on arrival at the course 'I did everything – I was on a mission to catch up with myself'. Living in a student billet she was free to work frenetically and, unlike most students, attended every day spending many hours in the machine room with technical experts Diana Thornton and Margaret Hall-Townley[46]. 'I just slotted in.' She also speaks of her head of department, Audrey Walker[16] and the 'landmark'

Opposite: *Bag of Winds,* 2003. Machine embroidery. Private collection. 90cm x 60cm (35in. x 24in.). Photo: James Newell

Left: *Lotus Eaters,* 2003. Machine embroidery. Private collection. 90cm x 60cm (35in. x 24in.). Photo: James Newell

Below left: *Argos I,* 2004. Machine embroidery. 90cm x 60cm (35in. x 24in.). Photo: James Newell

Below right: *Argos II,* 2004. Machine embroidery. 90cm x 60cm (35in. x 24in.). Photo: James Newell

critique which she still recalls as changing her perspective, and of Michael Brennand-Wood[40] whose dynamic presence and work provided abiding inspiration.

During these months she completed three major pieces one of which, *Eve Falling from Grace* 1988-9, she regards as one of the significant pieces in her career–indeed 'it established and generated a response; thereafter what I did was about confidence'. This large hanging typifies her early period of depicting a single figure surrounded by a jewel like space. Solidly machine stitched on a calico ground the innate tension of stitch results in a gently sculptural undulation of surface. Surprisingly, even though her pieces are often very large, she works directly onto the cloth with the fewest of initially placed lines and from the minimum of sketches.

Rayon, cotton and metallic threads are built up layer upon layer usually from the right side. Sometimes, when heavy rayon threads are desired, these have to be hand wound on to the bobbin/bottom spool and then, of necessity, are worked from the wrong side. So often ethereal, always a narrative, expressed in colour charged with at least one vibrant contrast, her works never fail to capture the beholder.

The course concluded; she left south London to return once again to her beloved Winchester, where she still lives. She was able to work by day in one of the newly opened Design Workshops/Studios. These were offered to new graduates as a half-way house. Loosely connected to the art school and supported initially by an enterprise scheme of £40 per week for a year and a modest rent of £25 per week in the two years she stayed thereafter, she learnt by trial and error how to work in the real world. Expectations at the time were very different. The main idea was to make pieces of embroidery with, at this stage, money not the main concern. True to character she worked incredibly hard producing enough work for a touring show, shared with a friend from the college, and culminating in another of her significant works *The Three Caryatids* 1989-90 purchased by the Whitworth Gallery in Manchester. Each panel conforming to her choice of a single figure in space and based on a theme from the subconscious. Regarded by her as a really important piece.

She was now approaching thirty, was happy, fulfilled and her esteem was growing.

In 1990 she married Matthew Koumis, with whom she was an integral part of Telos Art Publishing. The next five years involved a balance of time between the birth of two

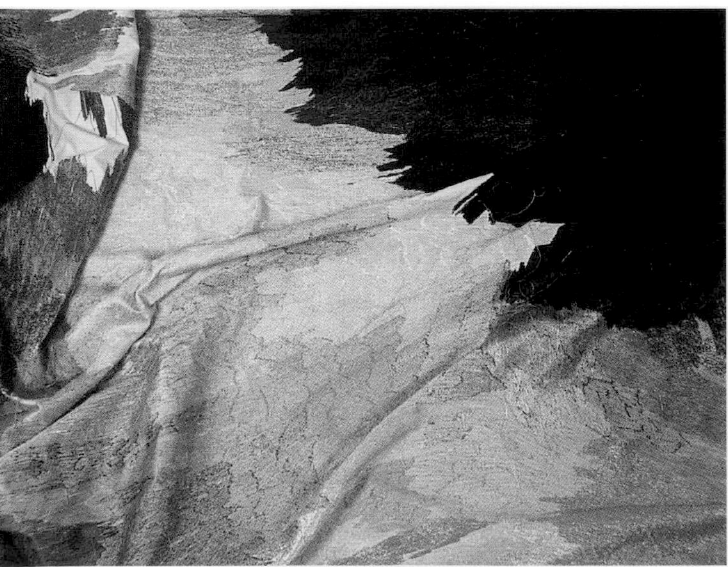

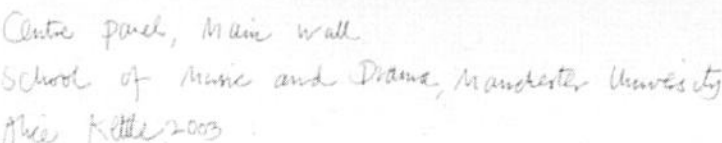

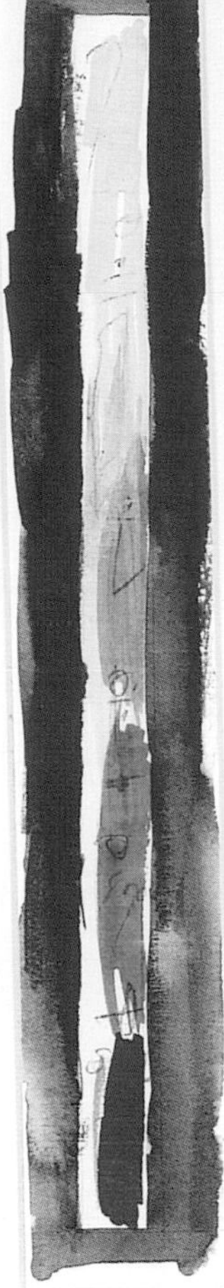

Opposite top: *Penelope's Bed,* 2003. Machine embroidery 90cm x 60cm (35in. x 24in.) Photo: James Newell

Opposite below: *Mythscapes Exhibition,* 2003, seen here on exhibition at Bankfield Museum, Halifax, England Scylla. 320cm (126in.)high x 40cm (16in.) diameter Charybdis 80 cm (31in.) diameter. Photo: Jerry Hardman Jones

Top left and above: Designs for a set of three panels in preparation for the School of Music and Drama Manchester 2004. Watercolour. Photo James Newell

Above left: Detail of embroidery in progress for a set of three panels for the School of Music and Drama Manchester, 2004-. Machine embroidery main panel 475cm x 175cm (187in. x 69in.). Photo: James Newell

daughters and her work. The first publication *Eye of the Needle* in 1995 was a profile on her own work. For many of the productions that followed, they shared the responsibility of running the company and Alice learnt how to do book graphics and layouts in order to produce, amongst others, the *Art Textiles of The World* series.

By 1991 she had finally completed *Creation*, a four part columnar work, which is now in the collection of Direzione Beni Culturali Regione Piedmonte in Turin. Still characteristically 'sculpted' in her own inimitable style, with her faithful Bernina 950 sewing machine, the magnificently lustrous surfaces of gold and pink uplift man from earth. Note too her first references to geometric shapes.

The subsequent years show an increasing involvement with large scale commissioned work. These major pieces involved designing appropriately and placing her stitched wall hangings within large, often public architectural spaces with all the inherent artistic and technical issues. The vast composite pieces *In Camera* for the High Court in Edinburgh 1996-97 show a development of the geometric form combined with an interpretation of the courtroom scene.

Above left: *Australian Landscape Series 1-1V,* 2000. Machine embroidery. Three hangings. National Library of Australia, Canberra each panel. 400cm x 185cm (157in. x 73in.), one panel (not seen) 400cm x 80cm (157in. x 31in.). Photo: Damian McDonald

Above right: *Australian Landscape Series I-IV,* 2000, detail of machine embroidery. Three hangings. National Library of Australia, Canberra. Each panel 400cm x 185cm (157in. x 73in.), one panel (not seen) 400cm x 80cm (157in. x 31in.). Photo: James Johnson

Below left: Design sheet for *In Camera,* 1996-7. Watercolour. Scottish High Court Edinburgh. Photo: James Johnson

Below right: *In Camera,* 1996-1997. Four machine embroidered panels in situ – Scottish High Court, Edinburgh – maximum dimensions 4.5m x 10m (14ft.9in. x 32ft.10in.).
Photo: Brian Fischbacher

Opposite top right: *In Camera,* detail of stitched technique, (opposite top left) *In Camera.* Four panels *in situ.* Scottish High Court, Edinburgh maximum dimensions 4.5m x 10m (14ft.9in. x 32ft.10in.). Photo James Johnson

Opposite below: *Eve Falling from Grace,* 1986. Private collection. 233cm x 157cm (92in. x62in.). Photo: James Johnson

In 2000 she completed the *Australian Landscape Series I-IV* for the National Library of Australia, a rendition of the powerful Australian land and skyscape into a palette of intense gold and blue.

A major solo touring show *Mythscapes* embarked upon in 2003, is a body of work based on Homer's epic poem *The Odyssey*. These pieces reflect a continuing interest in classicism together with a personal response to her intense attachment to Greece. These works which she regards as complex and important, 'pushed me into another place – I gave them all I'd got'.

In *Metamorphosis*, also completed in 2003, she feels she is working in a new direction, drawing, then folding the surface and redrawing a distorted image onto a new plane. Figures in recent works tend to be in groups and are more to do with real people as opposed to things symbolic.

She has always felt inspired by galleries and by travelling. She had one wonderful month in India after her Diploma course and with the stored memories she based six panels entitled *Glimpses of India* 1994-95 commissioned for the Curzon room on board the liner Oriana.

Ever more astonishing is to realise that these huge works akin to Medieval tapestries emerge from a workroom which is no more than a small, cold wooden shed at the bottom of the garden. To witness the shear physical management of the first of a set of three panels currently in preparation for the School of Music and Drama at Manchester University leaves one in total admiration. This simple space has one other saving grace in that it backs on to her allotment where she can take a break, dig, grow and reap her own vegetables just as she remembers her parents doing in the happy days in the garden of Winchester College.

The public face of major exhibitions and colossal works are also hiding the dependence on her work for a secure income. Her divorce in 2003 and need to maintain three young daughters make this an important challenge. The inner courage and strength, that once sustained her in her teens, will undoubtedly support this significant artist in the growth of her creativity. Could it be coincidence that her subjects are based on life's universal themes of suffering, struggle and hope, and as she expresses, 'a search for balance, a desire to understand the human condition.'

Footnote

64 *Sir Terence Conran 1931- Opened first Habitat store in Fulham Road in 1964. Furniture designer, entrepreneur, property developer, food guru and more. Loved by the 60s generation for enabling them to make their homes look different from those of their parents*

Photo: Jean-Christophe

RACHEL QUARMBY

1964	Born W. Yorkshire 24 April
1981 – 82	Batley College of Art Foundation Course
1982 – 86	Manchester Polytechnic BA Hons Embroidery
1986 – 87	Newcastle Polytechnic Business Management/Marketing
1986	Started embroidery business in England exhibiting and working to public and private commission Winner of the Embroiderers' Guild Lynette de Denne Bursary
1987	*Metamorphosis* textile sculpture Carlisle Library Cumbria
1988	*Twisting Flight* textile sculpture Oasis Park Swansea Featured *Architects Journal* August issue
1989	Contributor *Embroidery in Architecture* autumn issue *Embroidery*
1991	*Junk Sail Mobile* Jardine Matheson Headquarters London Textile Installation Children's A&E Hull Royal Infirmary Featured *Interior Design* April issue
1992	Textile Installation Eton Park Junior School Burton on Trent Moved to Paris Set Design and Interior Design for French TV and British Embassy
1993	Two suspended Sculptures Leeds Permanent Building Society HQ
1996	Commenced costume design for contemporary dance, cinema, opera, theatre and circus
1997	Patine for National Opera of Paris at the Garnier Leather and patine for Théâtre National de Chaillot
1998	Costume decoration and accessories in film *Astérix & Obélix contre César*. Leather costume accessories and patine Co-production Festspiele Bad Hersfeld Germany and Théâtre National de Chaillot. Acrobatic costumes after film *Mulan* Disneyland Paris
1999	African accessories aand costumes for *La Parade* Disneyland Paris Design and making contemporary dance costumes *Could you take some of my weight?* Design and making contemporary dance costumes *Jealousy* (dance school of Garnier Opera). Contemporary dance costumes Fureurs National Centre de Dance Angers Accessories, embroidery, patine *L'Avare* Théâtre National de Chaillot
2000	Costume decoration, patine, dyeing, leatherwork *Astérix & Obélix au Service de Cléopâtre*. Costumes for Tero Saarinen *Man in a Room* Venice Biennale. Circus costumes for Disneyland Paris
2001	Designing and making costumes for *Kaze* contemporary dance Finland Patine and accessories for la Comédie Francaise Assistant costumière at Théâtre de la Commune *L'Ecôle de Femmes*
2002	Costume design Opera of Gottenburg Sweden *Transfigured Night* Costumes for l'Opera de Rouen *La Force du Destin*
2003	Design and making contemporary dance costumes Soffio Compagnie Post-Retroguardia Assistant costumière for Lucile Hadzihalilovic's film *L'Ecole* Design and making costumes for ballet *Unison* Grand Théâtre Luxemborg
2004	Re-make of Costumes for Ballet National de Lorraine in *Could you take some of my Weight?* Costumes for Ballet National de Marseille in *The Captain*

Work in private and public collections include Drumcoon Art Education Centre Wigan: Kirklees Metropolitan Council W. Yorkshire: Shipley Art Gallery Gateshead.

Right: Embroidered Mobile 1989 200cm (78in.) long

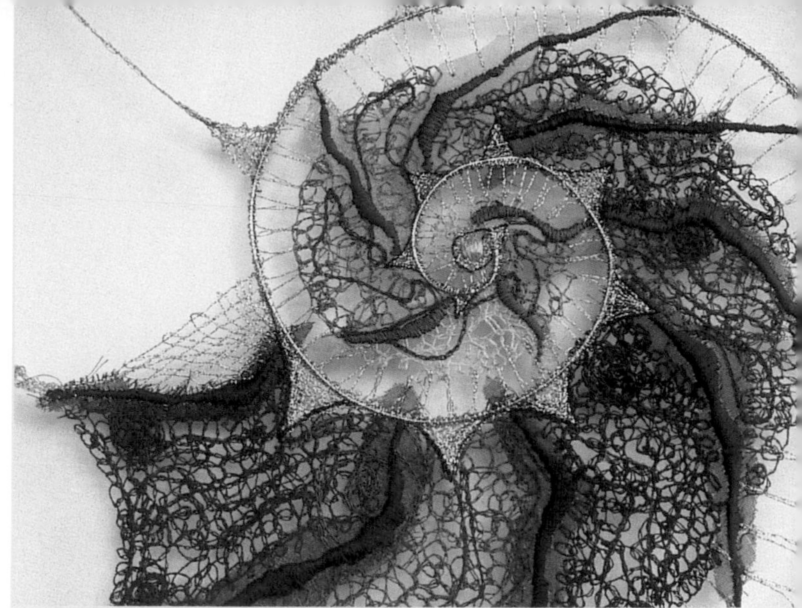

Rachel Quarmby

Rachel's twenty year career has been consistently underpinned by flair, enterprise and courage. The discipline and diversity of her training in embroidered and constructed textiles at Manchester Polytechnic undoubtedly formed the rock on which both parts of her career have been built. The first six years involved almost immediate success in a free-lance business responding to commissions for both public and private spaces and to making work for exhibition. In contrast the next thirteen years, though still involved in both design and making, have been spent pursuing a great diversity of costume projects within the world of theatre, film, circus and contemporary dance. Although the two parts of her life appear to be unconnected at first glance, they are both founded on the breadth of her early art school training. That established, it is also worth noting that, at the conclusion of her three year course, taking up a career in textiles was not an inevitability. A year out with ill health, together with a final grade that disappointed her, she was ready to do something else. However several of her embroidered panels, including *Fish* and *Butterflies*, sold at her degree show. 'That was the catalyst in giving me the idea that there was a possibility of making a living from what I enjoyed doing'. These early works were achieved technically by working with an Irish and a Cornely machine on vanishing muslin. These beautiful pieces evolved into powerful and personal images with her use of gestural marks in thread. Muslin of this sort is 'vanished' by means of a hot iron; hot enough to reduce the ground cloth to dust but not so hot that it melts the embroidery thread; in particular those with a metallic finish. The advantage of this muslin, over the cold water type more usually used to day, is that it will receive preliminary painted marks of any sort. Drawing on the water dissolvable type can only be done with felt tip pens.

Comforted and inspired by the early sales of her work she left art college, took a six month Business Studies

Above left: *Butterflies,* 1986. Machine embroidery on vanishing muslin. Private collection. 90cm x 55cm (35in. x 22in.). Photo: David Hankey

Above right: *Falling Fish,* 1986. Painting on canvas. Private collection

Opposite top: Untitled, 1986. Procion dyes on paper

Opposite below: *Fish,* 1986. Machine embroidery on vanishing muslin. Private collection. 70cm (28in.) square. Photo: David Hankey

course and with no knowledge of who might buy her work, set up on her own. No sooner had she received a grant for equipment and prepared her studio for work, she received a letter from Cumbria County Council and Northern Arts advising her that she had been short-listed for a project for Carlisle Library in Cumbria. Responding to this invitation to submit proposals she set about the lengthy process of research, prepared drawings and a model and succeeded in becoming the winning candidate. Not a wall panel but instead designing *Metamorphosis*; a piece in space. Taking a year to make, the twelve translucent dyed fabric shapes, stretched on tubular plastic, with highly embroidered streamers, created the illusion of movement and formed a spiral core in the heart of the building. Just two weeks after installation a photographic reproduction formed the front cover of the *Architects Journal*. From this point she says she never looked back. It was a period when the climate within the world of new buildings was encouraging clients to spend 1% of the budget on art. '1% for me was an enormous amount of money. From then on I was never without work until I left for France some six years later.' Amongst the numerous major projects in this period the one for the Jardine Matheson atrium is especially powerful. Thirteen sections suspended from painted metal mesh, in colours running from scarlet through to turquoise blue, are over brass-plated bright-mild steel tubing rods. Forming shapes initially reminiscent of fish fins they are in fact based instead on the sails of junk boats and bird wings. These small eastern sailing crafts had featured in the book loaned to her by the insurance company recounting their early history in the Far East. Suspended centrally, and somewhat helically, within a vast glass cylindrical space they gently move as a spiral suspended from a spinnaker sail attachment.

In 1991 the use of the old form of Procion dyes, which she had been applying regularly to fabrics through a mouth diffuser, took its toll resulting in an operation for bladder cancer. It was also a time when she and her husband, who had met and married as students, were drifting apart. Concurrent with this was the increasing awareness of the lone experience of making large works of art to commission. It is a fact that once the initial client contact has taken place and the brief agreed, work inevitably proceeds in isolation. This solitary state continues for rarely is there any feedback even after a piece is delivered. Large scale work means being consistently diligent, involves a huge responsibility to others and is therefore both daunting and physically exhausting. A new direction seemed timely.

She says 'It came in a whim. I was still married and my business was still running but I got in the car and drove to

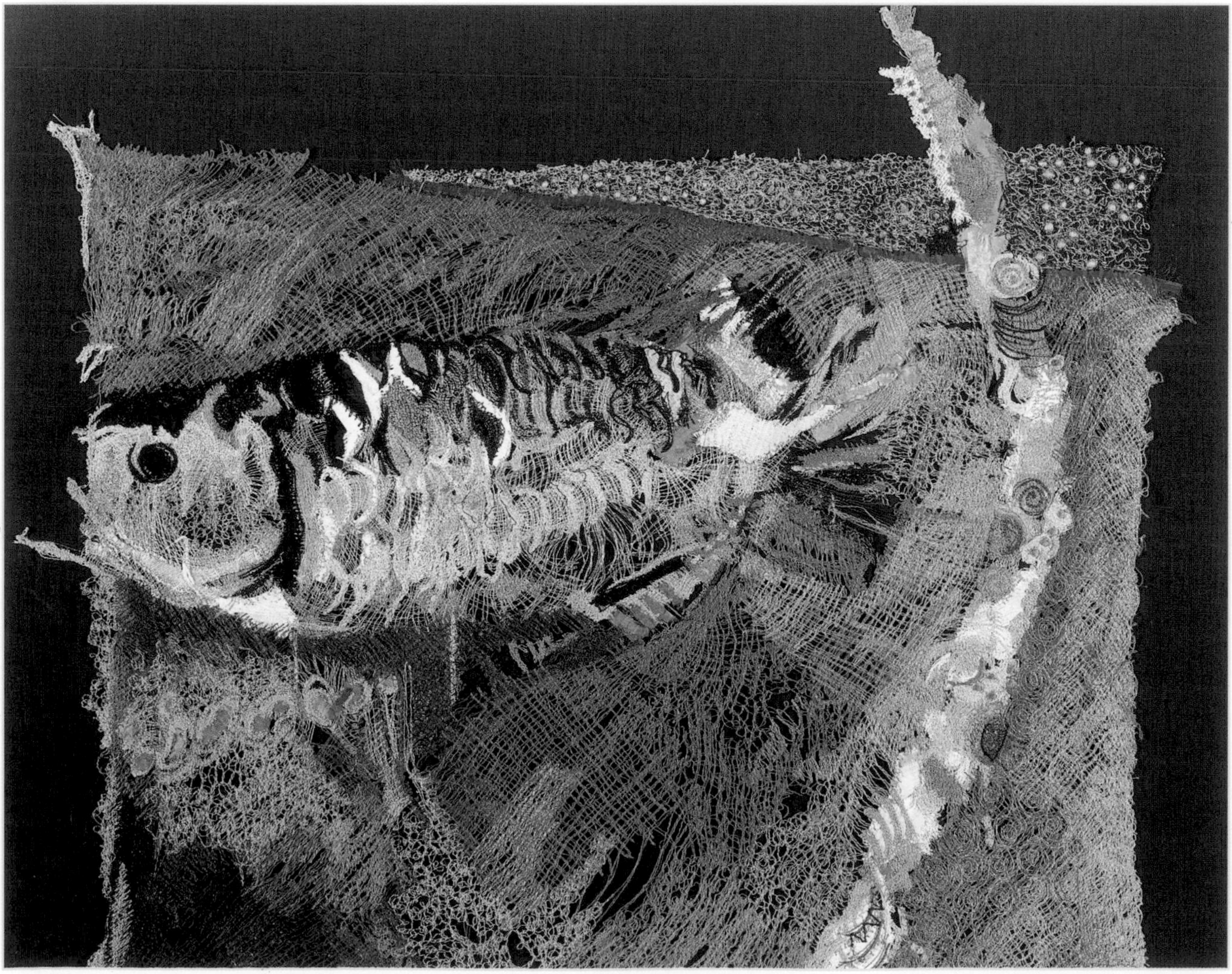

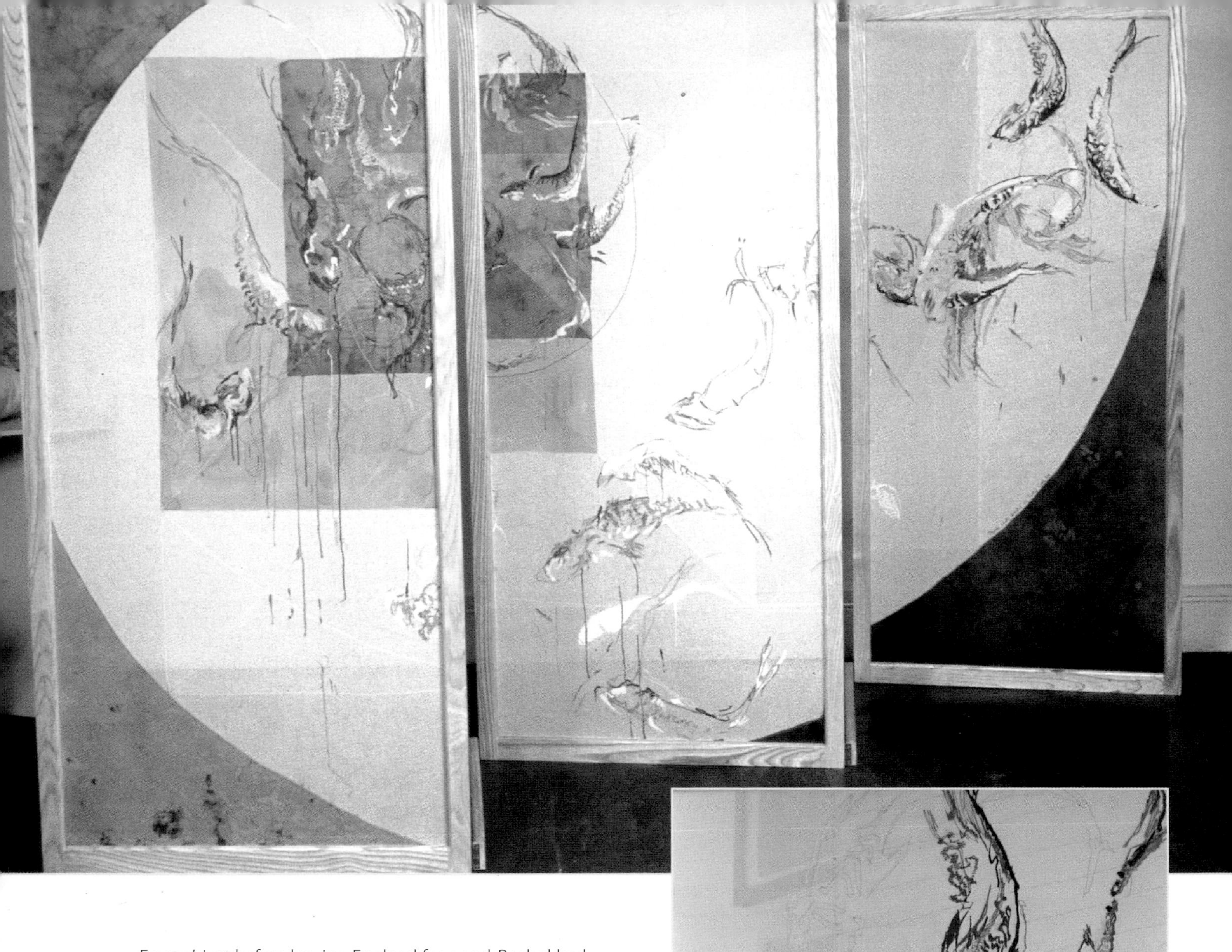

France'. Just before leaving England for good, Rachel had seen, and been inspired by, Archaos, an alternative French circus without animals. 'It triggered something in me and I knew I had to make a change'.

She did not speak French, stayed briefly with a friend till she found her own accommodation and, because of her early good fortune in England, she thought it would be easy to find work. This was not to be the case. She says that looking back 'sometimes making things difficult for yourself can actually be very positive in bringing the best out of you'. After helping a friend of a friend to make theatre costumes for two weeks when she felt in harmony with the transparency of fabrics and their movements, she dreamed of designing in this new field. It would still be the world of fabric and objects in space but now she would be making things for people with whom she could have a dialogue. It was to be a long slow journey of knocking on doors. She also learned that in France attitudes to work are the reverse of Britain. It is only when you stay in a job for a long time that you are considered competent; a

Opposite top: *Spiral Screen,* 1987. Machine embroidery

Opposite below: Detail, *Spiral Screen,* 1987. Machine embroidery

Left: *Metamorphosis,* 1987. Carlisle Library Twelve translucent dyed fabric shapes – suspended in the centre of the building – stretched on tubular plastic with highly embroidered streamers creating the illusion of movement

Bottom: Detail of *Metamorphosis,* 1987

Below: Light Fitting, Jardine House, 1990. Embroidery and perforated steel

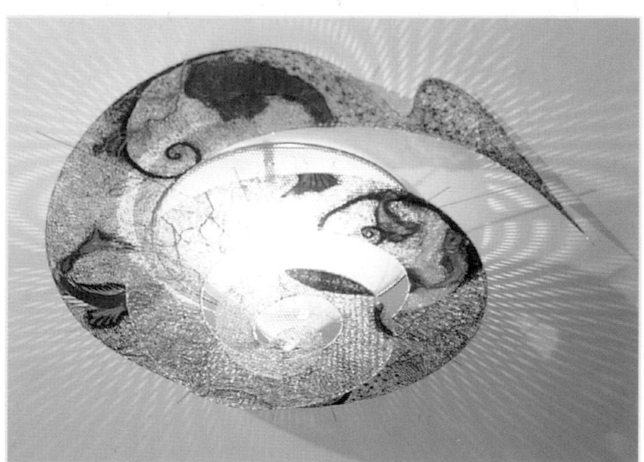

Left: *Junk Sail Mobile.* Suspended fabric sculpture in situ 1991 for Jardine Matheson. 26m (85ft 3in.)

Below: Research sheet for *Junk Sail Mobile,* 1991

Opposite top left: Preparation sheet for *Junk sail Mobile,* 1991

Opposite top right: Presentation sheet for *Junk Sail Mobile,* 1991

Opposite bottom left: Preparation sheet for *Junk sail Mobile,* 1991

Opposite bottom right: Artist's impression before fabrication of *Junk Sail Mobile,* 1991

diversity of experience is received with the reverse effect. Also now she was without her supportive parents. She acknowledges that her father, Arthur Quarmby, the eminent architect of underground houses, provided a role model in encouraging a belief in success. He always bought her the best art materials; when she was eight years old he gave her a sable brush, which she still has, and taught her how to care for it. She recalls always having good pencils and receiving a fine set of watercolours. He, together with her mother, a music teacher and someone who loved making things, enrolled Rachel in an adult two week watercolour course with a local artist when she was only thirteen. 'Dad always taught me about perspective and was also keen for me to look long enough at things in order to note the fall of light and the contrasts of tone'. Her skills in art at this early stage were also further nurtured by an exceptional art master at her all girls boarding school in Filey.

RACHEL QUARMBY

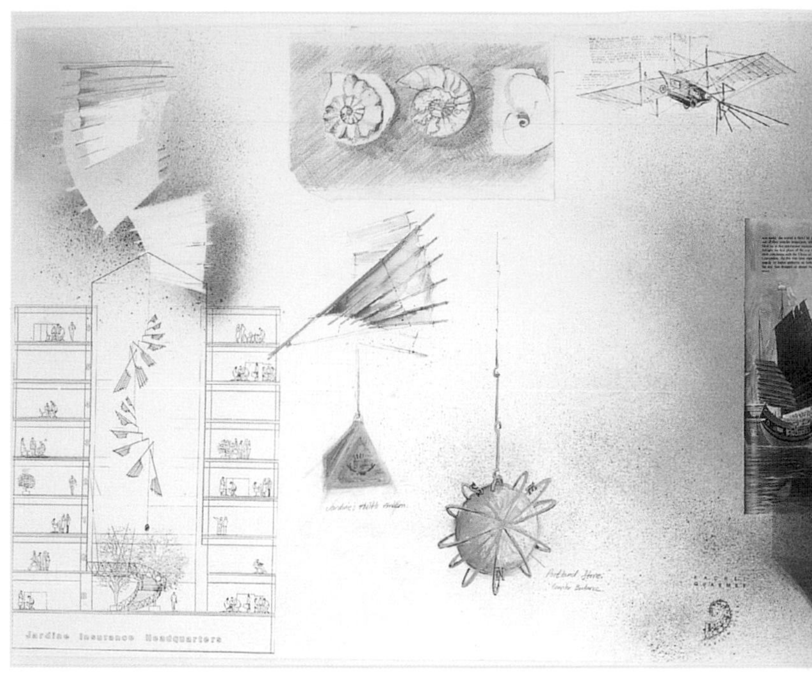
Jardine Insurance Headquarters
RACHEL QUARMBY

So here she was at twenty-eight, starting again in a foreign land, with the only familiar faces being a friend or two of her brother and her greatest skills seemingly being disregarded. A number of years were to pass undertaking modest projects which in turn helped her to learn how to get work in Paris; 'There is no escape from continually persisting in approaching person after person'. With her command of the language now much improved she finally got her foot in the door at the Opera Garnier. She was hired as an *accessoiriste* which meant she had to be able to make any stage props and accessories. Also at this period of 1996/7 she started to utilise what she had brought with her from her early training; the ability to artistically embellish, enrich, change by means of paint or dye, any cloth surface. In France this is referred to as patine and is something for which she is constantly in demand. A very important skill particularly for new costumes, which would otherwise look very raw on stage. To this she added the making of garments, which involved learning traditional sewing skills.

Sitting in her modest home in the Bagnolet district of east Paris, which she shares with her supportive partner Jean-Christophe, it is hard to imagine, twelve years on, the spread

Opposite above and below: *Explorations with Numbers*. Work sheet 34cm x 36cm (13in. x 14in.) with machine sample 29cm x 23cm (11in. x 9in.). Typical of the intrinsic way the artist works and experiments with sampling. Photos: David Hankey

Right: Drawing for a Stilt Costume together with a detail of the painted decoration on the actual garment. Photo: David Hankey

Below right: A typical design sheet as presented for work in the theatre

of her outside world of clients to which she responds; directors, designers, choreographers and performing artists. This world of action, of theatre, music and dance, can only be minimally absorbed by looking into project files that fill the shelves of her sewing area at the end of the sitting room. Stitched samples, of experiment and play, the sort that would have stemmed from earlier training, accompany many of the photographs and costume sketches long ago delivered.

It is a light airy space with large doors that open on to a tiny enclosed garden with room to sit. A large work table in the centre is flanked by the three machines she brought with her; the Bernina 801 sport, a basic trade industrial straight stitch machine and a trade overlocker. Her punishing schedule of long hours, temporarily reduced by impending arrival of a first baby, includes forthcoming designs of costumes for a Luxemburg contemporary Dance Company; design ideas for a new Norwegian choreographer for the Norway National Ballet in Oslo and finally reworking costumes designed for the Opera of Gothenburg soon to be staged at the Finnish Ballet and Opera House in Helsinki.

Productions are often overseas involving regular travel to Scandinavia; journeys which will be resumed in a few months time.

This gentle, modest, unmaterial personality belies a force and vision that must lie within. She says that looking at her output she does not feel that she fits into any particular category. 'If someone were to give me a workshop and tell me to go away and work for a year, a dream for many artists, I think I would be a bit stuck. I get my inspiration from the site and the client. I do better for a budget, a deadline, and someone who has a vision and needs to bring it to reality'.

Photo: Alan Gardiner

LOUISE GARDINER

1972	Born Cheshire 8 January
1990 – 1991	Foundation Course Distinction Manchester Metropolitan University
1991 – 1994	BA Hons. Textiles Goldsmiths' College School of Art London
1994	Selected by the Embroiderers' Guild for the Knitting and Stitching Show
1994 – 96	Living in Cheshire. Making and exhibiting
1994 – 2003	Freelance Artist and Illustrator. Initially organising solo shows and subsequently exhibiting venues nation-wide Lectures, workshops and presentations for a variety of groups including the Embroiderers' Guild. the WI. Age Concern 2002 project *Wearpurple.com. Cheshire Dance*. Children's Workshops and *The Big Draw* at The Guardian Newspaper
1994 – 2004	Freelance Artist Illustration and Design including commissions for The Guardian Newspaper. Selvedge Magazine. The National Pyramid Trust. Set Design BBC programme *The History of Toys*. Greeting Card design. Regular commissions for limited edition stationery. Show banners for Brunswig & Fils. Promotional material. Sign painting. Macclesfield NHS Hospital
1996	Look Out profile *Crafts* magazine Jan/Feb issue
1996 – 97	Travel to Australasia and Indonesia
1997	Two person show *Pots & People* The Fough Gallery Buxton. *Figuratively Speaking* Rufford Craft Centre Nottingham
1997 – 1998	Part-time Tutor at Manchester Metropolitan University
1997 – 2000	Interior Design Adviser and Showroom Assistant for Zoffany and Brunswig & Fils Chelsea Harbour Design Centre including Solo show
1998	Commission Four Panels Wetherspoons Brewery
1999 – 2001	Freelance Scenic Painter for *Sceneart* includes Six FlagsTheme Park Holland
2000 – 2001	MA Communication Design Manchester Metropolitan University
2001	Solo Exhibition The Corner House Manchester
2002	Solo Show Feeling Lucky The Arc Gallery Chester Contributed to *Figurative works* The Black Swan Gallery Frome Bath. Close Relations The Bluecoat Display Centre Liverpool. *Summer Fun* The Beatrice Royal Gallery Eastleigh Hampshire. *Happy Clapham* The Pond Gallery Clapham London. Artists' Team Member *The World's Largest Glitter Ball* construction Blackpool
2002 – 2004	Teaching Art and Design Sir John Deane's College, Northwich, Cheshire
2003	Profile *Embroidery* magazine Nov/Dec issue Contributed *Art of the Stitch* Williamson Art Gallery Birkenhead – touring to Dutch Textile Museum Tilberg Holland
2003 –	Works have been exhibited in shows which include Rufford Craft Centre Nottingham. The Knitting and Stitching Shows. The Embroiderers' Guild. Cambridge Contemporary Art.
2004	Commission for Gloucester Royal Hospital Moves to Bristol
2004 – 5	Embroiderers' Guild Scholar

Over 350 works in public and private collections. Features include Granada Television. A&I magazine. Manchester City Life. The Manchester Evening News. The Manchester Metro. *Selvedge* magazine. The Guardian Newspaper

Right: *Portabello* Commission for Selvedge magazine. 2004.
Machine embroidery with hand painting.
38cm x 30cm (15in. x 12in.) Photo: Mark Watson

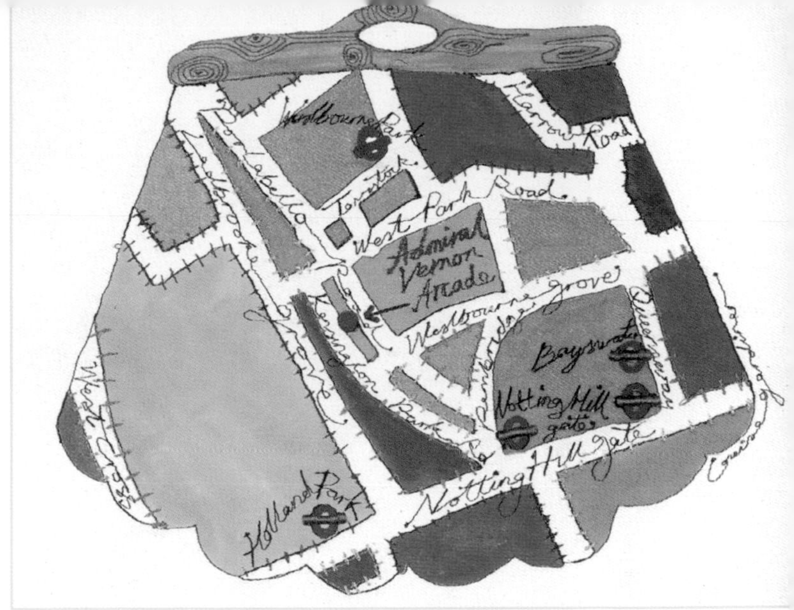

Louise Gardiner

To be in the company of Louise and her work is an exciting experience. She gives the feeling of being set in motion with little that could arrest an unending creation of delightfully descriptive machine embroidered pictures. This utterly personal style is founded on the ability to perceive, to quickly note on paper, to mentally retain and to respond with great directness onto fabric with colour and texture.

She speaks of her work with such passion and delight; a confidence that has been ten years in the making since tentatively finding her way through her three year textiles course at Goldsmiths' College. She is honest in admitting that she had selected that college 'because half of me was ambitious and wanted to go somewhere with an excellent reputation and the other half of me wanted to be in London and the two were in the same place.' It proved to be a tough experience because, for the first year, she really felt she was on the wrong course 'everyone else seemed to be so conceptual and my work was so labour intensive – everything around me made me wonder if I should have done textiles at all.' She came near to opting out and depriving the embroidery world of work that one day would, through her immaculate art and craftsmanship, exude humour, wit and charm. Aware too that her tutors did not consider her academically strong she knew that she had to find a practical alternative in time for her final exhibition. The resulting pictures, filled with scores of little figures, attracted a great deal of interest and admiration.

She discovered her subject through her empathy with people, especially the elderly, within an environment that she considered was both ordinary and anonymous. She described and contrasted similarity with individuality; dress, character, movement, style, walk and not least the bags they carried. She was responding to visual and emotional stimuli that were in direct contrast to all that she had previously experienced. Prior to her arrival in London for her BA Textiles

Above: Early sketches (1992) showing an interest and empathy for the elderly and the start of her fascination for the humour in the character of people. Photo: David Hankey

Left: Sketchbook drawings showing typical thumb nail sketches of observed movement. Photo: David Hankey

Opposite and over page: Large format drawings typical of those that precede many of the embroidereries. Pencil, pen and paint 85cm x 60cm (33in. x 24in.). Photo: David Hankey

course, life had been divided between an idyllic supportive parental farmstead home in Styal, Cheshire, and a well structured Foundation course in Manchester; both still valued by her.

Clearly, hidden strengths sustained her throughout this search. Motivation up to this point had been centred around her interest in History of Art, Critical Studies and Illustration. Until the discovery of this new subject matter her artistic energy had remained largely on hold – biding its time as it had been accustomed to doing from an even earlier age. Neither her convent school nor her mixed boarding school considered art as career material but this did not stop Louise being addicted to drawing 'even if it was only coke cans and kettles'. With no one to encourage her to draw imaginatively she feels that her work progressed little beyond basic recording with pencil.

The breakthrough seems to have occurred in her second college year with the use of a camera. 'Taking photographs of people in low lit shopping centres meant that I had to learn to look at strangers - up to now I had been spoilt with trees, cows and people I knew by name'. To avoid offence only back views and side views were photographed. These characters, without distinguishable features, easily developed into cut-outs, into repeated rows of men and women, into queues, into crowds; most often using the same figure in order to emphasise individuality. 'I've always loved taking photographs of people and sometimes I feel I could do just that. I started to lose myself in it'. It is clear that Louise believed that the college was expecting work that was motivated by social or feminist comment. Subconsciously, and in an effort to respond to the notional brief, a very personal iconography evolved. Though based on a combination of satire and

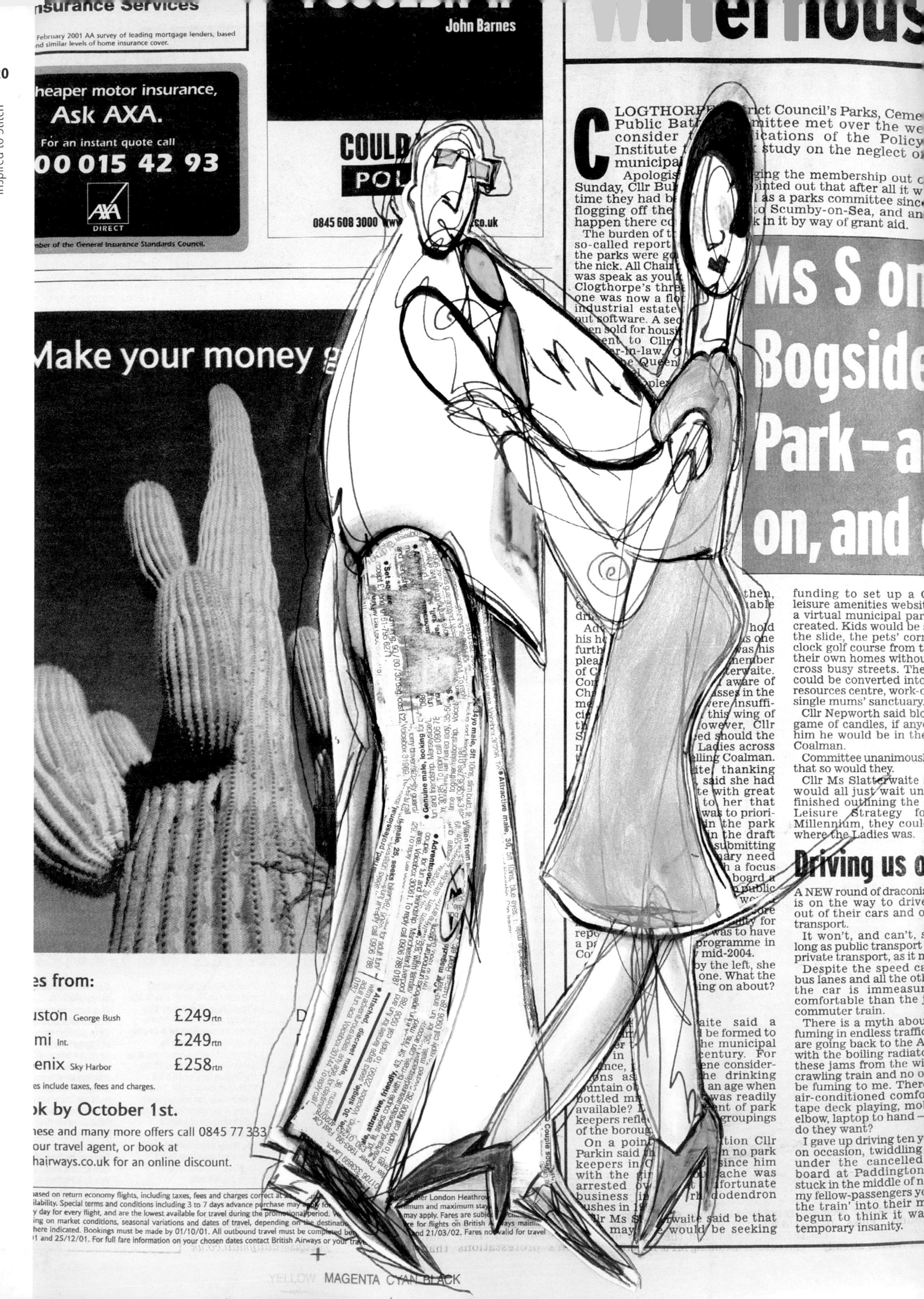
nsurance Services
February 2001 AA survey of leading mortgage lenders, based
nd similar levels of home insurance cover.
heaper motor insurance,
Ask AXA.
For an instant quote call
00 015 42 93
AXA
DIRECT
mber of the General Insurance Standards Council.
John Barnes
COULD
POL
0845 608 3000
co.uk
Make your money g
es from:
uston George Bush £249rtn
mi Int. £249rtn
enix Sky Harbor £258rtn
es include taxes, fees and charges.
ok by October 1st.
hese and many more offers call 0845 77 333
our travel agent, or book at
hairways.co.uk for an online discount.
Ms S on
Bogside
Park–a
on, and
Driving us o
LOGTHORPE
Public Bath
consider
Institute
municipa
Apologis
Sunday, Cllr Bu
time they had b
flogging off the
happen there c
The burden of t
so-called report
the parks were g
the nick. All Chair
was speak as you
Clogthorpe's thre
one was now a flo
industrial estate
out software.
funding to set up a
leisure amenities websit
a virtual municipal par
created. Kids would be
the slide, the pets' corr
clock golf course from t
their own homes withou
cross busy streets. The
could be converted into
resources centre, work-o
single mums' sanctuary.
Cllr Nepworth said blo
game of candles, if any
him he would be in the
Coalman.
Committee unanimousl
that so would they.
Cllr Ms Slatterwaite s
would all just wait un
finished outlining the
Leisure Strategy fo
Millennium, they coul
where the Ladies was.
A NEW round of draconia
is on the way to drive
out of their cars and o
transport.
It won't, and can't, s
long as public transport
private transport, as it m
Despite the speed ca
bus lanes and all the oth
the car is immeasur
comfortable than the j
commuter train.
There is a myth abou
fuming in endless traffic
are going back to the A
with the boiling radiato
these jams from the wi
crawling train and no o
be fuming to me. There
air-conditioned comfo
tape deck playing, mob
elbow, laptop to hand —
do they want?
I gave up driving ten ye
on occasion, twiddling
under the cancelled
board at Paddington
stuck in the middle of n
my fellow-passengers ye
the train' into their m
begun to think it was
temporary insanity.
YELLOW MAGENTA CYAN BLACK

Right: Machine stitched lines on cotton canvas prior to the addition of coloured acrylic paint by means of a fine brush. Photo: David Hankey

Below: *In the Clouds,* 2002. Machine stitching on cotton canvas with hand painting in acrylic 45cm x 40cm (18in. x 16in.) Photo: Mark Watson

pathos she is saying 'if you look carefully you will see the beautiful, the funny, the heart warming in everyone'. Her later work loses this sometimes darker side and moves towards the more obvious humour that currently pervades all she makes.

Photography gave the impetus and the energy. Images were processed and transposed to silk screens for printing onto canvas. These subjects were then enriched with machine embroidery and re-photographed for one or more repeats of the process.

This working method has now progressed. The camera has been exchanged for the immediacy of line drawing in pen or pencil directly from observation. Hundreds of examples exist in sketchbooks and on large sheets of paper. Rarely used as they were but instead were 'banked' in her memory for later retrieval. The resulting embroidery could be one of scores that she has to her credit. *Shop till you Drop* commissioned by The Guardian Newspaper is typical of her ability to combine the

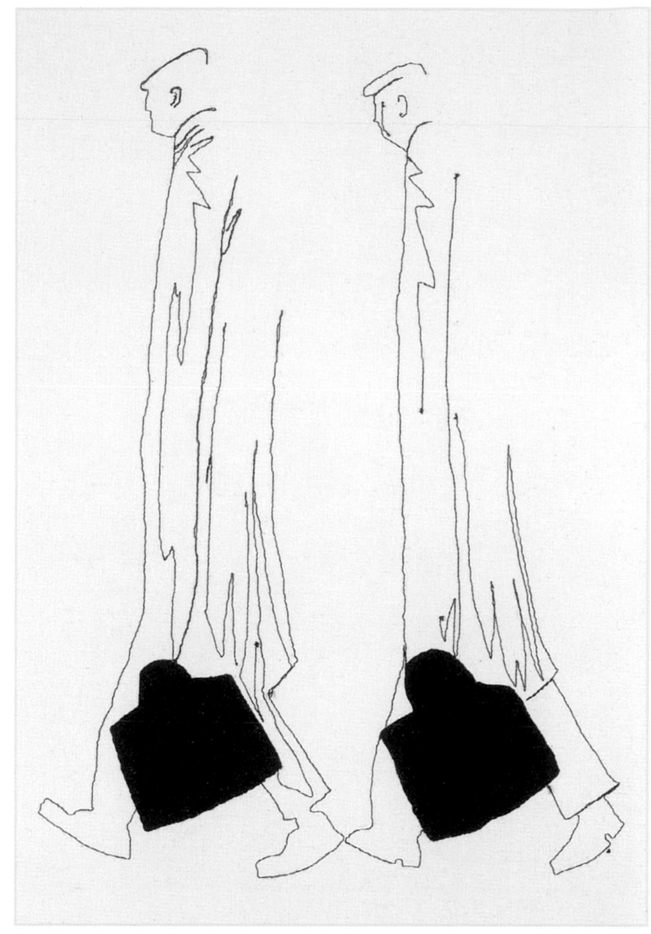

Left: *The Pyramid Trust,* 2003. An illustration for the Guardian newspaper. Machine line drawing with hand painting in acrylic colour. 26cm x 32cm (10in x 12½in.). Photo: Mark Watson

Below: *Groovy Gran,* 2003. An illustration commissioned by the Guardian newspaper. Machine line drawing with hand painting in acrylic colour. 26.5cm x 36cm (10½ x 14in.). Photo: Mark Watson

Opposite: *A Senior Moment,* 2004. Machine embroidery and acrylic paint. 54cm x 74cm (21in. x 29in.). Private collection. Photo: Mark Watson

techniques of embroidery with the skills of illustration. Her ultimate dream would be to run her own creative agency and gallery but in the meantime is proud to have been given orders for this broadsheet which include *Nan's World; Mothers are doing it for themselves; Earning and Learning; The Pyramid Trust* and *What's up with Modern art?*. She is a master at responding to a commission at very short notice.

Her early use of silk screen printing, now overtaken by the use of acrylic paint, is applied by fine brush directly onto the cotton canvas within the confines of the first stage of fine machine stitched outlines. Further intricate enrichment by machine embroidery then takes place to produce a decorative and descriptive whole.

Her spirit is admirably competitive. To watch the enthusiasm and passion with which she prepared her entry for a new poster for London Transport fully explains why her work is so appealing and visually complete. Tiny separate pencil drawn images on paper, initially temporarily tacked to the back of the canvas, have been transferred from the wrong side of the fabric by means of a fine black stitched machine line through the paper onto the cloth. She uses her Bernina sewing needle with the fluency of a fixed pen. The whole work no bigger than 60cm x 46cm (24in. x 18in.) includes fine detail with the potential to stand enlargement to enormous scale.

Through the demands of commission requirements she continues to advance technically. Thirty panels for Arts in Trust at the Gloucester Royal Hospital entitled *The Wacky Races* have been designed for the enjoyment of junior patients and staff. Beginning at the double doors of the theatre corridor and ending in the recovery rooms, fun images of animals and figures will be depicted. The young patient at this stage, being wheeled on a trolley, can compare their progress to those of the characters on the walls; all portrayed moving on some form of wheels from skateboards to trolleys and wheelchairs. To achieve these she starts with small scale drawings with a black fine liner. She then scans these and by means of Photoshop software she can play speedily with colour within the outlines. When satisfied a print is made as a record. From this stage procedure for each actual piece will be the same as that described for the competition piece. Then, in this case, each finished embroidery will be digitally photographed to a very high resolution by specialists, Indigo Art in Liverpool, who will then digitally print on to a cotton canvas with ink estimated to last seventy five years. Finally a coat of laminate or industrial varnish will be applied to produce a washable, durable surface. The final result is startlingly tactile and bearing all the character and vibrancy of stitch and texture. This illustrative use of the medium of embroidery allows the artist to retain

A Senior Moment.

the originals.

The descriptive nature of her work also enables a client, such as this hospital, to raise funds through the sale of limited edition prints and an accompanying story book.

A colossal output of both speculative and commissioned pieces, particularly in the last two years, has been produced outside the hours of a full time teaching post. She is hugely motivated 'because I have so much subject matter in my head'. Her studio work is solitary but she says that she makes

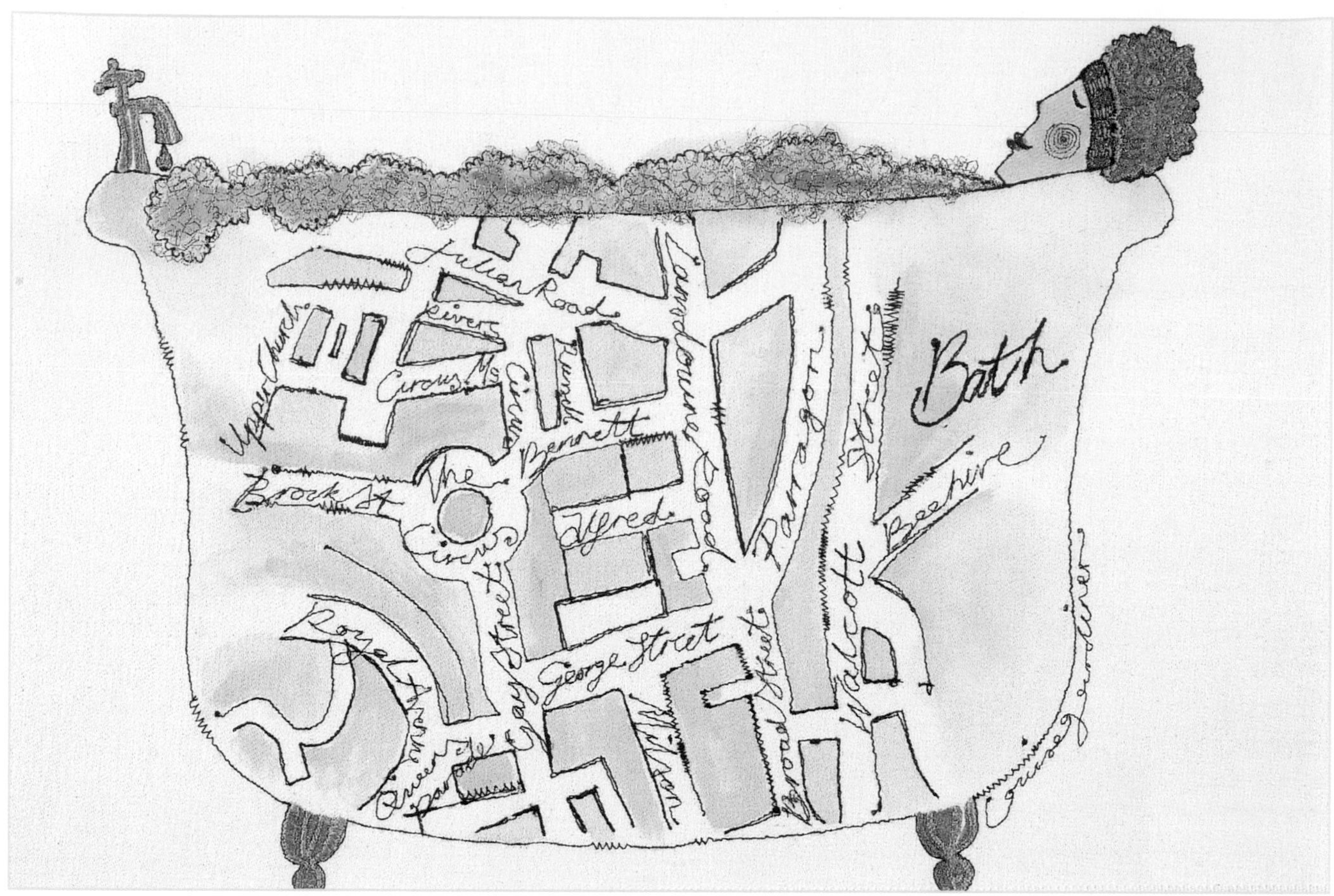

Opposite above left: *London Transport Open Spaces,* 2004. Competition for poster. Machine line drawing and hand painting in acrylic. 46cm x 60cm (18in. x 24in.). Photo: Mark Watson

Opposite above right: *Cha Cha Love,* 2004. Machine embroidery and acrylic paint. 54cm x 74cm (21in x 29in.). Private collection. Photo: Mark Watson

Opposite below left: *Shop till you Drop,* 2004. An illustration commissioned by the Guardian newspaper. Machine embroidery and acrylic paint. 25cm x 33cm (10in. x 13in.). Photo: Mark Watson

Opposite below right: *The Thoughtful Brothers,* 2004. Machine stitched lines with hand painting. Photo: Mark Watson

Above: *Bathing Belle,* 2004. Commissioned by Selvedge magazine. Machine embroidery with hand painting. 40cm x 33cm (16in x 13in.). Photo: Mark Watson

up for it the rest of the time by surrounding herself with people, even likening herself to the theatrical aspects of needing an audience to respond to her characters. (Drama, in which she also feels she could have trained, together with sport, was her other strong subject at school.)

'The subjects of my work reflect my continuous need to be in touch with my audience who I am determined to entertain and make smile. My art is my stage – I want to make people laugh about life as well as being sensitive and passionate about living'.

'I love working with others and I love teaching. Getting everyone to draw and to laugh – that's what makes me tick'. She often engages in workshops for Age Concern and the Embroiderers' Guild and has encouraged drawing through the Guardian newspaper project The Big Draw.

She is about to relocate from her parents home to Bristol where, near to her brother, she anticipates a diversification of interests. Unsure as to how she will earn her basic bread and butter yet determined that future teaching commitments should be above the level of the repetition of persuading and convincing pupils to be passionate about their work. Bringing drawing to either children with learning difficulties or to the elderly, along with a career in illustration, would be her goal. 'I want to keep putting something back'.

What is sure is that given new surroundings, Louise's masterly co-ordination of eye and hand combined with her enormous endeavour, she will respond and deliver with even greater result.

Where to See Embroidery

Aberdeen Art Gallery & Museum. Schoolhill, Aberdeen AB10 1FQ Embroidery C18-C20 Pictures. Samplers, Goldwork and Canvas Work. Costume collection 1820 to the present day. C17-C19 Lace. Tapestries and Woven Hangings

Allhallows Museum. High Street, Honiton, Devon EX14 1PG www.allhallowsmuseum.co.uk Honiton Lace

American Museum. Claverton Manor, Nr. Bath, Somerset BA2 7BD www.americanmuseum.org Quilt collection and C17-C19 textiles

Ashmolean Museum. Beaumont Street, Oxford OX1 2PH www.ashmol.ox.ac.uk Newbury Collection of Textiles

Aston Hall. Trinity Road, Aston, Birmingham B6 6JD Textiles C17-C19

Athelhampton House. Athelhampton, Dorchester, Dorset DT2 7LG Tapestry

Bankfield Museum. Boothtown Road, Halifax, West Yorkshire HX3 6HG An exceptional collection of textiles from around the world

Bath, Museum of Costume. Assembly Rooms, Bennett Street, Bath, Somerset BA1 2QH www.museumofcostume.co.uk Dress collection C16 to the present day. Reserve collection by appointment

Bradford Textile Archive. Bradford College, School of Art, Design and Textiles, Lister Building, Carlton Street, Bradford BD7 1AY www.textilearchive.bilk.ac.uk

Beamish Museum of Rural Life. Co. Durham DH9 0RG www.beamishmuseum.co.uk Quilts, Costume and other textiles

Belton House. Grantham, Lincolnshire NG32 2LS Tapestries

Blair Castle. Blair Atholl, Pitlochry, Perth and Kinross PH18 5TL Lace and Embroidery

Blaise Castle House Museum. Henbury, Bristol BS10 7QS Costume and accessories mainly Victorian.

Blenheim Palace. Woodstock, Oxfordshire OX20 1PX www.groups@blenheimpalace.com Tapestries

Blickling Hall. Blickling, Norfolk NR11 6NF Tapestries

Boscobel House. Brewood, Bishops Wood, Shropshire ST19 9AR Tapestries

Bowes Museum. Barnard Castle, Co. Durham DL12 9RZ Embroidery includes Samplers, Ecclesiastical and French Canvas Work seat covers. Reserve collection by appointment

Breamore House & Museum. Breamore, Nr. Fordingbridge, Hampshire SP6 2DF Tapestries and Crewel Work

British Museum. Great Russell Street, London WC1B 3DG www.thebritishmuseum.uk English and Ethnographic Embroidery

Brontë Parsonage Museum. Church Street, Haworth, Keighley, West Yorkshire BD22 8DR www.bronte.infobronte@bronte.org.uk Samplers and Costumes

Burrell Collection. Pollok Country Park, Glasgow G43 1AT Exceptional needlework room

Burton Court. Eardisland, Nr. Leominster, Herefordshire HR6 9DN Extensive collection of European and Oriental embroidery, costumes and fans

Boughton House. Kettering, Northampton NN14 1BJ Hungarian Flame Stitch chair covers in the Fourth State Room

Castle Museum. Nottingham NG1 6EL now holds the collection from the Museum of Costumes and Textiles, Nottingham www.aboutbritain.com/NottinghamCastleMuseumandArtGallery.htm

Cecil Higgins Art Gallery. Castle Lane, Bedford MK40 3RP www.cecilhigginsartgallery.org C18 and C19 textiles. Lace. Reserve collection by appointment

Charles Wade Costume Collection. The National Trust, Berrington Hall, Leominster, Herefordshire HR6 0DW C18 and C19 costume and accessories, military uniforms and ethnographic costume

Chastleton House. Chastleton, nr Moreton-in-Marsh, Oxfordshire GL56 0SU Crewel work bed hangings and covers, flame stitch wall coverings ,chair coverings many of which made specially for the house

Chavenage House. Chavenage, Tetbury, Gloucestershire GL8 8XP C17 Tapestries

Cheltenham Art Gallery and Museum. Clarence Street, Cheltenham, GL50 3JT www.cheltenham.artgallery.museum and www.artsandcraftsmuseum.org.uk The British Arts and Crafts Movement Collection. Oriental collection of costume. Reserve collection

Chertsey Museum. 33 Windsor Street, Chersey, Surrey KT16 8AT www.chertseymuseum.org.uk Dress and Accessories C18 to present day. Lace, Beadwork, Embroidery and Needlework Tools

Churchill House Museum & Hatton Gallery. Hereford

Museum, Broad Street, Hereford HR4 9AU Collection C18, C19, and C20 includes embroidery, costume, accessories, military uniforms, dolls and smocks available by appointment

Clandon. West Clandon, Guildford, Surrey GU4 7RQ Textiles and Carpets

Coliseum Museum and Art Gallery. Terrace Road, Aberystwyth, Ceredigion, Wales SY23 2AQ www.ceredigion.gov.uk/coliseum/

Constance Howard Resource and Research Centre in Textiles. Visual Arts Goldsmiths' College, Deptford Town Hall, New Cross, London SE14 6NW Embroidery Collection by appointment

Crafts Council. 44a Pentonville Road, London N1 9BY www.craftscouncil.org.uk. Loan collection

Crafts Study Centre, Institute of Art and Design, University College, Faulkener Road, Farnham, Surrey GU8 7SD

D-Day Museum. Clarence Esplanade, Southsea, Hampshire PO5 3NT Overlord Embroidery

Dean Clough. Halifax, W.Yorkshire HX3 5AX www.quiltersguild.org.uk The Quilters' Guild of the British Isles Collection in Room 90 on request

Discovery Museum. Blandford Square, Newcastle upon Tyne NE1 4JA Study Collection of Embroidery and Lace. Fashion in the N-East from 1750 to the present

Doddington Hall. Lincoln LN6 4RU www.doddingtonhall.free-online.co.uk Textiles

Durham Cathedral Treasures. The College, Durham DH1 3EH www.durhamcathedral.co.uk C10 Opus Anglicanum stole and maniple

Dorset County Museum. Dorchester. Dorset DT1 1XA www.dorsetcountymuseum.org

Dyrham Park. Dyrham, nr Chippenham, Gloucestershire SN14 8ER Many fine Textiles

East Riddlesden Hall. Bradford Road, Keighley, West Yorkshire BD20 5EL Furnished with textiles

Edmondsham House. Edmondsham, Wimborne, Dorset BH21 5RE Lace

Embroiderers' Guild. Apartment 41, Hampton Court Palace, Surrey, KT8 9AU www.embroiderersguild.com 11000 objects by appointment

Eyam Hall. Eyam, Hope Valley, Derbyshire S32 5QW www.eyamhall.co.uk C15 and C16 tapestries, C17 crewel work bed hangings

Fan Museum. 12 Crooms Hill, Greenwich, London SE10 8ER www.fan-museum.org.uk Over 3000 fans dating from the C11

Fashion and Textile Museum. 83 Bermondsey Street, London SE13XF www.ftmlondon.org

Fenton House. Windmill Hill, Hampstead, London NW3 6RT Needlework pictures of C17

Forde Abbey. Nr. Chard, Somerset TA20 4LU Mortlake Tapestries

Forge Mill Needle Museum. Needle Mill lane, Riverside, Redditch, Worcestershire B98 8HY Exhibitions of contemporary embroidery and displays of the process of needle manufacture

Fursdon. Fursdon, Cadbury,Thorverton, Exeter, Devon EX5 5JS www.fursdon.co.uk Costume collection

Gawthorpe Hall. Padiham, Nr. Burnley Lancashire BB12 8UA www.bronte-country.com/gawth1.html Finest Lace and Embroidery outside the V&A and includes The Rachel Kay-Shuttleworth Collection

Gilbert White's House. The Wakes, High Street, Selbourne, Hampshire GU34 3JH Embroidered bedhangings mid C18

Gunnersbury Park Museum. Gunnersbury Park, Popes Lane, London W3 8LQ Textile and Costume collection – C5000 items in reserve collection

Gwynedd Museum and Art Gallery. Fford Gwynedd, Bangor, Gwynedd LL57 1DT www.gwynedd.gov.uk

Hardwick Hall. Doe Lea, Chesterfield, Derbyshire S44 5QJ Very fine collection of Elizabethan embroidery and tapestry. Home of Bess of Hardwick

Holburne Museum of Art. Gt.Pulteney Street, Bath BA2 4DB www.bath.ac.uk/Holburne/

Hatfield House. Hatfield, Hertfordshire AL9 5NQ Tapestries and embroidery

Holkham Hall. Wells-next-the-Sea, Norfolk NR23 1AB Tapestries

Houghton Lodge Garden and Hydroponicum. Stockbridge, Hampshire SO20 6LQ Fine embroidery in the house

Hutton-in-the-Forest. Penrith, Cumbria CA11 9TH Embroidery C19

Kelmscott Manor. Kelmscott, nr Lechlade, Gloucestershire GL7 3HJ www.kelmscottmanor.co.uk Home of William Morris and full of embroidery

Killerton. Broadclyst, Exeter, Devon EX5 3LE Paulise de Bush costume collection displayed in period rooms

Knole House. Sevenoaks, Kent Tapestries, rugs, bedhangings and embroidered furniture

Lace Guild. The Hollies, 53 Audnam, Stourbridge, West Midlands DY8 4AE Lace collection. Library and reserve collection

Lady Lever Art Gallery. Port Sunlight Village, Port Sunlight, Wirral, Merseyside, CH62 5EQ Embroidered Pictures C17-C19, Embroidered caskets, mirror frames, bed furnishings, chair covers, samplers and costume

London Sewing Machine Museum. Wimbledon

Sewing Machine Co. Ltd., 312 Balham High Road, London SE17 7AA www.sewantique.com Over 600 industrial and domestic machines 1850-1950 and includes first Singer Machine

Longleat Warminster, Wiltshire BA12 7NW www.longleat.co.uk Embroidery room open to groups if booked

Luton Museum and Art Gallery. Wardown Park, Old Bedford Road, Luton LU2 7HA www.luton.gov.uk Lace Gallery. Reserve collection of lace, quilts, samplers

Manchester Metropolitan University Faculty of Art and Design, Textile/Fashion Department Archive, School of Design Cavendish Building, Cavendish Street, Manchester MI5 6BG. Database and Collection of student ecclesiastical works dating from mid 1960s - 1983/4. Specialist embroidery machines including Cornely, Irish and Schiffle also in archive

Manor House Museum. 5 Honey Hill, Bury St. Edmunds, Suffolk IP33 1HF www.stedmundsbury.gov.uk Textile and Costume collection including Irene Barnes 1930s Beaded Costume collection

Millennium Galleries. Arundel Gate, Sheffield S1 2PP www.sheffieldgalleries.org.uk

Montacute House. Montacute, Somerset TA15 6XP Tapestries and C17 Samplers

Muncaster Castle. Ravenglass, Cumbria CA18 1RQ Tapestries and a set of C16 Bed Valences

Museum of Domestic Design and Architecture (MoDA) Middlesex University, Cat Hill, Barnet, Hertfordshire EN4 8HT www.moda.mdx.ac.uk

Museum of Welsh Life. St Fagans, Cardiff CF5 PXB Quilts, costume and other textiles

Newby Hall. Ripon, North Yorkshire HG4 5AE Gobelin Tapestries with matching embroidered chair coverings

Normanby Hall. Normanby, North Lincolnshire DN15 9HU Costume galleries with reserve collection by appointment

Northampton Central Museum and Art Gallery. Guildhall Road, Northampton NN1 1DP www.northampton.gov.uk/museums Embroidered Shoes 1660 to present day.

Oxburgh Hall. Oxburgh, King's Lynn, Norfolk PE33 9PS Outstanding display of needlework done by Mary Queen of Scotts and Bess of Hardwick

Packwood House. Lapworth, Solihull, Warwickshire B94 6AT Textiles of C16

Paisley Museum and Art Galleries. High Street, Paisley, Renfrewshire PA1 2BA World's finest collection of over 1000 Paisley Shawls; items from Collection of Needlework Development Scheme

Palace House Gardens, Beaulieu. Beauleiu,Hampshire SO42 7ZN www.beaulieu.co.uk Embroidered Hangings by Belinda, Lady Montagu

Parham House. Parham Park, Nr. Pulborough, West Sussex RH20 4HS Significant embroidery collection

Pencarrow. Bodmin, Cornwall PL30 3AG www.pencarrow.co.uk Many examples of Needlework

Penshurst Place. Penshurst, Kent TN11 8DG Tapestries

Pickford's House Museum. 41 Friar Gate, Derby DE1 1DA www.derby.gov.uk/museums Historic costume collection

Platt Hall Gallery of Costume. Rusholme,Manchester M14 5LL www.cityartgalleries.org.uk Only open last Saturday of the month and other days for research by appointment

Quaker Exhibition Centre. Friends Meeting House, Stramongate, Kendal ,Cumbria LA9 4BH www.quaker-tapestry.co.uk

Rokeby Park. Rokeby, Barnard Castle, Co. Durham DL12 9RZ Anne Morritt C18 Needlepaintings

Rowley House Museum. Shrewsbury, Shropshire Temporarily closed but with good costume collection

Royal Museum. Chambers Street, Edinburgh EH1 1JF www.nms.ac.uk Middle Eastern and East Asian textiles

Royal School of Needlework. Apt.12a Hampton Court Palace, Surrey KT8 9AU www.royal-needlework.co.uk Courses, commercial workroom and Apprenticeship Scheme

Rufford Old Hall. Rufford, nr Ormskirk, Lancashire, L40 1SG Tapestries C16 aand C17

Salisbury and South Wiltshire Museum. The King's House, 65 The Close, Salisbury Wiltshire SP1 2EN www.salisburymuseum.org.uk Costume, Lace and Embroidery of south Wiltshire

Sandford Orcas Manor House. Nr. Sherborne, Dorset DT9 4SB Elizabethan Blackwork, Queen Anne embroidery, C18 Canvas Work and Samplers

Shambellie House Museum of Costume. New Abbey, Dumfries DG2 8HQ Period Clothes with Accessories 1850s-1950s in period settings. www.nms.ac.uk

Shipley Art Gallery. Prince Consort Road, Gateshead.NE8 43B www.twmuseums.org.uk

Shrewsbury Museum & Art Gallery (Rowley House) Barker Street, Shrewsbury SY1 1QH www.cogapp.com/uk

Silk Museum. Roe Street, Macclesfield SK11 6UT www.silk-macclesfield.org

Speke Hall. The Walk, Liverpool, Merseyside L24 1XD Wall Hangings/Tapestries

Springhill. 20 Springhill Road, Moneymore, Magherafelt, Co.Londonderry BT45 7NQ Colourful costume exhibition

Squerryes Court Manor House. Westerham, Kent TN16 1SJ www.squerryes.co.uk C18 English Tapestries and C18 Spanish embroidered pictures

Standen. West Hoathly Road, East Grinstead, West Sussex RH19 4NE Arts and Crafts Movement showpiece decorated throughout with fabrics, carpets and tapestries
Stonor Park. Stonor, Henley-on-Thames, Oxfordshire RG9 6HF www.stonor.com Tapestries
Stratfield Saye House. Basingstoke, Hampshire RG27 0AS Domestic embroidery includes a Portuguese Arraiolos embroidered carpet
Stourhead. Stourton, Warminster, Wiltshire BA12 6QD Needle paintings in the house
Sudeley Castle. Winchcombe, Gloucester GL54 5JD www.sudeleycastle.co.uk Stumpwork, Samplers, Lace
Sulgrave Manor. Sulgrave, Banbury, Oxfordshire OX17 2SD www.sulgravemanor.org.uk Embroidery
Sunderland Museum. Mowbray Park, Burdon Road, Sunderland, Tyne and Wear SR1 1PP Embroidery, Quilting, Knitting, Greek Embroidery and Study Collection
Tabley House Stately Home. Knutsford, Cheshire WA16 0HB Embroidery
Textile Conservation Centre, University of Southampton, Winchester Campus, Park Avenue, Winchester SO23 8DL www.wsa.soton.ac.uk/framesettcc.htm
Traquair House. Innerleithen, Peebleshire, Scotland EH44 6PW Embroideries of C17, early Textiles and Vestments
Trerice. Kestle Mill, nr Newquay, Cornwall TR8 4PG Needlework
Tullie House Museum & Art Gallery. Castle Street, Carlisle, Cumbria CA3 8TP www.tulliehouse.co.uk Costume and accessories circa 1750 to present. Quilts, samplers and Ayrshire work. Reserve collection by appointment
Upton House. nr Banbury, Warwickshire OX15 6HT Tapestries
Victoria & Albert Museum. Cromwell Road, London SW7 2RL www.vam.ac.uk Embroidery throughout the collections. Of special note are the Embroideries in The British Galleries and in The Student Study Room
Wemyss School of Needlework. Coaltown-of-Wemyss, Kirkaldy, Fife KY1 4NX Needlework from 1624 and Samplers made at the school from 1877 onwards
Whitworth Art Gallery. The University of Manchester, Oxford Road, Manchester ME15 6ER www.whitworth.man.ac.uk Worldwide Embroidery Collection
Wightwick Manor. Wightwick Bank, Wolverhampton, West Midlands WV6 8EE Fabrics of the Arts and Crafts Movement
William Morris Gallery. Lloyd Park, Forest Road, Walthamstow, London E17 4PP www.lbwf.gov.uk/wmg Works by Arts and Crafts Designers. Life and work of William Morris
Wolterton Hall. Erpingham, Norfolk Costume and Textile Collection Tapestries

Scottish Textile Heritage Online aims to provide information about the richness and diversity of Scottish textile heritage collections. Led by Heriot-Watt University it covers material within the six partner museums and archives of Heriot-Watt University, Dundee and Glasgow Universities, Scottish Borders Council, Glasgow School of Art and Paisley Museum and Art Galleries as well as providing links to significant collections held elsewhere in Scotland and the UK. Some 3000 catalogue entries have been compiled with over 400 supporting images and include works of Kath Whyte (1909-1996), the archives of J&P Coats Ltd and the Needlework Development Scheme www.scottishtextiles.org.uk

UMIST. Tela Project within Textiles Department. Significant Digital Resource for Textiles including contemporary designer/makers www.tela.umist.ac.uk

University of Leeds International Textile Archive (ULITA): St. Wilfred's Chapel, Maurice Keyworth Building, University of Leeds, Leeds, LS2 9JT www.leeds.ac.uk/collections/textilearchive.htm The collection consists of over 300,000 items, principally textiles including notable embroideries from China and the Eastern Mediterranean. 20,000 glass plate negatives and slides depicting textile machinery and designs
Art Guide. Comprehensive Internet guide to collections in Great Britain and Ireland www.cogapp.com/uk/intro.html
'62 Group Textile Artists www.62group.freeuk.com
Leeds University Artists database www.axisarstists.org.uk

Bibliography

Art Textiles of the World: Great Britain. Volume 1, ed. Mathew Koumis, Telos, 1996

Art Textiles of the World: Great Britain Volume 2, ed. Jennifer Harris, Telos, 1999

Audrey Walker (Ruthin Gallery catalogue) Beaney, Jan & Littlejohn, Jean, ***A Complete Guide to Creative Embroidery,*** Century, 1991, (BT Batsford, 1997)

Barry, Judy and Patten, Beryl ***The Rediscovery of Ritual; Embroidery and Architecture in the Nineteenth Century***. (Slide pack) 1996

Beaney, Jan, ***Stitches: New Approaches,*** Pelham Reprint, 1985, Batsford, 2004

Beaney, Jan & Littlejohn, Jean, ***A Complete Guide to Creative Embroidery,*** Century, 1991, (BT Batsford, 1997)

Beaney, Jan & Littlejohn, Jean, ***Stitch Magic,*** BT Batsford, 1992, 1998, 2002

Bromily Phelan, D., Haigh, J., and Jacobsson, H., ***Telling Tales with Threads: The Needle's Excellency,*** Holbourne Museum of Art, 2000

Burbidge, Pauline, ***Quilt Studio*** 2000 The Quilt Digest press USA

Clabburn, Pamela, ***The Needleworkers' Dictionary,*** Macmillan, 1976

The Crafts Council, ***Crafts Bimonthly*** (magazine)

Dean, Beryl, ***Ecclesiastical Embroidery***, Batsford, 1958

Dean, Beryl, ***Embroidery in Religion and Ceremonial*** Batsford, 1981

Dean, Beryl, ***Ideas for Church Embroidery***, Batsford, 1968

Dawson, Barbara, ***Metal Thread Embroidery,*** Batsford, 1968

Earnshaw, Pat, ***Lace Machines and Machine Made Laces Volume 2*** Gorse Publications, 1995

Embroiderers' Guild, ***Designer Textiles*** David & Charles, 1987

Embroiderers' Guild, ***Embroidery Bimonthly*** (magazine)

Gibson, Ann, ***Machine Stitched and Applied Machine Stitched Decoration on Dress 1828-1910.*** (Copies in the British Library and Manchester Metropolitan University)

Haigh, Janet, ***Crazy Patchwork***, Collins & Brown, 1998

Haigh, Janet, ***Japanese Inspirations,*** Collins & Brown, 1999

Howard, Constance, ***Twentieth Century Embroidery in Great Britain***, (four volumes published between 1981 and 1986 which take the form of a dictionary/reference with black and white photographs and eight colour pictures per volume). B.T.Batsford.

The International Association of Feltmakers, ***Echoes,*** (quarterly journal)

Jenkins, Simon, ***England's Thousand Best Churches*** Penguin Press, 1999

Lieberson, Marit and Knight, Anne, ***The Art of Zandra Rhodes***, 1984 (republished 2003)

Morrell, Anne. ***Contemporary Embroidery***, Studio Vista, 1994

Morrell, Anne, ***Contemporary Embroidery: exciting and innovative textile art***, Cassell, 1994

Parker, Rozsika, ***The Subversive Stitch: Embroidery and the Making of the Feminine*** Women's Press

Rawson, Philip, ***The Art of Drawing***, Prentice & Hall, 1983

Rawson, Philip, ***Seeing through Drawing,*** (to accompany TV series, BBC), 1978

Richardson, Sue (ed.), ***The Textile Directory***

Risley, Christine, ***Machine Embroidery: A Complete Guide*** Studio Vista, 1973

Ruthin Craft Centre, ***Alice Kettle***, 2003

Ruthin Craft Centre, ***Eleri Mills,*** 1995

Schoeser, Mary, 'English Church Embroidery 1833-1953', in ***The Watts Book of Embroidery***, 1998

Springall, Diana, ***Twelve British Embroiderers*** Gakken, Tokyo, 1984

Sutton, Ann, ***British Craft Textiles***, Collins, 1985

Telos, ***Eye of the Needle: The Textile Art of Alice Kettle*** Telos, 1995

Telos, ***Pauline Burbidge*** Portfolio Collection, Telos, 2004

Tucker, Dorothy, ***Embroidered Pictures,*** A & C Black, 1994

Warren, Verina, ***Landscape in Embroidery,*** Batsford, 1986

Whyte, Kathleen, ***Design in Embroidery,*** Batsford, 1969, (Four editions, 1983)

Endnotes

1 Or nué *Method whereby gold thread is laid on the surface of the cloth and couched down; in the Middle Ages with silk threads and in more recent times with floss or cotton. These stitches, often coloured, were spaced according to the desired effect of surface pattern.*

2 *Anthea Godfrey, BA Embroidery/Textiles, ATD. 1945- Fellow of the Royal Society of Arts. Past Chairman and Emeritus member of the Embroiderers' Guild. Highly respected teacher/lecturer worldwide. 1980-London College of Fashion. 1988 Nomination for Woman of the Year. Examiner for MA and BA Textiles. City & Guilds chief examiner for 'O' and 'A' level embroidery*

3 *Dorothy Allsopp ARCA ATD 1911-1999*
Work in the collection of the Victoria & Albert Museum. 1929-1931 Trained Chelsea School of Art 1931-1935. Royal College of Art. 1935-1949. West Hartlepool College of Art. Lecturer in women's crafts. 1949-1954 Expert in charge of Needlework Development Scheme – see note 22. 1954-1961 Hammersmith College of Art (now part of Chelsea School of Art) Senior Lecturer in Fashion/Textiles/Embroidery. 1961-1976 Inner London Education Authority Inspector, Fashion and Creative Studies. 1978 Chairman, City & Guilds of London Institute examination board in Creative Studies

4 *Iris Hills ARCA 1913-*
1932-1935 Trained Royal College of Art – Illustration/ Embroidery. 1935-1938 Bromley College of Art, part-time Lecturer in charge of 'Craft School'. 1946 Bromley College of Art, Lecturer in charge of embroidery. 1955-1961 Expert in charge of The Needlework Development Scheme-see note 22. 1961-1966 Hammersmith College of Art and Building, Senior Lecturer in Fashion/Embroidery/Textiles. 1965-1975 Chief Examiner for the City & Guilds of London Institute examinations in embroidery. 1967-1977 Worked for Inner London Education Authority.
Introduction to Embroidery, *published by Victoria & Albert Museum 1953*

5 *Tambour beading is produced on a round tambour frame consisting of two hoops of wood between which the fabric is stretched tight. It is necessary to support the frame to leave both hands free, one for operating the hook on top and one for controlling the thread beneath. The beads are first threaded onto a continuous thread and the work is done with the wrong side uppermost. The hooked tambour needle goes down through the ground fabric and each time it takes up a thread it leaves a bead secured.*

6 *Gustav Klimt 1862-1918 Painter of the Austrian Jugenstil*

7 *Eric Ravillious 1903-1942 Painter and designer*

8 *Hebe Cox 1909-1993*
1931-1934 Trained at Central School of Arts & Crafts. Adviser to National Federation of Women's Institutes. Founder member and trustee of the Crafts Centre of Great Britain (now the Crafts Council) Member of the Arts and Crafts Exhibition Society (now the Society of Designer-Craftsmen)
Simple Embroidery Designs. *Studio Vista 1948.* Embroidery Technique and Design. *Dryad 1954.* Canvas Embroidery. *Mills & Boon 1960. Contributor to,* Fifteen Craftsmen on their Crafts. *Sylvan Press 1945*

9 *Avril Colby 1900-1983*
Training in horticulture; interest in garden restoration; specialism in Patchwork: Worked for The Needlework Development Scheme22, National Federation of Women's Institutes and many private patrons and lectured widely
Patchwork. *Batsford 1958 (p/b ed. 1976).* Samplers. *Batsford 1964.* Patchwork Quilts. *Batsford 1965.* Quilting. *Batsford.1972.* Pincushions. *Batsford 1975.*

10 *Laura Ashley 1925-1986*
Noted for the fabrics and clothes marketed through the business set up with her husband Bernard in 1953. Laura Ashley Foundation continues

11 *Denys Short Sculptor 1927-*

12 *Pictures for Schools Exhibitions In 1947, a painter, Nan Youngman, conceived the idea of regular exhibitions from which local education authorities and members of the public could be encouraged to purchase work for schools. The shows were organised by members of The Society of*

Education Through Art who were prepared to accept embroidery and collage alongside drawings, paintings and prints. These annual exhibitions were highly regardedas a major marketing outlet and the shows had venues as varied as the Whitechapel Art Gallery. Embroiderers included in the earlier years were: Eirian Short, Christine Risley, Esther Grainger and later Audrey Walker and Richard Box.

13 *Jan Beaney NDD ATC 1938- See page 48*

14 *Julia Caprara NDD ATC 1939- Embroiderer exhibiting widely especially with '62 Group. Co Director and founder, with husband Alex, of Opus School of Textile Arts- Distance Learning, London: BA Hons in Embroidered Textiles; City & Guilds Embroidery; City & Guilds Patchwork and Quilting.*

15 *Earl of Longford 1906-2001*

16 *Audrey Walker 1924- See page 36*

17 *Harold Parker 1896-1980 Sculptor and Head of Department of Sculpture Goldsmiths' College School of Art. Most especially noted for the design of the farthing coin. Husband of Constance née Howard*

18 *Constance Parker (née Howard) MBE ARCA ATD FSDC 1910-2000 World-renowned teacher and lecturer of embroidery. Author of nine B.T.Batsford publications:* Design for Embroidery from Traditional English Sources *1956;* Inspiration for Embroidery *1966;* Embroidery and Colour *1976;* Constance Howard's Book of Stitches *1979;* Twentieth Century Embroidery in Great Britain *1981-86, four volumes*

19 *Christine Risley NDD MSIAD 1926 –2003 Well respected teacher and author specialising in machine embroidery. Lecturer, St. Martin's School of Art and Goldsmiths' College School of Art. Studio Vista Publications:* Machine Embroidery *1961;* Creative Embroidery *1969;* Machine Embroidery – a complete guide *1973 (pb 1981).*

20 *Margaret Kaye ARCA 1912-1991 Her bold fabric collage pictures, exhibited in galleries and illustrated in numerous publications, influenced many embroiderers of the 1950s and 1960s. Altar Frontal for Epiphany Chapel Winchester Cathedral 1962*

21 *Kathleen Whyte MBE DA 1907-1996 Most noted Scottish embroiderer. Head of the Department of Embroidery Glasgow School of Art 1948-1974 and author of* Design in Embroidery *1969 Batsford and three further editions. Founded the Glasgow School of Art Embroidery and Textile Group in 1956 eventually becoming the 167 Group now merged with Embryo and Seta Groups to become Edge (Textile Artists Scotland) in 2003. Obituary by Crissie White Crafts 1996 July/August issue*

22 *Needlework Development Scheme. Set up by J&P Coats Ltd of Paisley in 1934, and funded anonymously, for the purpose of improving technique and design through the loan collection, lectures and simple publications. Discontinued during the Second World War but re-opened in 1944 at the request of Glasgow School of Art. In 1946 an advisory committee was set up to ensure that embroidery collected was of the highest standard. The work was purchased both from pieces acquired from overseas as well as commissioned from Britain. Originally planned as a loan collection for the four Scottish art schools it was soon extended and by 1950 schools and colleges throughout Britain could borrow work free of charge. During 1949-1954 Dorothy Alsopp was 'expert in charge' and leaflets were published for all those who asked for them. She was succeeded in 1955-61 by Iris Hills. The scheme closed in 1961 and the collection divided between twenty-five institutions, including the art colleges at Dundee, Aberdeen, Glasgow and Edinburgh, the V&A, the Scottish National Museum, Paisley Museum & Art Galleries and the Embroiderers' Guild. Descriptions of all these disbursed collections are documented in the project database of Scottish Textile Heritage Online – see Chapter 'Where to see Embroidery' – which reunites the collection 'virtually' for the first time*

23 *The Embroiderers' Guild. Founded in 1906. Headquarters Apartment 41 Hampton Court Palace, Surrey, England*

24 *Royal School of Needlework. Founded 1872. Headquarters Apartment 12a Hampton Court Palace, Surrey, England*

25 *Jeff Koons 1955- American Post Modernism*

26 *Vera Sherman NDD 1917- Organiser of touring exhibitions of* 'Contemporary Hangings', 'Fabric and Thread' *and* 'Contemporary Pictures in Fabric and Thread' *from 1965-76.*
Author of Wall Hangings of Today *Mills & Boon London 1972*

27 *Piero della Francesca 1410/20-1492 Most popular painter of the quattrocento*

28 *Sir William Coldstream 1908-1987 Studied Slade School 1926-29. Founder member of the Euston Road School 1937-39. Official War artist 1943-45. Slade Professor University College London 1949-75. Responsible for the Coldstream report which radically changed Art education in colleges*

29 *Victor Pasmore 1908-1998 Painter of the most subtle landscapes and interiors seen in England since Steer or Whistler. Later to embrace constructivist movement. Influential teacher*

30 *Eirian Short 1924- See page 24*

31 *Margaret Nicholson 1913- See page 12*

32 *The '62 Group. Founded in 1962 with the intention of providing a professional addition to an organisation of predominantly amateurs and viewed at the time as an exhibiting branch of The Embroiderers' Guild, now a separate group*

33 *Jan Beaney 1938- See page 42*

34 *The Crafts Council 44a Pentonville Road London N1 9BY*

35 *Russell Brockbank 1913-1979 Art editor and cartoonist for* Punch *1949-60. Regular contributor to* The Motor

36 *Henri Matisse 1869-1954 French painter and sculptor. Principal artist of the Fauve group*
Marc Chagall 1887-1985 Russian painter whose main works in Britain, a complete series of stained-glass windows, can be seen in the church at Tudely in Kent

37 *Jean Littlejohn 1945- See page 72*

38 *Beryl Dean 1911-2001 MBE,ARCA, highly esteemed designer/maker of church vestments and renowned teacher.* An Appreciation of the Work of Beryl Dean *by Judy Barry, September issue* The World of Embroidery *2001. Profile* Twelve British Embroiderers *by Diana Springall 1984 Gakken Tokyo. Trained at Royal School of Needlework. 1930- Teaching Bromley College of Art; Royal College of Art; 1939-46 Eastbourne School of Art; 1952- Hammersmith College of Art and Building; Stanhope Institute London. Numerous major commissions most notably five panels Royal Chapel Windsor. Author many books most notable* Ecclesiastical Embroidery *1958 Batsford.* Ideas for Church Embroidery *1968 Batsford.* Embroidery for Religion & Ceremonial *1981.Batsford. ISBN0 71343325 6.*

39 *Pat Russell 1919- Prolific designer maker of church vestments, altar frontals and banners most usually carried out in fabric appliqué. Renowned for superb site-specific design and workmanship. Profile in* Twelve British Embroiderers *by Diana Springall Gakken Tokyo 1984. Author* Lettering in Embroidery *1971 Batsford ISBN 7134 2642*

40 *Hannah Frew Paterson 1931- Trained and lectured at Glasgow School of Art. Respected for her teaching and for many embroidered works of art for both ecclesiastical and secular application. Author of* Three-Dimensional Embroidery *1975 Reinhold . Profile in* Twelve British Embroiderers *by Diana Springall 1984 Gakken Tokyo*

41 *Barbara Dawson 1922- Particularly known for her accomplished use of gold and metal thread embroidery. Author* Metal thread Embroidery *1968 Batsford*

42 *Verina Warren 1946- Noted machine embroiderer of landscape scenes. Author* Landscape in Embroidery *1986 Batsford ISBN 0 7134 4567 X*

43 *Carol Naylor 1946- Lecturer Bishop Otter College 1972-1997, noted machine embroiderer and Vice Chairman of The Society of Designer Craftsmen*

44 *Margaret Hall-Townley 1946- Embroiderer, lecturer at Goldsmiths' College School of Art Department of Textiles and curator at the Constance Howard Resource & Research Centre in Textiles, Goldsmiths' College, London*

45 *Hugh Erhman of Hugh Ehrman Kits, 28a Kensington Church Street London W8*

46 *Janet Arnold*

47 Rouleau *is a hollow tube of fabric with edges turned in; particularly fashionable in shoulder straps of dresses of the 1930s and 1940s. Rouleaux first appeared in 19th century fashion trimmings*

48 Michael Haynes 1941- Founder, together with Judy Brittain, of Fosseway House Workshops and 401½ Workshops 403 Wandsworth Road London SW8 still owned and run by M.H.

49 Bill Gibb 1943-1988 Revolutionised British fashion in the 1970s and 1980s. Named Designer of the Year by Vogue in 1969. Sixtieth Anniversary exhibition Aberdeen Art Gallery 2004

50 Zandra Rhodes 1940- Fashion and textiles designer

51 Carding is the technique by which the unspun fibres of wool are passed between fine wire tines fixed to rollers or hand held boards. This removes impurities and leaves a fine film of wool with the fibres lying in one direction

52 Charles Poulsen 1952-. Sculptor working mainly in lead sheet for buildings and garden sculpture

53 Quilting: stitching by hand or machine to attach three or more layers of fabric together. Appliqué: applying pieces of fabric to another by means of stitch. Patchwork: areas of fabric seamed together with turnings

54 Judy Barry see page 60

55 Peter Clark 1944-. Illustrator and artist. Works exhibited with Rebecca Hossak Gallery and Charlotte Street Gallery London

56 Isabel Dibden Wright 1952- *Profile* Twelve British Embroiderers *Gakken Tokyo 1984. Author* Making your own Patchwork & Quilting *1994 New Holland. 1976 Senior Lecturer in Embroidery Manchester Metropolitan University formerly Manchester Polytechnic. External examiner BA.Hons 1991-95 Glasgow School of Art and 2002 University of Central England, Birmingham and Opus School of Textile Arts London. Work in public and private collections in the U.K. & overseas. Recent commissions include collection of pieces for Leicester Royal Infirmary's new Osborne Building. Former Chairman and Vice-Chairman of the '62 Group exhibiting 1975-1991. Founder member of Quilt Art exhibiting 1985-1991. Member of the British Quilt Study Group 1998-. Included in The Quilter's Guild slide Index.*

57 Anne Butler Morrell 1939- Leading figure in the world of embroidery. First artist to promote the abstract use of stitch. *Profile* Twelve British Embroiderers *1984 Gakken Tokyo. 1965-68 Lecturer Goldsmiths' College. 1968-92 Lecturer/Senior Lecturer/Principal Lecturer Manchester Regional College of Art Manchester Polytechnic/Manchester Metropolitan University. 1992 Appointed Professor of Embroidery. Work in numerous public and private collections. World renowned consultant in particular Calico Museum Ahmedabad India. Author of ten books most notable* Encyclopaedia of Embroidery Stitches *B T Batsford 1994 and by Arco USA ISBN 0 7134 3317 5.* Techniques of Indian Embroidery *B T Batsford 1994 and by Interweave USA ISBN 0 7134 6410 0.* Contemporary Embroidery *Cassell 1994 ISBN 0 289 80105 2.*

58 John Renshaw 1946- A practising artist with associated research interests situated at an interface between pedagogy and aspects of Fine Art practice, particularly drawing. 1975-81 Lecturer, Art and Design Foundation Course Stockport College. 1978-88 Visiting lecturer in Drawing and Visual Studies. Manchester Metropolitan University, Faculty of Art and Design, Department of Textiles and Fashion. 1981-86 Tutor in charge of Foundation studies Cheshire School of Art & Design Northwich. 1981-87 Lectures/workshops for Embroiderers' Guild and Cheshire Textile Group. 1986 - 87 Department of Education and Science Teacher Fellowship in Art Education ,Chester College and Cheshire Education Services. 1987 – Tutor in charge of Painting and Drawing. Currently Undergraduate Programme Leader for BA Hons Fine Art University College Chester. Author of numerous Seminar and Conference Papers that include *On the issue of Teaching Drawing and Painting* 1995 and *The Original Creative Principle* 2002 for National Society for Education in Art and Design . Works exhibited UK, Hong Kong, Canada, USA.

59 L.S.Lowry 1887-1976 Painter of industrial and slumscapes in his native Manchester. Known for his matchstick figures. Lived as a recluse. Elected to RA in 1962.

60 Silk felt is made from carded cocoon strippings for paper making. The process involves teasing out the fibres and placing them in little patches on a J-cloth. At this point other elements can be added followed by a second layer of felt to hold pieces in place. The cloth is then rolled up, together with the silk contents, and steeped in hot water for 30 seconds. This is then wrung out, ironed with a hot iron and left to dry at which point it is ready to receive drawing, sewing etc.

61 Discharge Printing: The printpaste, formaldehyde based, when applied to a surface previously dyed with Direct dye *replaces this original colour with the new pigment that has been added to the print paste. The new colour goes right into the cloth. Steam and heat are required to trigger the reaction. It makes it possible to apply light colours/ neutral/white to a dark background giving a 'deeper' and more varied texture.*

62 *Michael Brennand-Wood 1952- Visual artist, curator, lecturer, arts consultant. 1979- occupies central position in research, origination and advocacy of Contemporary International Textiles. Prolific artist exhibiting in galleries and museums worldwide. Work is in numerous private, public and corporate collections. Commissions UK and abroad.1987 won The Creative Concept Award. 1989 won The Fine Art Award Kyoto. 1990 RSA Art for Architecture Award. Extensive lecturing programme includes Senior Lecturer Goldsmiths' College London and many overseas countries. 1999 Major retrospective Bankfield Museum Halifax UK*

63 *Sally Freshwater 1958- Minimalist use of textiles often in large scale commissions for public places*

64 *Sir Terence Conran 1931- Opened first Habitat store in Fulham Road in 1964. Furniture designer, entrepreneur, property developer, food guru and more. Loved by the 60s generation for enabling them to make their homes look different from those of their parents*

Index